Baseball and American Culture

Baseball and American Culture

A History

John P. Rossi

ROWMAN & LITTLEFIELD
Lanham • Boulder • New York • London

Acquisitions Editor: Christen Karniski
Production Editor: Jessica McCleary
Cover Designer: Jason Enterline

Credits and acknowledgments of sources for material or information used with permission appear on the appropriate page within the text.

Published by Rowman & Littlefield
An imprint of The Rowman & Littlefield Publishing Group, Inc.
4501 Forbes Boulevard, Suite 200, Lanham, Maryland 20706
www.rowman.com

Unit A, Whitacre Mews, 26-34 Stannary Street, London SE11 4AB

British Library Cataloguing in Publication Information Available

Library of Congress Cataloging-in-Publication Data

Names: Rossi, John P., author.
Title: Baseball and American culture : a history / John P. Rossi.
Description: Lanham : Rowman & Littlefield, [2018] | Includes bibliographical references and index.
Identifiers: LCCN 2018016815 (print) | LCCN 2018019621 (ebook) | ISBN 9781538102893 (electronic) | ISBN 9781538102886 (hardback : alk. paper) | ISBN 9781538103289 (pbk.)
Subjects: LCSH: Baseball—Social aspects—United States. | Baseball—United States—History. | LCGFT: Textbooks.
Classification: LCC GV867.64 (ebook) | LCC GV867.64 .R67 2018 (print) | DDC 796.3570973—dc23
LC record available at https://lccn.loc.gov/2018016815

∞™ The paper used in this publication meets the minimum requirements of American National Standard for Information Sciences—Permanence of Paper for Printed Library Materials, ANSI/NISO Z39.48-1992.

Printed in the United States of America

To Caitilin Quinn Wilson, my granddaughter,
in hopes she, like her grandfather, will become a baseball fan.

Contents

Acknowledgments

This book would not have been possible for me to undertake without the help of a number of individuals. First and foremost, I owe my greatest debt to the secretary of the History Department at La Salle University, Lauren De Angelis. She was instrumental in my finishing the book. She read parts of the manuscript, checked notes, collected articles for me, and came to my rescue countless times when I encountered technical problems. Quite simply, the book would never have been completed without her help.

Two of the History Department's student assistants also contributed to this book. Juliana Mastroangelo read all 10 chapters, checking for continuity. Her keen eye uncovered a number of inconsistencies, for which I am deeply grateful. Molly Kitchell typed and retyped numerous drafts of various chapters. It was tedious work, but she did it beautifully. They were both a pleasure to work with and made my work much easier.

In gathering material and checking sources I had the support of the outstanding staff of La Salle's Connelly Library. In particular, I would like to single out Eithne Bearden, La Salle's excellent reference librarian, who came to my rescue several times by unearthing obscure material for me. I also wish to thank my friends and colleagues who put up with my constant chatter about the progress of the book. I am sure they quickly tired of hearing about baseball and American history. And that goes double for my wife, Frances, who bore with me as I traced the course of the book. She says it made her a baseball fan. I hope so.

Introduction

I first became a baseball fan when I was 10 years old, watching my hometown Phillies beat the Cincinnati Reds in a doubleheader on a rainy Sunday in May 1946. At first, I was a typical fan, blindly loyal to my Phillies, attaching myself to a handful of players whom I hero-worshipped: Richie Ashburn, Del Ennis—he was from my neighborhood in Philadelphia—Robin Roberts, and Andy Seminick. Sometime in the 1950s I began to collect any material I could find on the history of baseball. Alongside my graduate studies in history at Notre Dame and the University of Pennsylvania, I became fascinated by the connections between what happened in America's past and the development of the unique American sport of baseball. Aside from a few minor essays, I wrote little about baseball's past until I began teaching a course on baseball and American culture in the mid-1980s. Since then, as my wife said, my avocation gradually became something of a second vocation.

It is my belief that one can study American history through the development of baseball. Just about every theme in American life—immigration, industrialization, race relations, urbanization—is intimately linked and intertwined in America's history. As an example, the Irish and German immigrants of the mid-nineteenth century used baseball as a way of gaining acceptance from dominant groups in American society. Later, other ethnic outsiders would follow the same route in the first third of the twentieth century: Poles, Jews, Italians, and Latin Americans slightly later. We now accept that Jackie Robinson's breaking the race barrier in baseball played a significant part in ending segregation in the United States.

The first serious study of baseball appeared in 1960. Harold Seymour's *Baseball: The Early Years* demonstrated what a superb historian could do with the study of baseball's past. All serious study of baseball's past owes a major debt to Seymour. He pointed the direction that scholars could take if they wished to look at America's past through the lens of the sport known as early as the 1850s as the "national game."

Those who followed in Seymour's footsteps, David Voigt, John Thorn, Bill James, G. Edward White, Robert Burk, and Charles Alexander, to mention but a few, have carved out a rich field of scholarly study that continues to grow today. I would also like to salute those keen members of SABR, the Society for American Baseball Research, who continue to sharpen our knowledge of baseball's role in American life. Having taught baseball's history for more than 30 years, I have leaned heavily on their work, as well as the work of numerous others.

It is my hope in this book to connect the narrative of baseball history, which I regard as crucial, with readings that highlight one or more themes developed in its 10 chapters. I have tried to vary the readings so that they reflect what I consider the major cultural aspects of the sport. Each chapter also contains a number of questions designed to promote discussion.

Baseball may no longer be "America's game," but with roots that go back to the earliest days of the Republic, it is the only sport through which the student can delve deeply into the nation's past.

CHAPTER 1

Baseball's Origins

The Roots of American Baseball

Among America's sports, baseball is unique. It is the only form of recreation that literally grew up with the country. There is evidence of bat and ball games being played in the earliest days of the nation. During the past 175 years, the game has been imbedded in the very psyche of the nation. It is the only sport to produce serious literature, from Ring Lardner's humorous *You Know Me, Al*, to W. P. Kinsella's novel *Shoeless Joe*, the inspiration for the film *Field of Dreams*, to Bernard Malamud's *The Natural* and Mark Harris's *Bang the Drum Slowly*. With the exception of boxing, it is the only sport to achieve success in film. From *It Happens Every Spring* to *Major League*, baseball films have been critical and popular successes. Baseball also achieved mythic status with the poem "Casey at the Bat" and the song "Take Me Out to the Ball Game." Our very language abounds with baseball terminology: choke up, out in left field, cleanup hitter, strike out, grand slam, around the horn, and so forth.

The history of baseball has taken on mythic qualities. It was widely believed that, unlike other sports, it didn't evolve, but was invented one day in the summer of 1839—and not just by anyone, but by a hero from America's great test of survival, the Civil War. According to legend, Abner Doubleday, one day in the summer of 1839, drew up the rules for a new game while home in Cooperstown, New York, from West Point. From this point in the Garden of Eden, the game spread throughout the country. Some idea of the power of the Doubleday story can be inferred from the fact that it has been honored by the U.S. government with a postage stamp. When it came time to establish a shrine honoring America's unique sport, it was logically placed in Doubleday's hometown, Cooperstown. While scholarly research long ago undermined the Doubleday myth, its persistence tells us much about baseball's impact on the American psyche. The Doubleday tale also suited the American sense of nationalism. It was an American game, founded by Americans and played only by Americans. Reflecting this sense of uniqueness as early as 1856, baseball was labeled the "American game."[1]

The origins of baseball in America are much more complex. Bat and ball games had been played throughout history in various societies. The early colonists played versions of bat and ball games popular in England, with rounders and cricket being very popular by the late eighteenth and early nineteenth centuries. There is even a reference to a game of "base" being played by soldiers of the Continental Army at Valley Forge in 1778. Historians and baseball aficionados have unearthed references to bat and ball games in old newspapers, magazines, and books while searching for the sport's origin.

Something resembling baseball emerged in the early nineteenth century. It wasn't a game that was invented—there was no Doubleday Immaculate Conception—so much as an activity that evolved in different ways in different parts of the young nation. The game took root in the 1830s and 1840s, in the most populous area of the young nation, the Northeast, and was largely an urban phenomenon. Various versions of rounders were played regularly in cities, towns, and villages of the young nation. Cricket remained popular and was a serious rival to baseball until the 1860s.

American versions of rounders, often called "town ball" and "old cat," were the real inspiration for baseball. In variants of these games, a batter used a stick to hit a ball and then proceeded to run from one base to another (the number of bases varied). In "old cat" and "town ball," the number of players, the number of bases, and the size and shape of the field could vary, but batting, running, and catching the ball were common. Before long, the new game, already starting to be known as baseball—although spelled "base ball" until late in the nineteenth century—began to take on a more formal structure. Clubs and social organizations began to form their own teams, play nearby rivals, and formulate rules of play.

The innovative period for the new sport can be found in the 1830s and 1840s. The country was changing rapidly as a result of cheap transportation, especially the emergence of the railroad; the spread of education; and the growth of the newspaper, which spread stories of new ideas and concepts, and devoted considerable space to sports, especially horse racing, which was popular throughout the country. Cities were experiencing a huge expansion. In the 1840s, America's population grew by 36 percent, with cities and towns of more than 8,000 increasing by 90 percent. It was in these expanding urban areas that baseball took root.

The public, especially young males, sought an outlet for their energies and a way to spend their leisure time. At first, the new game of baseball drew most of its players from the ranks of shopkeepers, clerks, small manufacturers, and skilled craftsmen, people who would have the leisure time and money to invest in sport. Baseball also sought to emulate English cricket with its club tradition, which combined sport with a social occasion. It also provided healthy exercise, a way of overcoming the sedentary life, and promoted sportsmanship and even good citizenship. There was membership on teams—"gentlemen's clubs" was the preferred term—with contests played against rival clubs. Reflecting the nationalism of the time, Americans began considering baseball the "equal of cricket as a scientific game."

It is difficult to trace the precise process by which baseball developed—the official historian of baseball, John Thorn, has written that baseball started "in several places, more or less simultaneously."[2] By the 1840s, the level of play had become more sophisticated and the various forms of the game enormously popular. Almost every town and city of any consequence played some version of baseball. The game was played mostly by the better-off younger members of the middle class. Lower-class workingmen and laborers who had to work long hours—the work week in the middle years of the nineteenth century was 60 hours—did not have the opportunity to take off in the late afternoon for exercise, nor could they afford club dues. Despite that, baseball was broadly popular among working-class young men, who took every opportunity to play a version of the game. By one estimate, within a generation, two-thirds of the early baseball players came from a working-class background, while the remaining third was of the artisan class.

Many forms of baseball vied for popularity, with the rules varying from place to place. One of the oldest versions, the Philadelphia game, used an iron plate as a home base within a diamond-shaped playing field. The batter was retired if he was tagged out or the ball was thrown to the base ahead of him. In the Massachusetts game, the field was rectangular, with 10 to 14 players on defense, while bases or bounds, usually sticks, were located 60 feet apart at each corner of the field. The batter was out if he was hit with a ball while trying to reach base, called "soaking" and common to many versions of early baseball. These games clearly blended rounders with elements of town ball and versions of old cat.

The forerunner of modern baseball emerged from the version of baseball played in New York. The credit for this was long attributed to one man, Alexander Cartwright, a bank teller and volunteer fireman in New York. Historians of baseball once credited Cartwright with the decisive role in setting the rules of the game. That is no longer the case. Instead, Cartwright drew up a set of rules for his baseball club, the Knickerbockers, a gentleman's club made up of prosperous businessmen and merchants who desired vigorous leisure activity. They were also "men who were at liberty after three o'clock in the afternoon," unlike laborers, who would have no time during the week for recreation.[3]

It is now clear that Cartwright's claim to fame was to systematize what a number of his colleagues had been developing for some time. The scheme that emerged in 1845, attributed to Cartwright, borrowed concepts from various forms of baseball and was original only in the fact that it was codified and easy to follow. He adopted the diamond shape popular for the infield and placed the pitcher or bowler 45 feet from the batter. We have no clear evidence how far the bases were set apart, whether 75 or 90 feet. The bases were canvas bags, not sticks or stones, while home plate and the pitcher's plate were round iron disks. Cartwright did not specify the number of players, but nine quickly became commonplace. The players were distributed essentially as they are today, except for the shortstop, who moved about the infield. As in the other versions of baseball, the pitcher's job was to put the ball in play, not to get the batter out. He threw softly underhand. The batter was out if the ball was caught in the air or on the bounce, or if the fielder threw the ball to the base before the runner arrived there. The rules did away with soaking. Cartwright's rules ended the inning when three outs were made; the game was over when one side scored 21 runs, or "aces."

Cartwright's claim to baseball immortality is obviously greater than Doubleday's, but he too was not inventing anything. He was formalizing the ideas and plans of others. His association with baseball only lasted a few years after his codification of the rules. In 1849, he joined the rush to the California gold strike and then moved to Hawaii, where there is no evidence of his interest in baseball. It doesn't matter, however, Cartwright is still in baseball's Hall of Fame. As the great film director John Ford once noted, "When the legend becomes fact, print the legend."[4]

What came to be called the New York game spread throughout the North and East, perhaps reflecting the growing influence of New York City, the nation's largest metropolitan area, with a population of 516,000 in 1850, 176,000 more than the second-largest city, Philadelphia. New York was also at the center of a railroad hub and enjoyed the largest port traffic in the nation.

In 1858, with the spread in popularity of the New York game, a group of clubs met in New York to further codify the rules of the growing game. They organized as the National Association of Base Ball Players (NABBP) and, based on the experience of a decade of play, fine-tuned the baseball rules. They decided on nine innings for a game instead of awarding victory on the basis of a number of runs scored. They also standardized the size of the bat and ball. These changes proved successful because they gave the game a certain logic and simplicity. They were also easy to learn and relatively easy to master. Within a short period of time, the New York game was outstripping all other versions of baseball. Other forms of baseball continued to be played, especially in areas other than the Northeast, and cricket remained popular for some years, but they too soon gave way to the New York game.

One of the reasons for the popularity of baseball was the role played by the growing newspaper industry, which began carrying detailed, inning-by-inning scores of games. The rise of the cheap penny press led to increased sports coverage, gaining baseball a new audience. The weekly *New York Clipper*, founded in 1853, and the *Police Gazette* (1845) devoted considerable space to baseball. *Beadle's Dime Base-Ball Player*, a compendium of information about the sport, first appeared in 1860, and sold between 50,000 and 60,000 copies annually. Of crucial importance for the growing popularity of baseball was the role played by statistics. Baseball lent itself to recognizable statistical markers: hits, runs, errors, strikeouts, wins, losses, and so on, making it possible for debates and discussions about the game, still a source of its popularity today.

One of the key figures in spreading the new game's popularity was an English immigrant, Henry Chadwick.[5] Chadwick was born in England in 1824, and came to America as a young man. He was a fan of cricket but claimed he was converted to baseball when he first saw it played. Touching on the sense of uniqueness so appealing to Americans, he noted after seeing baseball that it was just the game for the American public. He became a celebrated sportswriter and, in 1860, is credited with inventing the "box score." Chadwick's idea was to provide a clear statistical breakdown of the game by showing the number of runs, hits, and outs recorded by each player. The box score, which might have been inspired by cricket scoring, caught on quickly because it was a simple way of showing what had happened in a particular game. It remains popular today. The idea of batting averages, runs scored, hits made, and pitcher's victories neatly outlined in the box score launched the statistical life of baseball, whereby players and teams may be compared in a way denied other sports. A glance at any sports page today shows the continuing popularity of baseball statistics. Baseball is the only sport, in fact, where statistics reveal anything important about the game. The best hitter has the highest batting average; the most powerful, the most home runs. Pitchers can be measured by wins, percentage of victories, earned runs allowed per nine innings, or games saved. Almost from the beginning, baseball was a mathematical wonder.

If Doubleday and Cartwright are largely mythic figures in baseball's development, Chadwick deserves recognition as one of the "fathers of baseball." He wrote sports for various New York newspapers, but more importantly, he edited the first true baseball guides: *Beadle's Dime Base-Ball Player* and *Spalding's Official Base Ball Guide*. Chadwick also wrote the first serious analysis of the sport: *The Game of Base Ball: How to Learn It, How to Play It, and How to Teach It* He not only wrote enthusiastically and expertly, but also literally preached the gospel of baseball.

There is abundant evidence of the popularity of the new game in the years before the Civil War. In 1858, an all-star game made up of the best players in the New York area was staged. Fifteen hundred spectators paid 50 cents to watch the game, producing gate receipts of $750, an enormous sum for the time—the equal to a year's salary for a professional man. Any doubts about the economic potential of the sport were removed.

Two years later, the Excelsior Club of Brooklyn undertook the first tour of a baseball nine, traveling by train throughout New York State and then down to Pennsylvania, Maryland, and Delaware, playing in front of large crowds already knowledgeable about baseball. Like the all-star game, the tour was a financial success. Taking the game nationally was becoming economically feasible now that the railway network was near completion. By the 1860s, there were more than 30,000 miles of railway track in the United States. The public could now undertake trips unthinkable in the recent past. A by-product of this was the spread in news about baseball and the ultimate growth in its popularity. Temperamentally, baseball suited the nation's mood. It was easy to follow; filled with action; and, in an age of growing nationalism, uniquely American.

Along with the growth of baseball, another aspect of the changing nature of the nation began in the 1840s. During that decade, the largest influx of immigrants in U.S. history took place. More than 1 million Irish and 1 million Germans entered the country from 1846 to 1855, bringing with them new attitudes, tastes, and standards. While seeking a better life, they also were searching for ways to identify with their new home. In a surprisingly short period of time, they and their children would adopt baseball as one way of showing their Americanism. The older generation of Americans hoped baseball would become for these immigrants what it was for them. They also hoped baseball would socialize these newcomers to America.[6]

A partial explanation of baseball's continued appeal to the older generation of Americans was largely nostalgic. Having played some form of baseball as children, they could, by watching the game, relive their youth. At this time, America was a nation of joiners. Fraternal organizations flourished throughout the country. These clubs or associations were a way for people often isolated to get together. Playing baseball games often served that purpose for both men and women.

THE EMERGENCE OF THE PROFESSIONAL GAME

The Civil War had a major impact on baseball. Team rosters were decimated as the nation went to war. Organized baseball was at a low ebb during the Civil War. While formal play seems to have reached new lows, baseball continued to be played. A painting exists showing a game of baseball being played in a prisoner of war camp in North Carolina. We know that contests were put on during the war, often for large crowds, hungry to see baseball played. On one occasion, a team from Philadelphia played a series of games against popular squads in New York, Brooklyn, and Newark. There is some evidence that President Abraham Lincoln and his young son, Tad, watched a game in Washington during the Civil War. Associating the martyred president with baseball was not that unusual.

In the 1940s, a popular sportswriter and broadcaster given to hyperbole, Bill Stern, would tell a dramatic story of Lincoln's assassination. As he lay dying, Stern would have Lincoln lean over and grasp the hand of the general trying to comfort him. "General, whatever happens don't let them destroy baseball," he said. After a dramatic pause, Stern would say that man was none other than Abner Doubleday, the man who invented baseball. Of course, the story was nonsense. Lincoln never recovered consciousness after he was shot, and Doubleday wasn't at his bedside. Once again, as with the story of baseball's "invention," myth trumped reality. Baseball was on its way to becoming as American as Plymouth Rock, the rolling Mississippi, and cowboys and Indians. The Civil War hurt baseball, but like future American conflicts, it couldn't kill the sport.[7]

Despite the crippling effects of the Civil War on baseball, the conflict played an important role in spreading the sport to all corners of the nation. Baseball was played by Northern soldiers in the prisoner of war camps throughout the South, helping to spread the popularity of the game that was little known below the Mason-Dixon line before the war. In a small but significant way baseball also helped to redefine the nation in the generation after the war. It quickly became the one sport that was played throughout the reunited country. Players from the border states, Maryland, Missouri, and even Washington, DC, began to show up on the roster of the National Association, the first professional baseball league, in the 1870s. Only a handful of ballplayers came from the Deep South in the 1870s but their numbers would increase over the next thirty years. A leading sports publication, *Wilke's Spirit*, argued that baseball "was destined to close National Wounds opened by the late war. It is no idle pastime which draws young men, separated by two thousand miles, together to contest in friendship, upon fields but lately crimsoned with their brothers' blood in mortal combat."[8]

Baseball was deeply embedded in the nation's popular culture after the Civil War. Not only was the game played in every corner of the nation, but also popular songs and dances drew on such baseball themes as "The Live Oak Polka" and "The Baseball Polka." A sure sign of baseball's growing significance was the fact that it began to be played on college campuses. Although there is clear evidence that baseball was played by colleges before the Civil War—the first recorded game was played by Amherst versus Williams College in 1859, which Amherst won, 73–32—the game only became the first truly intercollegiate sport between the 1870s and 1890s, when its popularity was challenged by the new game of football. Photographs of a game played by Wesleyan College in 1867, were published by the Society for American Baseball Research. The photos clearly show a game of baseball with the players at their regular positions. The pitcher is obviously using the underhand motion favored by the game at that time. There is an overwhelmingly male crowd standing along the foul lines.[9]

In the years after the Civil War, membership in the NABBP grew rapidly, until, by 1867, there were more than 200 registered clubs abiding by the association rules. Three years later, that number had increased to 350 clubs. Crowds grew larger. Baseball was becoming more popular. Enclosed grounds were erected to attract paying customers. There was money to be made in baseball, and in the boom and bust years after the Civil War it wasn't long before the economic possibilities of baseball were exploited. Baseball was entering what Harold Seymour called its twilight zone between amateurism and professionalism.[10]

At the same time, serious problems were emerging. Baseball's amateur tradition was giving way to professionalism. Intense rivalry between baseball clubs bred competition and the desire to win at all costs. It wasn't long before talented players were paid to play. Al Reach, one of the best players of his time, was lured to Philadelphia with the promise of a salary of $25 per week, a huge sum at a time when the average worker made about $500 a year. To keep up with the competition, the clubs resorted to professionals. A by-product of this professionalization was the tendency of players to jump from team to team, called "revolving," for higher play, something that would curse baseball in its early years.

Simultaneously, another theme that would plague early baseball also emerged: gambling, particularly the throwing of games. Where money was involved, there were always those looking for an edge. Alcoholism, the other great scourge of early baseball, would make its appearance a few years later. The end result of these problems was the ultimate breakup of the first serious baseball league. The governing body of the NABBP was too weak to deal with these problems, along with the failure of clubs to fulfill their schedule obligations—some teams simply stopped playing. In the midst of this chaos, the league dissolved in 1868.[11]

An interesting aspect of baseball's development was its adoption by African Americans. There were black teams throughout the nation, although they were refused recognition by organized baseball. An unwritten rule existed that African Americans could not play with whites or against white teams. The rule was occasionally winked at, but in the years after the Civil War, baseball perfectly mirrored the attitude of the country on racial matters. In 1867, the NABBP banned African American teams from its ranks on the specious grounds that "if colored teams were admitted, there would be some division of feeling . . . but by excluding them no injury would result." The New York club of the NABBP banned all clubs of "gentlemen of color." It was suggested that African Americans organize their own baseball association, a perfect reflection of the segregation of races—"separate but equal"—that the nation would thoroughly embrace in a few years.[12]

Baseball was still being played throughout the country, and there was a genuine appetite for the game. Into this gap, in 1869, emerged the first truly professional team, the Cincinnati Red Stockings. In a mixture of urban pride and the possibility of an economic bonanza, a group of Ohio businessman decided to build a winning team by employing professionals. They hired Harry Wright, a superb player, for an annual salary of $1,200, and gave him carte blanche to form a winning team. Wright signed his brother, George, a professional cricket player for the highly regarded Philadelphia Cricket Club, at a salary of $1,400. Eight other players were signed, with the entire payroll amounting to $9,300, a considerable sum in those days. These salaries compare favorably with a substantial middle-class income, which in the 1870s averaged approximately $1,000. The Cincinnati team was the first fully professional team, and its success pointed the direction of the future of baseball.

The question of baseball's impact on social mobility has fascinated historians of the game. There is no question that baseball was used by many young men as a way to rise on the social ladder. The salaries the best players received, usually under the table, would place them on a level with the average skilled laborer. Another factor at play was the prestige that went with a successful baseball career.

The Cincinnati team (they got their name from their red stockings) went on tour in 1869, taking on any challenger, even local favorite teams. By this time, every aspect of baseball play—hitting, pitching, and fielding—had become increasingly sophisticated. There were numerous clubs and players who played the sport at a high level. In spite of this, the Red Stockings swept through the country, defeating team after team with relative ease. Between 1869 and the early part of the next year, they won 84 (some sources argue the number was even higher) consecutive games, often by huge scores. It is estimated that in 1869 alone, traveling as far west as California, they played in front of 200,000 fans. They beat the best of the amateur clubs, losing their first game in June 1870, playing for a crowd estimated by the popular magazine *Harper's Weekly* at 10,000 to 15,000, to the Brooklyn Athletics, in extra innings by a score of 8–7. Tickets went for 50 cents, and the game brought in gate receipts of between $5,000 and $7,500. With money like this, baseball's future was clear. President Ulysses S. Grant arranged a meeting with the players when they were in Washington and congratulated them on their success. If politicians wanted to be associated with the game, it was a sure sign baseball had arrived.[13]

One unusual aspect of the Red Stockings' success was giving a definite form to the baseball uniform. A short-billed cap, a shirt with a turned-up collar, knickers-type pants, and colored stockings became the standard baseball uniform. A version of this type of uniform was widely adopted by other baseball teams in the late nineteenth century. It is a remarkable commentary on the traditionalism of baseball that this type of uniform didn't change radically for more than a century.[14]

By the 1870s, baseball equipment also began to resemble the modern game. Bats were longer, heavier than the modern bat, and with thicker handles to facilitate slapping at the pitch. The ball itself had shrunk from something resembling a modern softball to its present size of 9 to 9¼ inches in circumference and 5 to 5½ ounces in weight. The 1870s baseball consisted of a small core of hard rubber, surrounded with tightly wrapped wool and covered with two carefully stitched figure-eight pieces of horsehide, which gave the ball its distinctive look. Earlier baseballs had been stitched with a cover that looked like a peeled orange.

The game itself had become faster in every facet. The pitcher still threw underhand but no longer was simply having the batter put the ball in play. Instead, the pitcher was now trying to deceive the batter. One pitcher, Asa Brainerd, who pitched for the Red Stockings, developed a fastball delivered with a last-second snap of the wrist. Harry Wright perfected what he called his "dew drop," what today we would call a change-of-pace pitch. Batters still could call for their pitch whether high or low. Because batters stalled waiting for their pitch, by the 1870s umpires would begin to call strikes. Batters began to adjust their swing to avoid hitting soft fly balls, which were easy outs. They began to hit what were called "daisy cutters," hard ground balls that were difficult to field since only the pitcher and catcher wore gloves, and they were little more than leather gloves with the fingers cut out. The result was a lot of errors in a typical game, a fact of baseball life until the 1920s, when the baseball glove was perfected. By the 1870s, baseball was being played with such a high degree of professionalism that it was rare for one of the professional teams to lose to a team of amateurs. In 1871, the Boston Red Stockings, a first-class professional team, played 32 games against amateur opposition and won them all.[15]

A contributing factor to the popularity of baseball was the emergence of the modern sporting goods company. Two of the largest were built up by former players, A. G. Spalding and Al Reach. The industry contributed to the standardization of baseball equipment. By the late 1870s, the sporting goods industry was turning out a half-million bats, millions of balls, and thousands of uniforms. Baseball truly was a big business. During the next few years, baseball would follow the lead of other businesses in the nineteenth century and carry out a consolidation of teams and leagues, In a word, baseball became a trust.

THE FIRST MAJOR LEAGUE

It was clear to many involved in baseball that the NABBP needed reforming. The day of the amateur club was over. The game itself had become increasingly expensive as the cost of traveling, the salaries of the players, advertising games, and so forth demonstrated that baseball needed a steadier organization. After the 1870 season, Harry Wright led a group of owners who had become dissatisfied with the NABBP. They saw the potential of making a tidy profit off of the new game. In March 1871, team owners from 10 NABBP cities met in New York to form a new league, the National Association of Professional Base Ball Players (NAPBBP). The new key word was "professional," for the players themselves ran the league.

An entry fee of $10 was charged, and it was agreed that the scheduling of games would be handled by the teams. Each team would play every other team five times, and a pennant would be declared at the end of the season. The new association represented the most successful baseball clubs, including the New York Mutuals, Philadelphia Athletics, and Chicago White Stockings, but also teams from smaller cities: Fort Wayne, Indiana, Rockford, Illinois, and Troy, New York. Problems developed as a result.

The league suffered from the kind of chaos one would expect when the inmates run the asylum: Schedules weren't met, management was incompetent and "revolving" was a constant problem, and there were numerous gambling scandals. One of the biggest problems arose from the fact that teams could make more money playing unofficial or exhibition games than playing in the league itself. Despite these issues, the new league survived for a few years until a combination of mistakes destroyed it.

Things started out badly, and the new league was beset with birth pangs. Fort Wayne dropped out in mid-season 1871, to be replaced by the Brooklyn Eckfords, who themselves lasted only a year. The Chicago White Stockings, who boasted a new ballpark, had to leave the city when the Great Fire of 1871 burned them out of their home. Chicago, one of the hotbeds of baseball, was without a team for two years. Teams switched cities constantly, with only Boston, New York, and Philadelphia fielding a squad every year for the duration of the NAPBBP. In spite of the new league's problems, the quality of play was high, and fan interest surged in such cities as New York, Chicago, and Washington. The Boston team drew 70,000 fans in 1875, a remarkable figure for that era. Despite areas of success, the league was plagued by gambling scandals, especially incidents of players throwing games. Some of the baseball clubs were associated with corrupt political organizations. The infamous political boss of Tammany Hall, William Marcy Tweed, was part owner of the New York Mutuals.[16]

The league also suffered from the sale of alcohol at games, which led to rowdy fan behavior. It was common for fans to pour onto the field, fight with the players, and physically abuse the umpire. Umpire baiting had been rare in baseball. Now it began to be common. It was argued by Henry Chadwick and other sportswriters that baseball had to deal with these problems or the game would lose its hold on respectable fans.

Despite baseball's problems, it must be noted that the professionalism of the players grew, and the game had progressed. Players in the NAPBBP were clearly superior to their amateur counterparts. Familiar aspects of baseball like turning double plays became commonplace. Hitters were more scientific in their approach, waiting for a pitch to hit and trying, with great success, to place the ball beyond the fielders. Pitchers were mastering new pitches and learning to deceive the hitter. Some idea of the sophistication of play can be found in the fact that the number of runs scored declined from 13 per game to a little more than 10, a figure close to that of modern baseball. An outfielder demonstrated how strong his arm was by throwing a baseball 400 feet, 7½ inches, a record that lasted until the 1940s. The balance between offense and defense that emerged would stabilize baseball for the rest of the century.

The background of the players also was changing. Most players came from what was still the heart of baseball—the cities and towns of the Northeast—although the Midwest, especially Chicago, was producing a high quality of player. A. G. Spalding and Adrian "Cap" Anson, two of the dominant figures of early professional baseball, were midwesterners. But Philadelphia, New York, and Brooklyn alone placed 98 players on the league's roster. There were even a handful of foreign-born players: seven from England and five born in Ireland, the latter foreshadowing the first wave of Irish American players who would come to dominate the game in the next three decades. An Irish-born player, Tony Foley of County Cashel, briefly managed the Chicago White Stockings, a forerunner of the McGraws, Macks, and Hanlons who would dominate baseball managing by the late 1890s. For them, baseball was a vehicle for demonstrating their Americanism.[17] The WASP/Yankee character of baseball remained strong but was being challenged for the first time. The South and West were virtually unrepresented on the rosters of the league teams.

Harry Wright brought the best of his old Cincinnati team to Boston and dominated the new league. Boston finished third in the inaugural season behind Chicago and Philadelphia, and then won the championship easily for the next four seasons. At first, the championship season encompassed just 30 games, but by 1875 the teams were playing 80-game seasons. Lack of meaningful competition also hurt. In the league's final season, Boston began by winning their first 26 games and finished with a record of 71–8, an astonishing .890 winning percentage. Combined with the other ills that plagued the NAPBBP, it was only a matter of time before the league collapsed.

During the league's heyday, Wright and Spalding decided to take a page from the successful tours of the United States by leading English cricket players. In a burst of nationalism (and hopes of a financial killing) in the middle of the 1874 season, from July to September, they took a team of baseball players to England and Ireland for a series of 14 exhibitions and even played some matches against English cricket clubs. The Americans even won the cricket matches. English observers were amazed by the fielding prowess of their Yankee cousins and awed by the way the players drove the ball all over the cricket grounds. Wright and Spalding failed to convert the English to baseball, but, more importantly, the tour was a financial flop—Wright and Spalding lost $3,000, even if they achieved an artistic success. The English may have been blasé about baseball, but they saw that their American cousins were formidable athletes ready to challenge the mother country for sport domination.[18]

The tour also hurt baseball by taking players away in the middle of the season—but it did reveal something about the sport. Handled properly, there was money to be made in the game, but the old league would have to be scrapped and something more businesslike put in its place. By the 1875 season, the men who ran the old league were ready for something better—a league built on sound foundations run not by the players, but the businessmen who understood the complexity of the economic side of the sport. Baseball was ready for its next major step.

Questions for Consideration

1. Why and how did baseball take hold in the United States in the second quarter of the nineteenth century?
2. What were some of the sources of baseball's appeal to the public?
3. Discuss the "Doubleday myth" concerning the origins of baseball. Why did it take hold and last long after it was proven false?
4. What role did baseball play in forging an American identity?
5. Many individuals contributed to the growing popularity of baseball by the 1870s. Assess the role in this process of Alexander Cartwright, Henry Chadwick, and A. G. Spalding.
6. Discuss the pros and cons of considering Henry Chadwick the "father of baseball."
7. Discuss the impact of the Civil War on baseball. What can be said of the claim that baseball helped bring the nation together after the war?
8. What was the outcome of the first tour of baseball to England in the 1870s? Does the tour tell us something special about America at the time?
9. Trace the evolution of how baseball was played in the 1860s and 1870s. How do these changes help explain the growing popularity of the game?

Notes

1. For the most recent study of the origins of baseball, see John Thorn, *Baseball in the Garden of Eden: The Secret History of the Early Game* (New York: Simon & Schuster, 2011), especially chapters 1 and 2.

2. Thorn, *Baseball in the Garden of Eden*, 25.

3. Harold Seymour, *Baseball: The Early Years* (New York: Oxford University Press, 1960), 7. Thorn argues that other individuals, specifically William R. Wheaton and Daniel L. Adams, contemporaries of Cartwright in New York baseball circles, played a considerable role in systematizing the rules of the game. Thorn, *Baseball in the Garden of Eden*.

4. *The Man Who Shot Liberty Valance*, directed by John Ford (Hollywood: Paramount, 1962), VHS.

5. For Chadwick's significance, see Andrew J. Schiff, "Henry Chadwick: The Father of Baseball Was a Sportswriter," *National Pastime: A Review of Baseball History* 28 (2008): 37–48.

6. The class background of baseball players is analyzed in Melvin Adelman, *A Sporting Time: New York City and the Rise of Modern Athletics, 1820–1870* (Urbana: University of Illinois Press, 1986), 123–32.

7. George B. Kirsch, "Bats, Balls, and Bullets: Baseball in the Civil War," *Civil War Times* XXXVI, no. 2 (May 1998): 30–37.

8. Kirsch, "Bats, Balls, and Bullets," 31.

9. Ronald Smith, "The Rise of College Baseball," *Baseball History* I (1986): 23–41.

10. Seymour, *Baseball*.

11. Seymour, *Baseball*, chapter 5.

12. Thorn, *Baseball in the Garden of Eden*, 129.

13. George Bulkey, "The Day the Reds Lost," *National Pastime: A Review of Baseball History* 2 (Fall 1982): 5–10.

14. Bill James, *The New Bill James Historical Baseball Abstract* (New York: Free Press, 1998).

15. Peter Morris, *A Game of Inches: The Stories behind the Innovations That Shaped Baseball* (Chicago: Ivan R. Dee, 2006).

16. Seymour, *Baseball*, chapter 6.

17. Jerrold Casway, *Ed Delahanty in the Emerald Age of Baseball* (Notre Dame, IN: University of Notre Dame Press, 2004).

18. Neil Stout, "1874 Baseball: Not Cricket to the British," *Baseball Research Journal* (1985): 83–85.

FINAL DECISION OF THE SPECIAL BASEBALL COMMISSION

Edited by Henry Chadwick

New York, December 30, 1907

MR. JAMES E. SULLIVAN, Secretary, Special Base Ball Commission,
21 Warren St., New York City.

DEAR SULLIVAN,

On my earliest opportunity, after my recent return from Europe, I read, and read with much interest, the considerable mass of testimony bearing on the origin of Base Ball which you had sent to my office address during my absence. I cannot say that I find myself in accord with those who urge the American origin of the game as against its English origin as contended by Mr. Chadwick, on "patriotic ground." In my opinion we owe much to our Anglo-Saxon kinsmen for their example, which we have too tardily followed in fostering healthful field sports generally, and if the fact could be established by evidence that our national game, "Base Ball," was devised in England, I do not think that it would be any the less admirable nor welcome on that account. As a matter of fact, the game of ball, which I have always regarded as the distinctive English game, i.e., cricket, was brought to this country and had a respectable following here, which it has since maintained, long before any game of ball resembling our national game was played anywhere! Indeed, the earliest field sport that I remember was a game of cricket, played on an open field near Jamaica, L. I., where I was then attending school. Then, and ever since, I have heard cricket spoken of as the essentially English game, and, until my perusal of this testimony, my own belief had been that our game of Base Ball, substantially as played today, originated with the Knickerbocker club of New York, and it was frequently referred to as the "New York Ball Game."

"Final Decision of the Special Baseball Commission," *Spalding Guide 1908*, 45–48.

While "Father" Chadwick and I have not always agreed (I recall that he at first regarded as revolutionary the "Full Team Reserve Rule" and the alliance between professional Base Ball associations, both of which I devised in 1883, and I later modeled after the latter the Alliance of the A.A.U. reorganization), yet I always have had respect for his opinions and admiration for his inflexible honesty of purpose; and I have endeavored to give full weight to his contention that Base Ball is of English origin. It does seem to me, however, that in the last analysis, his contention is based chiefly upon the fact that, substantially, the same kind of implements are employed in the game of Base Ball as in the English game of "Rounders," to which he refers; for if the mere tossing or handling of some kind of ball, or striking it with some kind of stick, could be accepted as the origin of our game, then "Father" Chadwick would certainly have to go far back of Anglo-Saxon civilization, beyond Rome, beyond Greece, at least to the palmy days of the Chaldean Empire! Nor does it seem to me that he can any more successfully maintain the argument because of the employment, by the English schoolboy of the past, of the implements or materials of the game.

Surely there can be no question of the fact that Edison, Frank Sprague, and other pioneers in the electrical field were the inventors of useful devices and processes whereby electricity was harnessed for the use of man, although they did not invent electricity, nor do they, nor does anybody, know today what electricity is! As I understand it, the invention or the origination of anything practical or useful, whether it be in the domain of mechanics or field sports, is the creation of the device or the process from preexisting materials or elements; and in this sense I do not myself see how there can be any question that the game of Base Ball originated in the United States and not in England, where it certainly had never been played, in however crude a form, and was strange and unfamiliar when an American ball team first played it there.

As I have stated, my belief had been that our "National Game of Base Ball" originated with the Knickerbocker club, organized in New York in 1845, and which club published certain elementary rules that year; but, in the interesting and pertinent testimony for which we are indebted to Mr. A. G. Spalding, appears a circumstantial statement by a reputable gentleman, according to which the first known diagram of the diamond, indicating positions for the players, was drawn by Abner Doubleday in Cooperstown, N.Y., in 1839. Abner Doubleday subsequently graduated from West Point and entered the regular army, where, as captain of artillery, he sighted the first gun fired on the Union side (at Fort Sumter) in the Civil War. Later still, as major general, he was in command of the Union army at the close of the first day's fight in the battle of Gettysburg, and he died full of honors at Mendham, N.J., in 1893. It happened that he and I were members of the same veteran military organization, the crack Grand Army Post (Lafayette), and the duty developed upon me, as commander of that organization, to have charge of his obsequies, and to command the veteran military escort which served as guard of honor when his body lay in state, January 30, 1893, in the New York City Hall, prior to this interment in Arlington.

In the days when Abner Doubleday attended school in Cooperstown, it was a common thing for two dozen or more of school boys to join in a game of ball. Doubtless, as in my later experience, collisions between players in attempting to catch the batted ball were frequent, and injury due to this cause, or to the practice of putting out the runner by hitting him with the ball, occurred.

I can well understand how the orderly mind of the embryo West Pointer would devise a scheme for limiting the contestants on each side and allotting them to field positions, each with a certain amount of territory; also substituting the existing method of putting out the baserunner for the old one of "plugging" him with the ball.

True, it appears from the statement that Doubleday provided for 11 men on a side instead of nine, stationing the two extra men between first and second, and second and third bases, but this is a minor detail, and indeed, I have played, and doubtless other old players have, repeatedly with 11 on a side, placed almost identically in the manner indicated by Doubleday's diagram, although it is true that we so played after the number on each side had been fixed at nine, simply to admit to the game an additional number of those who wished to take part in it.

I am also much interested in the statement made by Mr. Curry, of the pioneer Knickerbocker club, and confirmed by Mr. Tassle, of the famous old Atlantic club of Brooklyn, that a diagram, showing the ball field laid out substantially as it is today, was brought to the field one afternoon by a Mr. Wadsworth. Mr. Curry says "the plan caused a great deal of talk, but finally, we agreed to try it." While he is not quoted as adding that they did both try and adopt it, it is apparent that such was the fact; as, from that day to this, the scheme of the game described by Mr. Curry has been continued with only slight variations in detail. It should be borne in mind that Mr. Curry was the first president of the old Knickerbocker club and participated in drafting the first published rules of the game.

It is possible that a connection more or less direct can be traced between the diagram drawn by Doubleday in 1839 and that presented to the Knickerbocker club by Wadsworth in 1845, or thereabouts, and I wrote several days ago for certain data bearing on this point, but as it has not yet come to hand I have decided to delay no longer sending in the kind of paper your letter calls for; promising to furnish you the indicated data when I obtain it, whatever it may be.

My deductions from the testimony submitted are:

First: That "Base Ball" had its origins in the United States.

Second: That the first scheme for playing it, according to the best evidence obtainable to date, was devised by Abner Doubleday at Cooperstown, N.Y., in 1839.

Yours very truly,
(Signature: A. G. Mills)

We the undersigned members of the Special Base Ball Commission unanimously agree with the decision as expressed and outlined in Mr. A. G. Mills's letter of December 30.

> (Signatures: Morgan Bulkeley,
> Nicholas E. Young, A. Reach, Wright.)

Senator Bulkeley, after affixing his signature, appended the following statement:

> I personally remember as a boy in East Haddam, Conn., before 1846, playing the game of One and Two Old Cat, and remember with great distinctness the early struggles in Brooklyn, N.Y., between the two rival clubs, the Atlantics and Excelsiors, and later the Stars, with Creighton as pitcher. This was some 10 to 15 years before the National organization. I was present, representing the Hartford club, at the formation of what is now the National League at the Grand Central Hotel, Broadway, New York City, about 1875 or 1876, and was its first president, with Nick Young, secretary.

> M. G. Bulkeley.

BATS, BALLS, AND BULLETS: BASEBALL AND THE CIVIL WAR

George B. Kirsch

A terrible tension clouded the early months of 1861. All over a partially divided America, people went about their lives with one eye fixed on the horizon of natural life, looking for signs of what was to be: the breakup of the Union? Peace? War? But life went on, and soon one of the newest but most dependable signs of spring appeared. In dozens of American cities and towns, baseball players set to work preparing their minds, bodies, and—in those days before stadiums, artificial turf, and professional groundskeepers—their grass and dirt playing fields for another season of play.

Then, in mid-April, just as the ball teams were getting warmed up, news of the firing on Fort Sumter in South Carolina sent shock waves through the North and South alike. It was war, time to take up swords and muskets, and lay aside bats and balls—or so it seemed at first. Instead, baseball went to war with the men in blue and gray, changed as they changed, and emerged stronger than ever to help reunite them in their own national game.

Legend assigns a Civil War connection of sorts to the very origins of baseball itself. Abner Doubleday, the Civil War general who some say aimed the first cannon in defense of Fort Sumter and who distinguished himself in the Battle of Gettysburg in 1863, is the central character in the myth of baseball's creation promulgated by the present-day professional baseball league, Major League Baseball, and the National Baseball Hall of Fame in Cooperstown, New York. According to a historical commission headed in 1907, by Abraham Mills, former president of professional baseball's National League, Doubleday invented the modern rules of the game in

George B. Kirsch, "Bats, Balls and Bullets: Baseball and the Civil War," *Civil War Times Illustrated* XXXVI, no. 2 (May 1998): 30–37. Used with permission of the *Civil War Times*. George B. Kirsch, a professor of history at Manhattan College, adapted this article from portions of his book, *The Creation of American Team Sports: Baseball and Cricket, 1838–72* (Champaign: University of Illinois Press, 1989).

1839, at Cooperstown. The tale rests entirely on the testimony of one Abner Graves, who recalled playing ball with Doubleday as a boy in that bucolic town in upstate New York. Albert G. Spalding, the noted baseball luminary and sporting goods magnate, fully endorsed Graves's story at the time but later admitted: "It certainly appeals to an American's pride to have had the great national game of Base Ball created and named by a major general in the United States Army."

Though the Doubleday–Cooperstown myth remains powerful in the American imagination, scholars have long since proven it false. Research has revealed that Doubleday enrolled as a cadet at West Point in the fall of 1838, and possibly never even visited Cooperstown. Although he may have played ball with Graves during his boyhood, in his published writings he never mentioned anything about a role in the creation of baseball. The Mills Commission's conclusion rested entirely on an elderly man's recollection of an event that had occurred 68 years earlier. And Graves's mental capacity at the time of his testimony is suspect; a few years later, he shot his wife and was committed to an institution. Furthermore, Mills had known Doubleday ever since the men served together in the Civil War, but his friend apparently had never said anything about his supposed brainstorm in Cooperstown.

If Abner Doubleday did not invent baseball, then who did? The answer is that no one person created the sport; rather, it evolved in stages from earlier bat-and-ball games, especially rounders, an English game often called "town ball" in the United States. New England varieties of town ball were called "roundball" or "base." The version of the sport that became widely known as the "Massachusetts game" matched sides of eight to 15 men on a square field with bases or tall stakes (as tall as five feet high) at each corner. The batter stood midway between first and fourth (home) base and tried to hit a ball made of yarn tightly wound around a lump of cork or rubber and covered with smooth calfskin. The cylindrical bat varied in length from three to three and a half feet and was often a portion of a rake or pitchfork handle. It normally was held in one hand. The pitcher threw the ball swiftly overhand, and the batter could strike the ball in any direction, there being no foul territory. After hitting the ball, the striker ran around the bases until he was put out or remained safely on a base. He could be retired if the catcher caught three balls he missed, if a fielder caught a ball he hit before it hit the ground, or if a fielder struck him with a thrown ball while he ran the bases (called "soaking" or "burning" the runner). Usually one out ended the inning, and the first team to score a previously agreed upon number of runs won the game.

Though the Massachusetts version of baseball thrived during the late 1850s, it faced a formidable rival in New York City's version of the game, which boomed in popularity after 1857. Modern baseball derives most immediately from the latter, specifically from the game created by the New York Knickerbocker Base Ball Club during the mid-1840s. Some baseball historians believe that a man named Alexander J. Cartwright first suggested that the Knickerbockers try aligning the bases along a diamond instead of a square and placing the batter at home plate. At the very least, Cartwright was the chief organizer of the club and the man responsible for codifying its first rules—namely, that the ball had to be pitched underhand, not overhand; that a ball knocked outside the area bounded by first and third bases was foul; and that a player was out if a ball he hit was caught on the fly or on the first bounce, or if a fielder touched him with the ball as he ran between bases. "Soaking" the runner was prohibited, three outs retired a side from the game, and 21 runs (called "aces") decided the game, provided each side had had an opportunity to make an equal number of outs. The Knickerbockers played their first intraclub games in the Murray Hill section of Manhattan, then moved to the Elysian Fields of Hoboken, New Jersey, in 1846. Their pastime spread very slowly until the late 1850s, when baseball mania swept across the greater New York City region.

At the time hostilities between North and South broke out in 1861, no one knew which form of the game would come to enjoy the greatest popularity, but it was already clear that there were striking parallels between team sports and war. During the late 1850s and early 1860s, the sporting press frequently pointed out the similarities. In wrapping up its review of the 1857 season, a journal called the *New York Clipper* remarked that the players "will be compelled to lay by their weapons of war, enter into winter quarters, there to discuss and lay plans for the proper conducting of next season's campaign." Yet sportswriters were acutely aware of the crucial differences between play and mortal struggle. "God forbid that any balls but those of the Cricket and Baseball field may be caught either on the fly or bound," read a March 1861 *Clipper* article, "and we trust that no arms but those of the flesh may be used to impel them, or stumps, but those of the wickets, injured by them."

After the struggle began, a Rochester reporter noted that "many of our first-class players are now engaged in the 'grand match' against the rebellious 'side,' and have already made a 'score' which, in after years, they will be proud to look upon." Another remarked,

> Cricket and Baseball clubs . . . are now enlisted in a different sort of exercise, the rifle or gun taking the place of the bat, while the play ball gives place to the leaden messenger of death. . . . Men who have heretofore made their mark in friendly strife for superiority in various games are now beating off the rebels who would dismember the glorious "United of States."

In April, a Union soldier encamped with his regiment at Culpeper Court House, Virginia, reported, "If General Grant does not send them to have a match with Gen. Lee, they are willing to have another friendly match, but if he does, the blue coats think that the leaden balls will be much harder to stop than if thrown by friendly hands on the club grounds."

Soldier-athletes also believed that baseball was useful in preparing them for the more deadly contests of the battlefield. The *Rochester Express* noted that with "the serious matter of war . . . upon our hands . . . physical education and the development of muscle should be engendered by indulgence in baseball."

Thousands of Northern baseball club members enlisted in the Union army, and few volunteered for the Confederate cause. The sportsmen who marched off to war took with them their love of play—and sometimes their bats and balls. Military authorities permitted recreation for soldiers at appropriate times and places because it provided useful diversion. The U.S. Sanitary Commission recommended that to preserve the health of soldiers, "when practicable, amusement, sports, and gymnastic exercises should be favored among the men." Baseball was listed among the approved pastimes. Officers encouraged sport to relieve the boredom of camp life. Organized games also helped to motivate men during training, to foster group cohesion and loyalty, and to improve recruits' physical fitness.

The *Clipper* praised the practice of athletic games in camp, noting the "beneficial effect they have on the spirits and health, and how they tend to alleviate the monotony of camp life." The journal also remarked that sports had helped create "a wholesome rivalry between companies and regiments, and augment the *esprit de corps* of the same, to an extent that to those who have not witnessed it would appear marvelous." Baseball was even allowed in certain prison camps. A prominent Southern game, for example, originated at Johnson's Island, Ohio, where inmates learned the New York game while being held in Union forces.

Baseball-playing soldiers improvised makeshift grounds for their games, constructed rudimentary equipment, and arranged contests both in camp and even perilously close to enemy positions. One enthusiast sent the *Clipper* the score of a match played on the parade ground of the "Mozart Regiment Row in Secessia" in October 1861. He wanted to report the sports news to civilians on the home front, "lest you imagine that the 'sacred soil' yields only to the tramp of the soldier; that its hills echo only the booming gun, and the dying shriek." The game, he wrote, totally "erased from their minds all the absorbing topics of the day."

Soldiers played both the Massachusetts and New York versions of the game, arranging pickup games within their own regiments or challenging rival units. According to an often-repeated story, on Christmas 1862, more than 40,000 Union soldiers witnessed an encounter between the 165th New York Infantry and an all-star squad that included future National League president A. G. Mills. While it is possible that the game actually occurred, the size of the crowd had undoubtedly been exaggerated.

Generally, the men sported within the relative security of their encampments, though sometimes they violated army regulations and competed outside their fortifications and beyond their picket lines. George H. Putnam remembered a contest among Union troops in Texas that was aborted by a surprise enemy assault. "Suddenly there came a scattering fire, of which the three fielders caught the brunt," he wrote, "the center field was hit and was captured, the left and right field managed to get into out lines." The Northern soldiers repulsed the Confederate attack, "but we had lost not only our center field but . . . the only baseball in Alexandria."

While baseball enthusiasts enjoyed their favorite sport in army camps, the game suffered some understandable setbacks on the home front. With so many sportsmen off at war, and with civilian anxieties focused on battlefield news, interest in playful contests naturally waned. Yet the sport persisted, and even progressed, under the trying conditions. In a review of the 1861 season in the New York City area, the *Clipper* reported, "The game has too strong a foothold in popularity to be frowned out of favor by the lowering brow of 'grim-visaged war.'"

The New York form of the game gained momentum in New England when a tour by the Brooklyn Excelsiors excited Boston's sporting fraternity. In Philadelphia, baseball overtook cricket in popularity during the early 1860s. Near the end of the war, the Federal capital experienced a baseball revival, thanks in part to resident New Yorkers who worked in the U.S. Treasury Department and played for the National and Union clubs on the grounds behind the White House. In the South, the Union conquest of New Orleans took baseball back deep into Dixie, where the war had virtually snuffed out the sport before it could become firmly established. And in the West, a contingent of "Rocky Mountain Boys" played the New York game in Denver in 1862.

As it was before the war, the Middle Atlantic region was at the core of baseball fever. New York, New Jersey, and Pennsylvania inaugurated the sport's first championship system, as well as several intercity all-star contests and club tours. The early 1860s also ushered in an era of commercialism and professionalism, as William H. Cammeyer of Brooklyn and other entrepreneurs enclosed fields and charged admission fees. Before and during the Civil War, amateur clubs offered various forms of compensation—direct payments, jobs, or gifts—to premier players such as James Creighton and Al Reach. The National Association of Base Ball Players, founded in 1857, continued to supervise interclub play and experiment with the sport's rules, endorsing the New York rules even as the New England game remained popular among soldiers. In 1863, a national sporting weekly edited by a George Wilkes, *Wilkes' Spirit of the Times*, grandly proclaimed, "The National Association game has won for itself the almost unanimous approval of all who take any interest in the sport; and the clubs who adopt any other style of playing are, every day, becoming small by degrees, and beautifully less."

The most striking evidence of baseball's capacity to flourish amid the adversity of war was the first invasion of Philadelphia players into the New York City area, in 1862. When a select "nine" competed before about 15,000 spectators in a series of games against Newark, New York, and Brooklyn teams, *Wilkes' Spirit* reported that the Philadelphia challenges awakened in New York "the old *furore* for the game that marked the years 1857–8 and 9." The paper noted that the victory of the guests over a New York team at Hoboken did more to create interest in the game in that city than five ordinary seasons' play would have done. Teams from Brooklyn and New York returned the visit later in the summer [and] generated excitement in their contests with the local teams: the Olympics, Adriatics, Athletics, and Keystones. The following year the Athletics won two of six games against tough opponents and established themselves as contenders for baseball's championship. By the end of the war, trips by Brooklyn, New York, and New Jersey clubs to Philadelphia were commonplace. Some of the matches were arranged to benefit the U.S. Sanitary Commission.

The tours succeeded despite the atmosphere of crisis that pervaded the entire region so near to the seat of war. In most cases, the war did not detract from the excitement of the contests, and there is little evidence that citizens disapproved of men who played ball instead of serving in the army. Understandably, though, military news sometimes completely overshadowed baseball. When Brooklyn's crack Atlantics swept a series in Philadelphia in August 1864, few fans attended, and there was little additional interest. The *Clipper* explained that the local citizens "were absorbed in the important subject of resisting the rebel invasion of the State, and this and the preparations to respond to the governor's call for 30,000 militia materially interfered with the sensation their visit would otherwise have created." Most of the Philadelphia clubs could not play many of their best men, the journal reported, because they had responded "to the call of duty."

The return of peace to the United States in 1865 ignited a new baseball boom, prompting the *Newark Daily Advertiser* to announce that the sport "is rightfully called the national game of America." Veterans played a key role in spreading the sport around the nation after the war. "When soldiers were off duty," declared the *Clipper* in 1865, "base ball was naturalized in nearly every state in the Union, and thus extended in popularity."

Regional rivalries, tours by prominent clubs, and intersectional matches helped smooth relations between North and South immediately after the Civil War. "Maryland [was] fast being reconstructed on this base-is," punned the *Clipper* in 1865. The game was even taking hold in Richmond, Virginia, the former capital of the Confederacy. "Base ball fever," the *Clipper* reported, "is rapidly assuming the form of an epidemic among the constructed and reconstructed denizens of the former stronghold of the extinct Davisocracy." But the journal followed up this news with a rebuke of the Richmond club for refusing the challenge of that city's Union team, made up mostly of businessmen and federal officials. "We regret to learn of such petty feeling and sectional animosity being evinced by any party of Southern gentlemen calling themselves ballplayers," the journal opined. "Our national game is intended to be national in every sense of the word, and, until this example was set by the Richmond club, nothing of a sectional character has emanated from a single club in the country."

Northern and Southern journalists believed the tours of the great Eastern ball clubs would help heal the bitter wounds of war. When the Nationals of Washington, DC, visited Brooklyn in July 1866, the Excelsiors treated them to a lavish dinner, even though a National Association of Base Ball Players rule prohibited expensive entertainment. The *Clipper* argued that the Brooklynites' extravagance showed Southerners that

> the ballplayers' "policy of reconstruction" is one marked by true fraternal regard, irrespective of all political opinions or sectional feelings, the National Association knowing . . . "no North, no South, no East, no West," but simply the interest and welfare of the game itself, and the cultivation of kindly feelings between the different clubs.

When the Nationals stopped at Louisville in 1867, however, *Wilkes' Spirit* reported, "a crowd of the most unruly partisan boors and rowdy boys" extended the so-called invading Yankees a greeting "not at all in accordance with the reputation for chivalric sentiments which the Southern cities have hitherto claimed." The journal singled out the women spectators for special criticism and urged that sectional feelings be kept out of the game. "The Nationals . . . though from the shores of the Potomac, had too much of the North about them apparently to merit the favor of Southern women," the journal remarked.

During the summer of 1868, the Philadelphia Athletics received a warmer reception in Louisville. For Philadelphia's part, the Pennsylvania city's *Sunday Mercury* defended the Louisville players' gray uniforms, which "had been held up to scorn, and those who wear it denounced as rebels." The paper reported that the choice of uniform color did not necessarily indicate the players had sided with the South in the war, and even if it did, it "had got nothing to do with our national game." The article's author concluded, "If Jefferson Davis . . . was to meet me on the ball field, and salute me as a gentleman, I would endeavor to prove to him that I was one." When a New Orleans newspaper announced the upcoming trip of its Southern Club to Memphis and St. Louis with players who had organized while prisoners of war at Johnson's Island, its editor wondered, along with his Northern counterparts, "would it not be pleasant to see the hatchet buried in the great national game, 'spite of the efforts of politicians to keep up ill feeling between the sections?" *Wilkes' Spirit*, reporting on the New York Mutual Club's December 1869 excursion to New Orleans, observed,

> This national game seems destined to close the national wounds opened by the late war. It is no idle pastime which draws young men, separated by 2,000 miles, together to contest in friendship, upon fields but lately crimsoned with their brothers' blood in mortal combat.

Of course baseball alone could not heal the wounds of the Civil War, but it did help reunite the nation, establishing itself as a popular institution in the social and cultural worlds of the American people. Publicists relished the sport's success and promoted it as a democratic game that offered all classes and ethnic groups an opportunity to play, if not in a stadium, then at least on a sandlot. Baseball had become the national pastime, and the stage was set for the game's glory years—and the glory years of the nation itself.

CHAPTER 2

Baseball Becomes a Business, 1876–1890

Baseball Takes Hold

The National Association had advanced baseball to a point where it was the most popular professional sport in the United States. Baseball was one of the ways Americans defined themselves in the years after the Civil War. Poet Walt Whitman, always searching for the democratic essence of American life, wrote, "Baseball is our game—the American game I connect to our national character." Fellow author Mark Twain put matters in a bolder way. He saw baseball in those years as the "very symbol, the outward and visible expression of all the drive and push and struggle of the raging, tearing, booming nineteenth century."[1] Both men were right—the religion of baseball was being spread by the new telegraph lines, the new sports weeklies, and growing national press to every corner of the nation.

At the same time, professional baseball was in trouble. The National Association was failing not so much as a sport, but as a business. The potential profitability of baseball was not being exploited. Given the commercial bent of the nation in the years after the Civil War, that situation couldn't last for long. With the National Association in trouble, the man who took baseball to a new level stepped in. William Hulbert was a classic example of the nineteenth-century man on the make. A coal dealer, a member of the Chicago Board of Trade, and a fanatical Chicago booster, he once bragged that he would rather be a "lamppost in Chicago than a millionaire anywhere else."[2] Hulbert was jealous of the way eastern interests had dominated professional baseball and wanted to shift the sport's center of gravity to the West and, in the process, bring new levels of prosperity to baseball.

Disgusted by the failings of the National Association and sensing the potential of a reformed baseball league, after the 1875 season Hulbert contacted like-minded businessmen about creating a better-run organization of teams. With the active support of A. G. Spalding, who was interested in exchanging his player's credentials for a more profitable business role, Hulbert convened a meeting in New York in February 1876, to form a new league. This new league would be run by hardheaded businessmen, not players. To make clear that businessmen and not players were running his new organization, he labeled it the National League of Professional Baseball Clubs, soon shortened to just the National League.

To avoid the problems that had plagued the National Association, Hulbert insisted on firm rules on institutional issues. League membership was set at $100 instead of the paltry $10 of the National Association. Scheduling would be handled by the league, not the individual clubs. Any team that failed to fulfill its schedule—one of the curses of the National Association—would be ousted from the league. A side benefit of Hulbert's insistence on fulfilling the schedule was the fact that a real pennant winner would clearly emerge.

The clubs in the new league agreed to honor one another's contracts. In this way it was hoped there would be no more jumping from club to club—then called hippodroming—which had been commonplace in the past.[3] Hippodroming was a serious matter. One player, George Wright, in a four-year period, jumped clubs six times. Only cities with a population base of at least 75,000 could join the new league. To attract a more respectable, middle-class audience, the admission price was set at 50 cents, and to maintain the loyalty of the clubs, the visiting team would receive 30 percent of the gate. To deal with rowdy fan behavior, the sale of alcoholic beverages at the games was banned. As a further demonstration of respectability, no games would be played on Sunday. Any club that failed to abide by these rules would be expelled.

These rules showed that Hulbert was concerned with changing the image of professional baseball. By charging a half-dollar admission, even for those seats along the first-base and third-base lines, called bleaching boards because of their exposure to the sun—thus the origin of the term "bleachers"—and starting the game at 3:30 in the afternoon, Hulbert hoped to keep the number of the rough classes from marring the image of the new league.

To give the new organization added validity, Hulbert ensured that the president of the National League would be an easterner. He picked Morgan Bulkeley, a well-known Republican and a prominent businessman from Connecticut, the owner of the huge Aetna Insurance Company, as the first president of the National League. Bulkeley possessed good political connections. He would later serve as governor and senator from Connecticut, and, at least in the beginning, provided the new league with a positive image. After one year, Bulkeley, while remaining active in baseball, stepped down as president, and Hulbert took over and guided the National League through its difficult early years. Interestingly, Bulkeley was elected as one of the founding members of Baseball's Hall of Fame, while the real architect of the league, Hulbert, wasn't named until 1995.

Hulbert's actions are an almost perfect reflection of the new attitude toward business that flourished in the post–Civil War era—ruthless competition, rationalizing business practices, and a smart emphasis on the bottom line. In his own way, he was simply following the "root hog or die" economic attitude of the era and applying the Social Darwinist principles of John D. Rockefeller and Andrew Carnegie to the business of baseball.

The early years of the National League were rocky. The season lasted from late April to the third week of October and encompassed 70 league games. This provided ample time for exhibitions against local teams, which was a lucrative way for the National League squads to make money during the season. These games were often better attended and more profitable than league games. Part of the way through the initial season, with Hulbert's Chicago White Stockings team holding a commanding lead in the pennant chase, the New York and Philadelphia teams decided to abandon their last western trip. The Philadelphia team had played poorly and was unable to compete with the popularity of the nation's centennial celebration in the city. Hulbert felt it was necessary to uphold the new league's charter, and the two teams representing the two largest cities in the nation were expelled from the National League.

Hulbert's decision crippled the National League by robbing it of the two eastern anchors. But it was a necessary step toward showing that teams would have to abide by the rules. The 1877 and 1878 seasons were a testing time for professional baseball, with Hulbert forced to shift franchises to such marginal cities as Providence or Worcester, Massachusetts, to keep the National League functioning. Few teams showed a profit, partly as a result of the economic depression that began in 1873, and lasted into the early 1880s. To cement the image he wanted his new league to project, Hulbert also struck at one of the major banes of the National Association—throwing games at the behest of gamblers. In 1878, reacting to evidence that four players from the Louisville team had conspired to throw games, he banned them and refused to reinstate them, even when his action doomed the Louisville franchise.

Hulbert died of heart disease in 1882 but by that time the new league had started to prosper. In 1883, New York and Philadelphia returned to the fold. Now at eight teams and with a reasonable balance, the National League entered its first sustained period of prosperity. Arthur Soden, owner of the successful Boston franchise, along with Hulbert, one of the leading figures in the success of the National League, took over as president for one year before passing on the position to A. G. Mills, known as the "Bismarck of Baseball" because of his key role as counsel to Hulbert.

The success of the National League whetted the appetite of other baseball people who believed there were enough talented players available to form a new league. In 1882, just as the National League began to turn a profit, a group led by independent baseball executives in St. Louis, Cincinnati, and New York met and formed a new league, the American Association. One of its founders was Al Spink of St. Louis, who would go on to found the most successful baseball publication in history, the *Sporting News*, long self-proclaimed as the "Bible of Baseball." Starting with six teams in key baseball towns like Philadelphia, New York, and Baltimore, the American Association went into head-to-head competition with the National League. It had certain advantages, one of which was the fact that its teams represented a larger population base than the National League.

The American Association teams played an 80-game schedule, which meant plenty of lucrative exhibition games. The association's owners took a more liberal attitude toward the social and entertainment side of baseball. Unlike the National League, they agreed to serve alcohol at their games. They also played Sunday baseball and charged a low admission price of 25 cents. Largely because of these changes, the new league drew larger crowds than the National League, which got the older leagues' attention. One of the key franchises was created in St. Louis, called the Brown Stockings or simply the Browns, and run by an eccentric saloonkeeper and baseball enthusiast, Chris von der Ahe. Von der Ahe, a forerunner of such baseball showmen as Bill Veeck, knew next to nothing about baseball. He loved being the head of his team, known as "Der Poss Bresident," and set out to win fans by entertaining them. He set up a beer garden at his ballpark, would put on circus shows at the games, and would even conduct the team's band. After every game, pushing a wheelbarrow with the day's receipts, he led a group of cheering fans to the bank.

The American Association was a success, attesting to the popularity of baseball in the 1880s and the prosperity of the decade. Its success also attracted the attention of the National League owners, who decided the best approach would be to negotiate some kind of agreement. At a time when jumping from team to team was still common, the existence of two leagues gave players leverage to force salary increases, something the businessmen running baseball feared would jeopardize their profits. Meetings between leaders of the two leagues in February 1883 led to the signing of a peace treaty. This so-called National Agreement required each club to respect one another's contracts and established a minimum salary of $1,000 for its players. The two leagues agreed to compromise on their differences because of the establishment of yet a third league, the Union League, for the 1884 season.

The Union League was an attempt to cash in on the prosperity baseball had achieved to this point. The new league was poorly financed and badly administered, with franchises in bad sites, like Altoona, which had a limited population, and Washington, DC, which had yet to show it was a big-league baseball city. After one season, the new league collapsed. One by-product of this competition for players was a groundbreaking decision to expand the reservation of players under contract. This so-called reserve clause would be considered one of the keys to the success of baseball during the next century and would also serve as one of the game's most controversial elements.[4]

BASEBALL'S FIRST GOLDEN AGE

The idea of reserving the services of players to one team emerged in the late 1870s, as a way to stop jumping, which had a tendency to drive up players' salaries. Teams had used the blacklist as a way of controlling players who jumped; however, given the impact competition had on team profits, some owners would sign jumpers despite promises to honor the blacklist. In the late 1870s, Arthur Soden had floated the idea of writing a reservation into the players' contracts.[5] This "reserve clause" would be automatically renewed from season to season unless the player retired or was released by his club. The idea caught on. Beginning in 1879, at a time when teams carried approximately 15 players, each team would be allowed to reserve the rights to five players. Within a short period of time, the number was expanded to 11 and, finally, in 1889, written into every player's contract.

One of the reasons the National League eagerly sought a compromise with the American Association was that the new league threatened to sign its players. The reserve clause showed how the baseball owners reflected the business mentality of the times. Despite the talk of Darwinist rugged competition bringing out the best in everyone, baseball owners, like businessmen throughout the nation, sought to control costs by mergers. Professional baseball was becoming a cartel where the owners regulated every aspect of the business side of the sport. At the heart of this cartelization was the reserve clause. Initially, players didn't recognize its significance—some even regarded it as a source of pride—but it didn't take them long to understand that they had been reduced to something like pampered serfs. As long as the game was prosperous and salaries slowly rose, baseball players were content, but when hard times came and the baseball clubs sought to contain costs, the players would attempt to revolt. In essence, the foundation of the owner's power was the reserve clause and the reason why, in the future, they wouldn't consider any revision of it.

There was little protest during the decade of the 80s about economic issues in baseball because the sport was enjoying a period of sustained prosperity. It is not by accident that some historians have called these years baseball's first "Golden Age." Baseball clubs were uniformly prosperous during the 1880s. In

1889, it was estimated that professional baseball grossed $750,000, an enormous sum for those days and one that dwarfed the income of any other sport in the nineteenth century. Players' wages rose slowly until the average reached $1,600 per year, with some stars, like Cap Anson and Mike "King" Kelly, earning more than $5,000.

Foreshadowing what would become common in the future, baseball players and some other sports celebrities were able to earn extra money endorsing products, usually tobacco. At the same time, many players worked during the offseason, a phenomenon that persisted in baseball until the big contracts of the 1970s transformed the salary structure. Players drifted to such unskilled jobs as bartenders, pool hall attendants, carpenters, and teamsters. By the 1880s, an industrial worker's wage averaged about $650 a year. With baseball players able to make three times that income, even though a career barely exceeded an average of six years, it is no wonder many young men wanted to play baseball and saw the game as an excellent opportunity for upward mobility.

A consequence of the increasing professionalism of baseball was a startling rise in the quality of play. The decade of the 1880s produced the modern game as played today. The 1880s were perhaps the most innovative years in baseball history. A list of the most significant changes introduced easily demonstrates this. The first postseason playoff series were played in the 1880s. Pitchers were allowed to throw overhand, which changed the nature of the game forever. Overhand pitches could be delivered with greater speed, and the ball could be made to move in different ways. Practically every recognizable pitch thrown today was being used by the end of the 1880s: curveballs, sliders (then often called nickel curves), changeups, and even screwballs. To balance offense and defense, the pitcher's mound, then really a box, was moved back five feet to 50 feet. A walk was finally defined as four balls. Batters could no longer signal where they wanted the pitch thrown. Teams used the hit-and-run play in the 1880s, contrary to the view that it was introduced by the famous Baltimore Orioles team of the 1890s. Just about every defensive player now wore a glove. Even if skimpy by modern standards, gloves brought about a decline in errors and better defense in general. Defense also was stressed, and the infielders now tended to play where they are positioned in today's game. Such concepts as fielders backing up one another and the use of relays from the outfield became commonplace. Artistically, baseball was rapidly becoming the beautiful, even scientific, game that won the hearts of American fans.[6]

Some idea of how "modern" the game of the 1880s was can be attained by comparing batting and pitching averages in the span of a century. In 1887, the ERA in the American Association was 4.29. The association batting average was .273. For the National League that year, the figures were comparable: 4.05 and .261, respectively. A century later, similar statistics prevailed. For the National

League, they were 4.08 and .261, for the American League, 4.46 and .265. There is no greater commentary on how the game had modernized in the 1880s than those figures. No other sport could show that kind of consistency during a century of play.

The eight years after the founding of the American Association in 1882 saw baseball rise to new levels of popularity. Generally, most clubs made a profit in the 1880s, sums that in the late nineteenth century would be considered enormous. The rivalry of the two leagues, despite often-bitter disputes, brought out the competitive best in the game. The postseason meeting of the league champions, for instance, proved successful, even if the games were played with something approaching a war. The American Association owners, in particular, wanted to show that their brand of baseball was clearly superior. To ensure real competition, the players were guaranteed extra pay for playing. Chris von der Ahe, in 1886, gave his share of the proceeds, $15,000, to the players. Played every year from 1884 to 1890, the postseason series increased interest in baseball. The National League prevailed in four of the series, with the American Association winning two. One series, in 1890, ended in a tie. The concept would be revived again in the 1890s and then come into full fruition in 1903.

Given the coverage provided to baseball by the newspapers and the popularity of various sports publications, baseball in the 1880s truly became the national game, followed avidly by fans in every part of the country. One by-product of that was the creation of the first true sports superstars. The sport had few rivals for popularity. In John L. Sullivan, boxing had produced the first sports hero widely known throughout the country after he was recognized as the heavyweight champion of the world in 1882. Boxing's reputation for violence and roughness limited its potential as a sport. Other heroes, like Buffalo Bill or General Custer, came from outside the world of sport. Baseball, which had grown up with the country, now reached a wide audience and began to focus on its best players.

Baseball players were lionized as never before in the 1880s. Probably the most popular player of the decade, and the one deserving the epithet of "superstar," was Adrian "Cap" Anson. A rugged six-footer, he played professional baseball for 22 years. He was the first player to accumulate 3,000 hits and ended his career with a lifetime batting average of .334. He managed for 19 years and was a brilliant innovator, using such concepts as instituting spring training to tutor his players, rotating his pitchers, and making use of various signals to move his players around. His hitting prowess and commanding demeanor made him a hero in baseball circles.

Unfortunately, there is a darker side to Anson's reputation. He played a key role in segregating baseball. In 1883, he threatened to take his team off the field if his opponents, the Toledo team, fielded an African American player.

Anson was a catalyst of the move to ban African Americans from professional baseball. That didn't mean African Americans ceased playing baseball. They formed their own teams and played exhibitions as a way of making money. In 1887, the last year African Americans played in the white leagues, a colored league was organized with teams in those cities with large African American populations, in New York, Philadelphia, and Baltimore, among others. The league quickly collapsed, but it was the forerunner of attempts to create African American baseball on par with the major leagues. This was one of the many efforts by the African American community, forced by segregation, to organize a parallel society to white America. By the end of the decade, it was clear that baseball had followed the rest of the nation in adopting a strict policy of segregation.[7]

If Anson was the face of professional baseball in the 1880s, the most popular and unusual player was Mike "King" Kelly. At 5-foot-10, 170 pounds, he was a rawboned, immensely talented player who possessed that indefinable quality, charisma. Fast and quick, he played in the major leagues for 16 years. His best seasons were with Chicago, where he won two batting titles, one with a .388 average. But what set him apart was his flair for baseball—and unfortunately for life. He loved to run the bases, and as soon as he got on first, fans would start cheering, "Slide, Kelly, slide," as he took off for second. He is credited with inventing the hook slide as a way of avoiding the fielder's tag. But like a great deal of early baseball, this is probably more myth than reality. What is real is that he was sold to Boston in 1887, for the then-unheard-of sum of $10,000. There, he was an instant hero to the large Irish community. He made $5,000 at his peak but ended his career because of baseball's greatest curse of the nineteenth century: alcoholism. He died at 37, the first but not the last of the great baseball players to fall victim to alcoholism.

An interesting commentary on Kelly's popularity, as well as that of John L. Sullivan, is that it came at a time when there was a strong anti-Irish and anti-Catholic bias in the country. The last two decades of the nineteenth century saw the rise of a powerful nativist movement, the American Protective Society, which was determined to end Catholic influence in the United States and specifically targeted Irish Catholics because of their large numbers in the major cities of the nation. The popularity of Irish athletes like Kelly and Sullivan helped undermine this anti-Catholic sentiment, as did the record of success of many Irish in baseball, where they became prominent in the 1880s and 1890s. Baseball proved a convenient avenue for acceptance in the United States, a process that would later pan out for other immigrant groups—Italians, Jews, and Poles—as they entered the country.[8]

If you created an all-star team from the ranks of the great players of the 1880s, that team would be a match of the best in baseball history. First basemen

Dan Brouthers, Roger Connor and outfielders Peter Browning (who is associated with the development of the Louisville Slugger bat) and Sam Thompson would be stars in any era. The same is true, if not more so, with regard to the great pitchers: John Clarkson, Pud Galvin, and Tim Keefe, all of whom won 300 games. Buck Ewing set the standard for catchers for years and is often credited with being the first to use the crouch. All were lionized by the fans of the 1880s and have been named to the Hall of Fame.

A testament to baseball's popularity in the last years of the nineteenth century was the amazing success of the poem "Casey at the Bat." Written by a Harvard graduate, Ernest Lawrence Thayer, the poem first appeared in William Randolph Hearst's paper, the *San Francisco Examiner*, in June 1888. But the poem got its start as the most famous sport ballad in American history when monologist De Wolf Hopper recited it for a crowd of players from the Chicago White Stockings and New York Giants two months later.

"Casey at the Bat" is a classic example of the ballads that captured the nation's attention in the days before the movies, radio, or television. Like "The Face on the Bar Room Floor," "The Shooting of Dan McGrew," and the tale of Paul Bunyan, it enthralled the nation. The poem cleverly captured the baseball craze gripping the nation with its evocation of the hopes of fans and the ultimate letdown when "mighty Casey has struck out." Hopper recited it over and over again for the rest of his life. There is even an early talking film version in which the aged Hopper recited "Casey" in the late 1920s.

Thayer, who got the grand sum of $5 for his poem, came to detest it, telling anyone who asked that he never wanted to be reminded of it. An interesting sidelight on the huge success of the poem is the large number of Irish names of the players mentioned, clearly a reflection of the Gaelic influence on baseball at the time. There has been an attempt to identify the "mighty Casey." Thayer never revealed who it was, but given that he was from Boston and Mike Kelly played there in 1887–1888, and fit the image of the braggart Casey, it is a safe guess he was the model.[9]

BASEBALL TURNS MILITANT

The National League and American Association lived in uneasy peace because both organizations prospered during the 1880s. A sure sign of baseball's prosperity was the construction of new, more elaborate ballparks. Chicago's Lakefront Park was able to hold 10,000 spectators. The Polo Grounds, in New York, was constructed in an oval format, which would distinguish it throughout its long history, and it became a popular gathering spot in New York. The most impressive of the new ballparks was built in Philadelphia by A. J. Reach for more than $100,000 in 1887. It was the first to be constructed of brick and reinforced steel, and was used by the Phillies for more than 50 years.[10]

Despite their solid financial standing, some of the more aggressive owners in the National League were looking for a way to undermine their rivals and get control of the best players in the American Association. After the collapse of the Union League, baseball owners got together and decided to limit the top salary paid to any player at $2,000, as one way of controlling costs. That same year, a group of the game's best-known players, including such stars as Roger Connor, Tim Keefe, and Buck Ewing, met to organize what would become known as the "Brotherhood of Professional Base Ball Players." They elected John Montgomery Ward, the driving force behind the movement, as their president.

Ward was careful to avoid using the word "union" to describe his organization, given the negative view of unions as conspiracies in the late nineteenth century. Brotherhood had a friendly quality to it. Ward was a talented shortstop and, unusual for his time, a lawyer with a degree from Columbia. The organization claimed 200 members, although the real figure was somewhere between 70 and 120. Ward wanted the Brotherhood to present a united front in dealing with the owners with regard to salary issues and the blacklisting of players.

At first, relations between the Players Association and the owners were positive, but the players won few concessions. Then, in 1888 A. G. Spalding organized a tour to show the world America's new game of baseball. Accompanied by some of the best players in the game, one of whom was Ward, Spalding barnstormed the western United States, crossed the Pacific, and played games in India, Ceylon, and Egypt, where they staged a game near the Sphinx. The tour then moved on to Italy, France, and England, among other places. Spalding had an ulterior purpose. As the leading manufacturer of sporting goods, he hoped to find new markets for his products, succeeding in Australia, where he eventually opened three stores. The tour was an artistic success but also a financial failure, with just about everyone losing money. A banquet at Delmonico's restaurant in New York for the returning players heralded the tour, in classic nineteenth-century nationalist terms, as yet another example of American greatness.[11] This wouldn't be the last time the baseball magnates tried to show the American game to the world.

After the 1913 season, a group of players from the two leagues undertook another tour to expose baseball to the uninitiated, playing games in Asia, the Middle East, and Italy, and ending up with a game in London in front of a large crowd, including King George V. The tour was an artistic success and made some money for the players and owners. The teams returned home shortly before the outbreak of World War I aboard the liner RMS *Lusitania*, which would meet a sad fate the next year. These tours and others like them reflected a combination of naivete and chauvinism. Just seeing the American game played would win new fans throughout the world. It didn't work that way. None of the baseball tours created a new home for a game that was as uniquely American as crackers, cowboys, and the Liberty Bell.

During the course of the tour, the National League owners, now commonly referred to as "magnates," testifying to the big-business side of baseball, decided to institute a new set of rules, especially as related to salaries. They created a scale devised by John Brush, one of the most aggressive of the baseball owners. The Brush scale set up five categories for the players, with the highest pay being set at $2,500, and then four further declining steps at $250 intervals. It was the way labor relations were conducted at a time when workers had little or no bargaining power. The Brush plan outraged the players.[12]

With player anger growing throughout the 1889 season, Ward reacted by approaching businessmen who wanted to cash in on this lucrative sport. The leader of the group was a prosperous traction magnate, Albert L. Johnson of Cleveland. In just a few months, Johnson and Ward organized a new league that would challenge the existing structure of baseball on the grounds that the National League and American Association had "broken faith" with the ballplayers. Spalding, speaking for the owners, branded the Brotherhood an "oath bound, secret organization of strikers."[13] Arguing that there were millions to be made in baseball, Johnson had no difficulty lining up other businessmen to support the new baseball organization, which was christened the Players League. The new league also promised a better brand of baseball and a fairer deal for the players. Each player was given a contract for three years based on their 1889 salary. The reserve clause would not operate, and players would be guaranteed a role in all baseball playing and financial decisions. To keep owners and players happy, gate receipts would be shared on a 50–50 basis.

Teams were placed in those cities where baseball had proven popular and where the new league could confront the older leagues with a direct challenge. Ward targeted the National League as the stronger of the two baseball organizations and as a way of keeping the American Association quiet. He hoped the baseball establishment would accept the Players League and negotiate a fairer contract as a way of keeping their players. The baseball establishment was outraged, labeling the Players League as an example of "outlaw" baseball. They were shocked when some 90 players jumped to the new league, notably such prominent figures as Connie Mack, Charles Comiskey, and Ed Delahanty.

The strategy of the National League owners, led by Spalding, was to accuse the Players League of trying to create a union, widely seen as an un-American idea. By harping on the union concept and accusing Ward and his people of going on strike against baseball, Spalding was capitalizing on the fear of labor that prevailed in the late nineteenth century. The 1880s had witnessed a series of violent episodes, of which the Haymarket Affair in 1886 and the Molly Maguire attacks on coal mine owners were the most famous. Linking the players to strikers was a shrewd move on Spalding's part and helped undermine sympathy for the new league. Some of the magnates threatened to sue the players for breach of contract, although this was seen as being potentially dangerous given the nature of the baseball contract in which there was no mutuality of rights. A club could cancel a player's contract with just 10 days' notice, while a player was bound to the club by the reserve clause for life.

The Players League confronted baseball with its first existential crisis. The events of 1884 had shown that there wasn't enough talent or money to conduct three leagues. Now, despite baseball turning a sizeable profit, another challenge by a third league might bring about economic doom for everyone. The idea of a players' revolt and the challenge of a third league was followed avidly by sports fans and given extensive coverage in the growing number of sports publications, often with the same kind of emotional response that characterized the 1981 and 1994 baseball strikes. The 1890 season was a disaster for the business of baseball. The three leagues often went head-to-head in the same cities, scheduling games at the same time. Just about everyone lost money, and it was clear before the season was half over that the Players League would not survive. In the fall, the Players League owners sued for peace. Negotiations dragged on, with some of the Players League owners being allowed to buy into or merge with existing clubs. Any idea of punishing the players was dropped because they were seen as too value a commodity. Players returned to their former clubs on various terms. The reserve clause was restored.[14]

The real victor in this disaster for baseball was the National League. As the older and better administered of the two major leagues, the National League survived the collapse of the Players League. The American Association, even though it lost fewer players to the upstart league, was seriously weakened. Its base was much weaker than the National League to start with. Teams in places like Louisville, Columbus, Rochester, and Syracuse could not compete with the National League, which, by 1890, had solidified its position in urban areas with large populations: New York, Brooklyn (not yet incorporated into New York), Philadelphia, Chicago, and Boston.

A dispute between the two surviving leagues concerning the rights to players released when the Players League disbanded led to yet another conflict during the 1891 season. The American Association, already weakened by the Players League challenge, threatened to move teams into National League cities. After the 1891 season, they withdrew from the National Agreement and sought to sign National League players. Economically, both leagues suffered in 1891. Jumping, the curse of baseball in the past, was back, but this time the National League was strong enough to withstand a challenge. Peace talks began during the season, and it was decided that the two leagues would merge into a single 12-team organization. The four strongest American Association teams, Baltimore, Washington, St. Louis, and Louisville, joined the expanded league, now named the National League and American Association of Professional Base Ball Clubs. The players left over from the four collapsed American Association teams were gobbled up cheaply by the remaining clubs.

Professional baseball had survived its first real crisis with the sport intact, but the price was high. For the first, but not last, time, baseball had broken faith with its fans. The owners had shown who ran the game and revealed once and for all that baseball was a business, as well as the most popular form of sports entertainment in the country.

Questions for Consideration

1. What was the significance for the United States of the growing professionalization of baseball in the last quarter of the nineteenth century?
2. Discuss the role played by William Hulbert and A. G. Spalding in gaining recognition for baseball as America's most popular sport.
3. How did baseball in the late nineteenth century reflect some of the ethnic changes occurring in the United States? What role did sport play in helping to create an American identity for these groups?
4. How did baseball deal with the issue of race in the United States in the years after the Civil War?
5. Why did the National League succeed in the 1880s when other baseball leagues failed? Why was it able to prevail over the Union League, Players League, and American Association?
6. Discuss John Montgomery Ward's plan for the Players League. Why did it ultimately fail?
7. Make the connection between baseball and economic developments in the United States in the years after the Civil War. How did baseball reflect these economic changes?
8. Why was the concept of the reserve clause so important for the development of baseball from the 1870s onward? Was it necessary for the growth and expansion of professionalism in baseball?

Notes

1. The Whitman quote is a paraphrase of what he wrote about baseball's future in the United States. It is quoted in the film *Bull Durham* by the character played by Susan Sarandon. The Mark Twain quote comes from Lewis Carlson, "The Universal Athletic Sport of the World," *American History Illustrated* 19, no. 2 (April 1984): 37.

2. William E. Akin, "Hulbert, William Ambrose," in David L. Porter, ed., *Biographical Dictionary of American Sports: Baseball*, 3 vols. (Westport, CT: Greenwood Press, 2000), 716.

3. Michael Haupert, "William Hulbert and the Birth of the National League," *Baseball Research Journal* 44, no. 1 (Spring 2015): 83–92.

4. Harold Seymour, *Baseball: The Early Years* (New York: Oxford University Press, 1960) discusses the development of the idea of the reserve clause.

5. Frederick Ivor-Campbell, "Arthur Soden," *Baseball's First Stars* (Cleveland, OH: Society for American Baseball Research, 1996).

6. For the innovative changes in baseball, see Peter Morris, *A Game of Inches: The Stories behind the Innovations That Shaped Baseball* (Chicago: Ivan R. Dee, 2006).

7. Jerry Malloy, "Out at Home: Baseball Draws the Color Line," *National Pastime: A Review of Baseball History* 4 (Spring 1985): 15–30, and Jerry Malloy, ed., *Sol White's History of Colored Baseball* (Lincoln: University of Nebraska Press, 1995).

8. John Rossi, "Early Irish Influences on the Development of Baseball," *Eire/Ireland* (Summer 1988).

9. T. P. Coffin, *The Old Ball Game: Baseball in Fact and Fiction* (New York: Herder and Herder, 1971); Charles O'Brien, ed., *American Ballads: Naughty, Ribald, and Classic* (New York: Red Seal, 1952).

10. Philip Lowry, *Green Cathedrals* (New York: Walker and Company, 2006).

11. Peter Levine, "Business, Missionary Motives behind the 1888–1889 World Tour," *Baseball Research Journal* 13 (1984): 60–63, covers the tour in depth.

12. John Thorn, *Baseball in the Garden of Eden: The Secret History of the Early Game* (New York: Simon & Schuster, 2011).

13. Seymour, *Baseball*, 226–27.

14. A good overview of the Players League dispute can be found in Leonard Koppett, *Koppett's Concise History of Major League Baseball* (Philadelphia: Temple University Press, 1998).

OUT AT HOME:
BASEBALL DRAWS THE COLOR LINE

Jerry Malloy

The year 1887 was a watershed year for both the International League and organized baseball, as it marked the origin of the color line. As the season opened, the
black player had plenty of reason to hope he would be able to ply his trade in an
atmosphere of relative tolerance; by the middle of the season, however, he would
watch helplessly as the IL drew up a written color ban designed to deprive him of
his livelihood; and by the time the league held its offseason meetings, it became
obvious that Jim Crow was closing in on a total victory.

Yet before baseball became the victim of its own prejudice, there was a period of uncertainty and fluidity, however brief, during which it seemed by no means
inevitable that men would be denied access to organized baseball due solely to
skin pigmentation. It was not an interlude of total racial harmony, but a degree
of toleration obtained that would become unimaginable in just a few short years.
This is the story of a handful of black baseball players who, in the span of a single
season, playing in a prestigious league, witnessed the abrupt conversion of hope
and optimism into defeat and despair. These men, in the most direct and personal
manner, would realize that the black American baseball player soon would be
ruled "out at home."

I

The International League is the oldest minor league in organized baseball. Founded
in 1884, as the "Eastern" League, it would be realigned and renamed frequently

Jerry Malloy, "Out at Home: Baseball Draws the Color Line," *National Pastime: A Review of Baseball
History* 2 (Fall 1983): 81–83. Edited and published with permission of the Society for American Baseball
Research. Special thanks to Celia Tan.

during its early period. The IL was not immune to the shifting sands of financial support that plagued both the minor and major leagues (not to mention individual franchises) during the nineteenth century. In 1887, the league took the risk of adding Newark and Jersey City to a circuit that was otherwise clustered in upstate New York and southern Ontario. This arrangement proved to be financially unworkable. Transportation costs alone would doom the experiment after one season. The New Jersey franchises were simply too far away from Binghamton, Buffalo, Oswego, Rochester, Syracuse, and Utica in New York, and Hamilton and Toronto in Ontario.

But, of course, no one knew this when the 1887 season opened. Fans in Newark were particularly excited, because their "Little Giants" were a new team and an instant contender. A large measure of their eager anticipation was due to the unprecedented "color battery" signed by the team. The pitcher was George Stovey, and the catcher was Moses Fleetwood Walker.

"Fleet" Walker was born in Mt. Pleasant, Ohio, on the route of the Underground Railroad, on October 7, 1857. The son of a physician, he was raised in nearby Steubenville. At the age of 20 he entered the college preparatory program of Oberlin College, the first school in the United States to adopt an official admissions policy of nondiscrimination by sex, race, or creed. He was enrolled as a freshman in 1878, and attended Oberlin for three years. He was a good but not outstanding student in a rigorous liberal arts program. Walker also attended the University of Michigan for two years, although probably more for his athletic than scholastic attainments. He did not obtain a degree from either institution, but his educational background was extremely sophisticated for a nineteenth-century professional baseball player of whatever ethnic origin.

While at Oberlin, Walker attracted the attention of William Voltz, former sportswriter for the Cleveland *Plain Dealer*, who had been enlisted to form a professional baseball team to be based in Toledo. Walker was the second player signed by the team, which entered the Northwestern League in 1883. Toledo captured the league championship in its first year.

The following year Toledo was invited to join the American Association, a major rival of the more established National League. Walker was one of the few players to be retained as Toledo made the jump to the big league. Thus did Moses Fleetwood Walker become the first to play Major League Baseball, 64 years before Jackie Robinson. Walker played in 42 games that season, batting .263 in 152 at-bats. His brother, Welday Wilberforce Walker, who was two years younger than Fleet, also played outfield in five games, filling in for injured players. Welday was 4-for-18 at the plate.

While at Toledo, Fleet Walker was the batterymate of Hank O'Day, who later became a famous umpire, and Tony Mullane, who could pitch with either hand and became the winningest pitcher, with 285 victories, outside the Hall of Fame. G. L. Mercereau, the team's batboy, many years later recalled the sight of Walker catching barehanded, as was common in those days, with his fingers split open and bleeding. Catchers would welcome swelling in their hands to provide a cushion against the pain.

The color of Walker's skin occasionally provoked another, more lasting, kind of pain. The Toledo *Blade*, on May 5, 1884, reported that Walker was "hissed . . . and insulted . . . because he was colored," causing him to commit five errors in a game in Louisville. Late in the season the team travelled to Richmond, Virginia, where manager Charley Morton received a letter threatening bloodshed, according to Lee Allen, by "75 determined men [who] have sworn to mob Walker if he comes on the ground in a suit." The letter, which Morton released to the press, was signed by four men who were "determined" not to sign their real names. Confrontation was avoided, for Walker had been released by the team due to his injuries before the trip to Richmond.

Walker started the 1885 season with Cleveland in the Western League, but the league folded in June. He played the remainder of 1885 and all of 1886 for the Waterbury, Connecticut, team in the Eastern League. While at Waterbury, he was referred to as "the people's choice" and was briefly managed by Charley Hackett, who later moved on to Newark. When Newark was accepted into the International League in 1887, Hackett signed Walker to play for him.

So, in 1887, Walker was beginning his fifth season in integrated professional baseball. Tall, lean, and handsome, the 30-year-old catcher was an established veteran noted for his steady, dependable play and described, literally, as a gentleman and a scholar. Later in the season, when the Hamilton *Spectator* printed a disparaging item about "the coon catcher of the Newarks," the *Sporting News* ran a typical response in defense of Walker: "It is a pretty small paper that will publish a paragraph of that kind about a member of a visiting club, and the man who wrote it is without doubt Walker's inferior in education, refinement, and manliness."

One of the reasons that Charley Hackett was so pleased to have signed Walker was that his catcher would assist in the development of one of his new pitchers, a Negro named George Washington Stovey. A 165-pound southpaw, Stovey had pitched for Jersey City in the Eastern League in 1886. Sol White, in his *History of Colored Baseball*, stated that Stovey "struck out 22 of the Bridgeport [Connecticut] Eastern League team in 1886 and lost his game." The *Sporting News* that year called Stovey "a good one, and if the team would support him they would make a far better showing. His manner of covering first from the box is wonderful."

A dispute arose between the Jersey City and Newark clubs prior to the 1887 season concerning the rights to sign Stovey. One of the directors of the Jersey City team tried to use his leverage as the owner of Newark's Wright Street grounds to force Newark into surrendering Stovey. But, as the *Sporting Life* Newark correspondent wrote, "On sober second thought I presume he came to the conclusion that it was far better that the [Jersey City] club should lose Stovey than that he should lose the rent of the grounds."

Newark planned to mute Stovey's "headstrong obstinance" with the easygoing stability of Fleet Walker. That the strategy did not always work is indicated by an account in the Newark *Daily Journal* of a July game against Hamilton:

> That Newark won the game [14–10] is a wonder, for Stovey was very wild at times, [and] Walker had several passed balls. . . . Whether it was that he did not think he was being properly supported, or did not like the umpire's decisions on balls and strikes, the deponent saith not, but Stovey several times displayed his temper and fired the ball at the plate regardless of what was to become of everything that stood before him. Walker got tired of the business after awhile and showed it plainly by his manner. Stovey should remember that the spectators do not like to see such exhibitions of temper, and it is hoped that he will not offend again.

Either despite or because of his surly disposition, George Stovey had a great season in 1887. His 35 wins is a single-season record that still stands in the International League. George Stovey was well on his way to establishing his reputation as the greatest Negro pitcher of the nineteenth century.

The promotional value of having the only all-Negro battery in organized baseball was not lost upon the press. Newspapers employed various euphemisms of the day for "Negro" to refer to Newark's "colored," "Cuban," "Spanish," "mulatto," "African," and even "Arabian" battery.

The Newark correspondent for *Sporting Life* asked, "By the way, what do you think of our 'storm battery,' Stovey and Walker? Verily they are dark horses and ought to be a drawing card. No rainchecks given when they play." Later he wrote that, "Our 'Spanish beauties,' Stovey and Walker, will make the biggest kind of drawing card." Drawing card they may have been, but Stovey and Walker were not signed by Newark for promotional gimmickry, but because they were talented athletes who could help their team win.

Nor were other teams reluctant to improve themselves by hiring black players. . . . For Buffalo had retained the services of Frank Grant, the greatest black baseball player of the nineteenth century.

Frank Grant was beginning the second of a record three-consecutive years on the same integrated baseball team. Born in 1867, he began his career in his hometown of Pittsfield, Massachusetts, then moved on to Plattsburgh, New York. In 1886, he entered organized baseball, playing for Meriden, Connecticut, in the Eastern League until the team folded in July. Thereupon, he and two white teammates signed with the Buffalo Bisons, where he led the team in hitting. By the age of 20, Grant was already known as "the Black Dunlap," a singularly flattering sobriquet referring to Fred "Sure Shot" Dunlap, the first player to sign for $10,000 a season, and acknowledged as the greatest second baseman of his era. Sol White called Frank Grant "the greatest ballplayer of his age," without reference to race.

In 1887, Grant would lead the International League in hitting with a .366 average. Press accounts abound with comments about his fielding skills, especially his extraordinary range. After a series of preseason exhibition games against Pittsburgh's National League team, "Hustling Horace" Phillips, the Pittsburgh manager, complained about Buffalo's use of Grant as a "star." The Rochester *Union* quoted Phillips as saying that, "This accounts for the amount of ground [Grant] is allowed to cover . . . and no attention is paid to such a thing as running all over another man's territory." Criticizing an infielder for his excessive range smacks of praising with faint damns. Grant's talent and flamboyance made him popular not only in Buffalo, but also throughout the IL.

In 1890, Grant would play his last season on an integrated team for Harrisburg, Pennsylvania, of the Eastern Interstate League. His arrival was delayed by several weeks due to a court battle with another team over the right to his services. The Harrisburg *Patriot* described Grant's long-awaited appearance:

> Long before it was time for the game to begin, it was whispered around the crowd that Grant would arrive on the 3:20 train and play third base. Everybody was anxious to see him come, and there was a general stretch of necks toward the new bridge, all being eager to get a sight at the most famous colored ballplayer in the business. At 3:45 o'clock an open carriage was seen coming over the bridge with two men in it. Jim Russ's famous trotter was drawing it at a 2:20 speed, and as it approached nearer, the face of Grant was recognized as being one of the men. "There he comes," went through the crowd like magnetism, and three cheers went up. Grant was soon in the players' dressing room, and in five minutes he appeared on the diamond in a Harrisburg uniform. A great shout went up from the immense crowd to receive him, in recognition of which he politely raised his cap.

Fred Dunlap should have been proud had he ever been called "the White Grant." Yet Grant in his later years passed into such obscurity that no one knew where or when he died (last year an obituary in the New York *Age* was located, revealing that Grant had died in New York on June 5, 1937).

Meanwhile, in Binghamton, Bud Fowler, had spent the winter working in a local barbershop. At age 33, Fowler was the elder statesman of Negro ballplayers. In 1872, only one year after the founding of the first professional baseball league, Bud Fowler was playing professionally for a white team in New Castle, Pennsylvania. Lee Allen, while historian of baseball's Hall of Fame, discovered that Fowler, whose real name was John Jackson, was born in Cooperstown, New York, in about 1854, the son of itinerant hops-pickers. Thus, Fowler was the greatest baseball player to be born at the future site of the Hall of Fame.

As was the case with many minor-league players of his time, Fowler's career took him hopscotching across the country. In 1884 and 1885, he played for teams in Stillwater, Minnesota; Keokuk, Iowa; and Pueblo, Colorado. He played the entire 1886 season in Topeka, Kansas, in the Western League, where he hit .309. A Negro newspaper in Chicago, the *Observer*, proudly described Fowler as "the best second baseman in the Western League."

Binghamton signed Fowler for 1887. The *Sportsman's Referee* wrote that Fowler "has two joints where an ordinary person has one. Fowler is a great ballplayer." According to *Sporting Life's* Binghamton correspondent:

> Fowler is a dandy in every respect. Some say that Fowler is a colored man, but we account for his dark complexion by the fact that . . . in chasing after balls [he] has become tanned from constant and ceaseless exposure to the sun. This theory has the essential features of a chestnut, as it bears resemblance to Buffalo's claim that Grant is of Spanish descent.

Fowler's career in the International League would be brief. The financially troubled Bings would release him in July to cut their payroll. But during this half-season, a friendly rivalry existed between Fowler and Grant. Not so friendly were some of the tactics used by opposing baserunners and pitchers. In 1889, an unidentified International League player told the *Sporting News*:

> While I myself am prejudiced against playing in a team with a colored player, still I could not help pitying some of the poor black fellows that played in the International League. Fowler used to play second base with the lower part of his legs encased in wooden guards. He knew that about every player that came down to second base on a steal had it in for him and would, if possible, throw the spikes into him. He was a good player but left the base every time there was a close play in order to get away from the spikes.
>
> I have seen him muff balls intentionally, so that he would not have to try to touch runners, fearing that they might injure him. Grant was the same way. Why, the runners chased him off second base. They went down so often trying to break his legs or injure them that he gave up his infield position the latter part of last season [i.e., 1888] and played right field. This is not all.
>
> About half the pitchers try their best to hit these colored players when [they are] at the bat. . . . One of the International League pitchers pitched for Grant's head all the time. He never put a ball over the

> plate but sent them in straight and true right at Grant. Do what he
> would he could not hit the Buffalo man, and he [Grant] trotted down
> to first on called balls all the time.

The International League season was getting underway. In preseason exhibitions against major-league teams, Grant's play was frequently described as "brilliant." *Sporting Life* cited the "brilliant work of Grant," his "number of difficult one-handed catches," and his "special fielding displays" in successive games in April. Even in an 18–4 loss to Philadelphia, "Grant, the colored second baseman, was the lion of the afternoon. His exhibition was unusually brilliant."

Stovey got off to a shaky start, as Newark lost to Brooklyn 12–4 in the team's exhibition opener. "Walker was clever—exceedingly clever behind the bat," wrote the Newark *Daily Journal*, "yet threw the ball wildly several times." A few days later, though, Newark's "colored battery" performed magnificently in a 3–2 loss at the Polo Grounds to the New York Giants, the favorite National League team of the Newark fans (hence the nickname "Little Giants"). Stovey was "remarkably effective," and Walker threw out the Giants' John Montgomery Ward at second base, "something that but few catchers have been able to accomplish." The play of Stovey and Walker impressed the New York sportswriters, as well as New York Giants' Captain Ward and manager Jim Mutrie, who, according to White, "made an offer to buy the release of the 'Spanish Battery,' but [Newark] manager Hackett informed him that they were not on sale."

Walker, too, impressed fans and writers with his defensive skill and baserunning. In a game against Buffalo, "Walker was like a fence behind the home plate. . . . [T]here might have been a river 10 feet behind him and not a ball would have gone into it." Waxing poetic, one scribe wrote:

> There is a catcher named Walker
> Who behind the bat is a corker,
> He throws to a base
> With ease and with grace
> And steals 'round the bags like a stalker.

Who were the other black ballplayers in the IL? Oswego, unsuccessful in signing George Williams away from the Cuban Giants, added Randolph Jackson, a second baseman from Ilion, New York, to their roster after a recommendation from Bud Fowler. (Ilion is near Cooperstown; Fowler's real name was John Jackson—coincidence?) He played his first game on May 28. In a 5–4 loss to Newark he "played a remarkable game and hit for a double and single, besides making the finest catch ever made on the grounds," wrote *Sporting Life*. Jackson played only three more games before the Oswego franchise folded on May 31, 1887.

Binghamton, which already had Bud Fowler, added a black pitcher named Renfroe (whose first name was unknown). Renfroe had pitched for the Memphis team in the Southern League of Colored Base Ballists in 1886, where "he won every game he pitched but one, averaging 12 strikeouts a game for nine games. In his first game against Chattanooga he struck out the first nine men who came to bat," wrote the Memphis *Appeal;* "he has great speed and a very deceptive downshoot." Renfroe pitched his first game for Binghamton on May 30, a 14–9 victory over Utica, before several thousand fans.

"How far will this mania for engaging colored players go?" asked *Sporting Life.* "At the present rate of progress the International League may ere many moons change its title to 'Colored League.'" During the last few days in May, seven blacks were playing in the league: Walker and Stovey for Newark, Fowler and Renfroe for Binghamton, Grant for Buffalo, Jackson for Oswego, and Robert Higgins.

V

July 14, 1887, would be a day that Tommy Daly would never forget. Three thousand fans went to Newark's Wright Street grounds to watch an exhibition game between the Little Giants and the most glamorous team in baseball: Adrian D. (Cap) Anson's Chicago White Stockings. Daly, who was from Newark, was in his first season with the White Stockings, forerunners of today's Cubs. Before the game he was presented with gifts from his admirers in Newark. George Stovey would remember the day, too. As for Moses Fleetwood Walker, there may have been a sense of déjà vu—for Walker had crossed paths with Anson before.

Anson, who was the first white child born among the Pottawatomie Indians in Marshalltown, Iowa, played for Rockford and the Philadelphia Athletics in all five years of the National Association and 22 seasons for Chicago in the National League, hitting over .300 in all but two. He also managed the Sox for 19 years. From 1880 through 1886, Anson's White Stockings finished first five times and second once. Outspoken, gruff, truculent, and haughty, Anson gained the respect, if not the esteem, of his players, as well as opponents and fans throughout the nation. Cigars and candy were named after him, and little boys would treasure their Anson-model baseball bats as their most prized possessions. He was a brilliant tactician with a flair for the dramatic. In 1888, for example, he commemorated the opening of the Republican National Convention in Chicago by suiting up his players in black, swallowtail coats.

In addition to becoming the first player to get 3,000 hits, Anson was the first to write his autobiography. *A Ball Player's Career,* published in 1900, does not explicitly delineate Anson's views on race relations. It does, however, devote several pages to his stormy relationship with the White Stockings' mascot, Clarence Duval, who despite Anson's vehement objections was allowed to take part in the round-the-world tour following the 1888 season. Anson referred to Duval as "a little darkey," "a coon," and "a no account nigger."

In 1884, when Walker was playing for Toledo, Anson brought his White Stockings into town for an exhibition. Anson threatened to pull his team off the field unless Walker was removed. But Toledo's manager, Charley Morton, refused to comply with Anson's demand, and Walker was allowed to play. Years later *Sporting Life* would write:

> The joke of the affair was that up to the time Anson made his "bluff" the Toledo people had no intention of catching Walker, who was laid up with a sore hand, but when Anson said he wouldn't play with Walker, the Toledo people made up their minds that Walker would catch or there wouldn't be any game.

But by 1887, times had changed, and there was no backing Anson down. The Newark press had publicized that Anson's White Stockings would face Newark's black Stovey. But on the day of the game, it was Hughes and Cantz who formed the Little Giants' battery. "Three thousand souls were made glad," glowed the *Daily Journal* after Newark's surprise 9–4 victory, "while nine were made sad." The *Evening News* attributed Stovey's absence to illness, but the Toronto *World* got it right in reporting that, "Hackett intended to putting Stovey in the box against the Chicagos, but Anson objected to his playing on account of his color."

On the same day that Anson succeeded in removing the "colored battery," the directors of the International League met in Buffalo to transfer the ailing Utica franchise to Wilkes-Barre, Pennsylvania. It must have pleased Anson to read in the next day's Newark *Daily Journal*:

> THE COLOR LINE DRAWN IN BASEBALL
> The International League directors held a secret meeting at the Genesee House yesterday, and the question of colored players was freely discussed. Several representatives declared that many of the best players in the league are anxious to leave on account of the colored element, and the board finally directed Secretary White to approve of no more contracts with colored men.

Whether or not there was a direct connection between Anson's opposition to playing Stovey and Walker, and, on the same day, the International League's decision to draw the color line is lost in history. For example, was the league responding to threats by Anson not to play lucrative exhibitions with teams of any league that permitted Negro players? Interestingly, of the six teams which voted to install a color barrier—Binghamton, Hamilton, Jersey City, Rochester, Toronto, and Utica—none had a black player; the four teams voting against it—Buffalo, Oswego, Newark, and Syracuse—each had at least one.

In 1907, Sol White excoriated Anson for possessing "all the venom of a hate which would be worthy of a Tillman or a Vardaman of the present day." (Benjamin R.Tillman was a senator from South Carolina, while James K. Vardaman was governor of Mississippi. Both were ardent segregationists.)

> Just why Adrian C. Anson . . . was so strongly opposed to colored players on white teams cannot be explained. He repugnant feeling, shown at every opportunity, toward colored ballplayers, was a source of comment throughout every league in the country, and his opposition, with his great popularity and power in baseball circles, hastened the exclusion of the black man from the white leagues.

Subsequent historians have followed Sol White's lead and portrayed Anson as the meistersinger of a chorus of racism who, virtually unaided, disqualified an entire race from baseball. Scapegoats are convenient, but Robert Peterson undoubtedly is correct:

> Whatever its origin, Anson's animus toward Negroes was strong and obvious. But that he had the power and popularity to force Negroes out of baseball almost single-handedly, as White suggests, is to credit him with more influence than he had, or for that matter, than he needed.

The International League's written color line was not the first one drawn. In 1867, the National Association of Base Ball Players, the loosely organized body which regulated amateur baseball, prohibited its members from accepting blacks. The officers candidly explained their reason: "If colored clubs were admitted there would be in all probability some division of feeling, whereas, by excluding them no injury could result to anybody and the possibility of any rupture being created on political grounds would be avoided."

This 1867 ban shows that even if blacks were not playing baseball then, there were ample indications that they would be soon. But the NABBP would soon disappear, as baseball's rapidly growing popularity fostered professionalism. Also, its measure was preventative rather than corrective: It was not intended to disqualify players who had previously been sanctioned. And, since it applied only to amateurs, it was not intended to deprive anyone of his livelihood.

"We think," wrote the Binghamton *Daily Leader*, "the International League made a monkey of itself when it undertook to draw the color line"; and later the editor wondered "if the International League proposes to exclude colored people from attendance at the games." Welday Walker used a similar line of reasoning in March 1888. Having read an incorrect report that the Tri-State League, formerly the Ohio State League, of which Welday Walker was a member, had prohibited the signing of Negros, he wrote a letter to league president W. H. McDermitt. Denouncing any color line as "a disgrace to the present age," he argued that if Negroes were to be barred as players, then they should also be denied access to the stands.

The sporting press stated its admiration for the talents of the black players who would be excluded. "Grant, Stovey, Walker, and Higgins," wrote *Sporting Life*, "all are good players and behave like gentlemen, and it is a pity that the line should have been drawn against them." That paper's Syracuse correspondent wrote, "Dod gast the measly rule that deprives a club as of good a man as Bob Higgins." Said the Newark *Daily Journal*, "It is safe to say that Moses F. Walker is mentally and morally the equal of any director who voted for the resolution."

Color line or no color line, the season wore on. Buffalo and Newark remained in contention until late in the season. Newark fell victim to injuries, including one to Fleet Walker. Grant's play deteriorated, although he finished the year leading the league in hitting. Toronto, which overcame internal strife of its own, came from the back of the pack, winning 22 of its last 26 games; they may have been aided by manager Charley Cushman's innovative device of having his infielders wear gloves on their left hands. On September 17, Toronto swept a doubleheader from Newark at home before 8,000 fans to take first place. One week later they clinched their first International League title. To commemorate the triumphant season, the Canadian Pacific Railway shipped a 160-foot-tall pine, "the second-tallest in America," across the continent. Atop this pole would fly the 1887 International League pennant.

Before the season ended there was one further flareup of racial prejudice that received national attention. On Sunday, September 11, Chris von der Ahe, owner of the St. Louis Browns, canceled an exhibition game that was scheduled for that day in West Farms, New York, against the Cuban Giants. Led by its colorful and eccentric owner, and its multitalented manager-first baseman, Charles Comiskey, the Browns were the Chicago White Stockings of the American Association. At 10 o'clock in the morning von der Ahe notified a crowd of 7,000 disappointed fans that his team was too crippled by injuries to compete. The real reason, though, was a letter von der Ahe had received the night before, signed by all but two of his players (Comiskey was one of the two):

> Dear Sir: We, the undersigned members of the St. Louis Base Ball Club, do not agree to play against Negroes tomorrow. We will cheerfully play against white people at any time and think by refusing to play, we are only doing what is right, taking everything into consideration and the shape the team is in at present.

VI

There was considerable speculation throughout the offseason that the International League would rescind its color line, or at least modify it to allow each club one Negro. At a meeting at the Rossin House in Toronto on November 16, 1887, the league dissolved itself and reorganized under the title International Association. Buffalo and Syracuse, anxious to retain Grant and Higgins, led the fight to eliminate the color line.

While the subject of the color line was not included in the minutes of the proceedings, the issue apparently was not quite "forgotten." An informal agreement among the leaders provided a cautious retreat. By the end of the month, Grant was signed by Buffalo, and Higgins was retained by Syracuse for 1888. Fleet Walker, who was working in a Newark factory crating sewing machines for the export trade, remained uncommitted on an offer by Worcester, as he waited "until he finds whether colored players are wanted in the International League [sic]. He is very much a gentleman and is unwilling to force himself where he is not wanted." His doubts assuaged, he signed, by the end of November, with Syracuse, where in 1888, he would once again join a black pitcher. The Syracuse directors had fired manager Joe Simmons and replaced him with Charley Hackett. Thus, Walker would be playing for his third team with Hackett as manager. He looked forward to the next season, exercising his throwing arm by tossing a claw hammer into the air and catching it.

Frank Grant would have a typical season in Buffalo in 1888, where he was moved to the outfield to avoid spike wounds. For the third straight year his batting average (.346) was the highest on the team. Bob Higgins, the agent and victim of too much history, would, according to *Sporting Life*, "give up his $200 a month and return to his barbershop in Memphis, Tennessee," despite compiling a 20–7 record.

Fleet Walker, catching 76 games and stealing 30 bases, became a member of a second championship team, the first since Toledo in 1883. But his season was blighted by a third distasteful encounter with Anson. In an exhibition game at Syracuse on September 27, 1888, Walker was not permitted to play against the White Stockings. Anson's policy of refusing to allow blacks on the same field with him had become so well-known and accepted that the incident was not even reported in the white press. The Indianapolis *World* noted the incident, which by now apparently was of interest only to black readers.

Fowler, Grant, and Stovey played many more seasons, some with integrated teams, some on all-Negro teams in white leagues in organized baseball, some on independent Negro teams. Fowler and Grant stayed one step ahead of the color line as it proceeded westward.

Fleet Walker continued to play for Syracuse in 1889, where he would be the last black in the International League until Jackie Robinson. Walker's career as a professional ballplayer ended in the relative obscurity of Terre Haute, Indiana (1890), and Oconto, Wisconsin (1891).

In the spring of 1891, Walker was accused of murdering a convicted burglar by the name of Patrick Murphy outside a bar in Syracuse. When he was found not guilty "immediately a shout of approval, accompanied by clapping of hands and stamping of feet, rose from the spectators," according to *Sporting Life*. His baseball career over, he returned to Ohio and embarked on various careers. He owned or operated the Cadiz, Ohio, opera house, and several motion picture houses, during which time he claimed several inventions in the motion picture industry. He was also the editor of a newspaper, the *Equator*, with the assistance of his brother Welday.

In 1908, he published a 47-page booklet entitled *Our Home Colony: A Treatise on the Past, Present, and Future of the Negro Race in America*. According to the former catcher, "The only practical and permanent solution of the present and future race troubles in the United States is entire separation by emigration of the Negro from America." Following the example of Liberia, "The Negro race can find superior advantages, and better opportunities . . . among people of their own race, for developing the innate powers of mind and body." The achievement of racial equality "is contrary to everything in the nature of man, and [it is] almost criminal to attempt to harmonize these two diverse peoples while living under the same government." The past 40 years, he wrote, have shown "that instead of improving we are experiencing the development of a real caste spirit in the United States."

Fleet Walker died of pneumonia in Cleveland at age 66, on May 11, 1924, and was buried in Union Cemetery in Steubenville, Ohio. His brother Welday died in Steubenville 13 years later at the age of 77.

VII

In *The Strange Career of Jim Crow*, historian C. Vann Woodward identifies the late 1880s as a "twilight zone that lies between living memory and written history," when "for a time old and new rubbed shoulders—and so did black and white—in a manner that differed significantly from Jim Crow of the future or slavery of the past." He continued:

> A great deal of variety and inconsistency prevailed in race relations from state to state and within a state. It was a time of experiment, testing, and uncertainty—quite different from the time of repression and rigid uniformity that was to come toward the end of the century. Alternatives were still open and real choices had to be made.

Sol White and his contemporaries lived through such a transition period, and he identified the turning point as 1887. Twenty years later he noted the deterioration of the black ballplayer's situation. Although White could hope that one day the black would be able to "walk hand-in-hand with the opposite race in the greatest of all American games—base ball," he was not optimistic:

> As it is, the field for the colored professional is limited to a very narrow scope in the baseball world. When he looks into the future he sees no place for him. . . . Consequently, he loses interest. He knows that, so far shall I go, and no farther, and, as it is with the profession, so it is with his ability.

The "strange careers" of Moses Walker, George Stovey, Frank Grant, Bud Fowler, Robert Higgins, Sol White, et al., provide a microcosmic view of the development of race relations in the society at large, as outlined by Woodward. The events of 1887 offer further evidence of the old saw that sport does not develop character—it reveals it.

CASEY AT THE BAT

Ernest Lawrence Thayer

The outlook wasn't brilliant for the Mudville nine that day;
The score stood four to two, with but one inning more to play,
And then when Cooney died at first, and Barrows did the same,
A pall-like silence fell upon the patrons of the game.

A straggling few got up to go in deep despair.
The rest clung to that hope which springs eternal in the human breast;
They thought, "If only Casey could but get a whack at that—
We'd put up even money now, with Casey at the bat."

But Flynn preceded Casey, as did also Jimmy Blake,
And the former was a hoodoo, while the latter was a cake;
So upon that stricken multitude grim melancholy sat;
For there seemed but little chance of Casey getting to the bat.

But Flynn let drive a single, to the wonderment of all,
And Blake, the much despised, tore the cover off the ball;
And when the dust had lifted, and men saw what had occurred,
There was Jimmy safe at second and Flynn a-hugging third.

Then from five thousand throats and more there rose a lusty yell;
It rumbled through the valley, it rattled in the dell;
It pounded on the mountain and recoiled upon the flat,
For Casey, mighty Casey, was advancing to the bat.

Ernest Lawrence Thayer, "Casey at the Bat," *San Francisco Examiner*, June 3, 1888.

There was ease in Casey's manner as he stepped into his place;
There was pride in Casey's bearing and a smile lit Casey's face.
And when, responding to the cheers, he lightly doffed his hat,
No stranger in the crowd could doubt 'twas Casey at the bat.

Ten thousand eyes were on him as he rubbed his hands with dirt.
Five thousand tongues applauded when he wiped them on his shirt.
Then while the writhing pitcher ground the ball into his hip,
Defiance flashed in Casey's eye, a sneer curled Casey's lip.

And now the leather-covered sphere came hurtling through the air,
And Casey stood a-watching it in haughty grandeur there.
Close by the sturdy batsman the ball unheeded sped
"That ain't my style," said Casey. "Strike one!" the umpire said.

From the benches, black with people, there went up a muffled roar,
Like the beating of the storm-waves on a stern and distant shore;
"Kill him! Kill the umpire!" shouted someone on the stand;
And it's likely they'd have killed him had not Casey raised his hand.

With a smile of Christian charity great Casey's visage shone;
He stilled the rising tumult; he bade the game go on;
He signaled to the pitcher, and once more the dun sphere flew;
But Casey still ignored it, and the umpire said, "Strike two!"

"Fraud!" cried the maddened thousands, and echo answered, "Fraud!"
But one scornful look from Casey and the audience was awed.
They saw his face grow stern and cold, they saw his muscles strain,
And they knew that Casey wouldn't let that ball go by again.

The sneer has fled from Casey's lip, the teeth are clenched in hate;
He pounds with cruel violence his bat upon the plate.
And now the pitcher holds the ball, and now he lets it go,
And now the air is shattered by the force of Casey's blow.

Oh, somewhere in this favored land the sun is shining bright,
The band is playing somewhere, and somewhere hearts are light,
And somewhere men are laughing, and little children shout;
But there is no joy in Mudville—mighty Casey has struck out.

CHAPTER 3

Monopoly Baseball and the Rise of the American League, 1891–1908

Baseball's Not So "Gay Nineties"

The decade of the 1890s proved crucial for the development of professional baseball. For all practical purposes, the trends that began in the 1880s saw the final formulation of the game on the field: the setting of the pitching distance to 60 feet, six inches. Later, two changes would complete the modern structure of the game. A pitcher's mound approximating the modern mound would emerge in the first years of the new decade. Rules limited the mound to no higher than 15 inches. Along with throwing overhand and the newly established pitching distance, these modifications reinforced the dominance of defense, that is, pitching, for the next 20 years. At the same time, the National League, later joined by the American, would count all foul balls as strikes. Heretofore, a ball that rolled foul before passing first or third base did not count. As a result, by the beginning of the new century, the professional level of play closely approximated modern standards. At the same time, the business side of baseball reflected the features of modern capitalism: ruthless competition and managerial control of the product and players in every form. The games "magnates" may not have been "robber barons," but they were ruthless businessmen who ran their sport for profit.[1]

It is also important to note that the 1890s caused problems for baseball in another sense. The decade saw the worst depression in American history, an economic slump that left scars on baseball for two decades and eventually caused a new restructuring of the game. The unemployment rate rose from a low of 4 percent in 1890 to a high of 18.4 percent four years later, the highest in U.S. history and a figure not topped until the Great Depression of the 1930s. Historians are not in complete agreement as to what caused the economic slump to be so severe. But it is safe to say that the depression of the 1890s was the result of many factors.

Agricultural prices, which had risen to all-time-high levels in the 1880s, suddenly collapsed through overexpansion. The price of wheat, corn, and cotton hit low levels. The railroad building boom that characterized the post–Civil War period came to a sudden halt. Excessive building of railroads led to the bankruptcy of some of the major lines: the Union Pacific and the Northern Pacific, among others. The banking industry, which was basically unregulated at the time, saw more than 500 banks close their doors in the early 1890s, causing widespread panic. Baseball's problems in the 1890s once again show that the sport was an expression of much that was happening in the nation.

The newly reformed National League now had 12 teams, in cities that had supported major-league-quality baseball in the past and would again in the future (except for Louisville). The magnates were happy with their handiwork. They now not only controlled all the best sites for baseball, but also the destinies of the players. The players now would be easy to control, which meant salaries would be dictated by the magnates. The $3000 to $4000 salaries of the players' revolt were a thing of the past. Now, $2,400 had become the established maximum. Any player protesting could be blacklisted. In 1893, the Phillies had an outfield consisting of three future Hall of Famers—Billy Hamilton, Sam Thompson, and Ed Delahanty—and paid each just $1,800.[2]

The new National League showed an attendance increase in 1892 and 1893, although attendance still fell below the 3 million mark set by the National League and the American Association in 1889. To boost attendance, the magnates decided to revive the idea of a playoff. In 1892, they devised the concept of a split season, with the winner of the first half playing the second-half champion. That idea didn't work out well. The Boston Beaneaters easily won the first half and finished second to the Cleveland Spiders in the second half. In the playoffs, Boston swept Cleveland in four games, which gave rise to suspicions that Boston had coasted in the second half of the season. More importantly, given the reputation in the past for players throwing games or just letting down, the public and some of the sporting press believed some kind of fix had been planned.

For the owners, the most important aspect of the split schedule was the decline in attendance for the second half of the season. Some kind of meaningful postseason playoff format had to be devised to maintain fan interest. That problem proved easier to solve than the inherent lack of competition in a 12-team league. Between 1892 and the breakup of the 12-team concept after the 1899 season, Boston won four titles, the Baltimore Orioles three, and Brooklyn, then known as the Bridegrooms, one. Most seasons, some teams were out of the pennant race within a matter of weeks, with the result that attendance plummeted. In 1899, for instance, Cleveland established a record for futility that has been unchallenged in baseball history: They won 20 games and lost 134. Season attendance was 6,100, with the team averaging 145 for home games. Along with the lack of competition, the depression of the 1890s drove down baseball attendance. In no year of the decade did the new league match the figures reached in 1889.

One imaginative attempt to drum up interest occurred in 1894. A Pittsburgh businessman and former owner of the Pittsburgh team, William Temple, with a fan's interest in baseball, offered to donate a silver trophy to the winner of a playoff. Nicknamed the Temple Cup, much like the Davis Cup in tennis or the Stanley Cup in hockey, Temple's idea was put into operation after the 1894 season. The silver cup, worth about $800, would be awarded to the winning team and given permanently to the first team to win three championships. The idea was to have the winner of the pennant play the second-place team in a postseason championship. Since the players' salaries stopped at the end of the season, they offered a share of the playoff money: 60 percent to the winners and 40 percent to the losers as a way to ensure genuine competition. It appears that, among themselves, the players decided to make the split 50–50.[3]

The National League owners liked the idea in principle, as it revived the successful World Series play with the American Association in the 1880s. The plan worked for a couple of seasons. In 1894, the Orioles won the pennant, only to have the New York Giants sweep them in four consecutive games. Attendance was good, at 56,000, so it looked like the Temple idea worked. The next season, the Orioles won the pennant again and this time lost to Cleveland, four games to one. Baltimore finally won the Temple Cup in 1896, beating Cleveland handily, but attendance had dropped sharply to 12,000 from the high in 1894. Fans were losing interest in this playoff format. In the last year of the Temple Cup series, 1897, Baltimore, the runner-up, defeated Boston, with the last game played for a hometown crowd of just 750 fans.[4]

The failure of the Temple Cup is an interesting commentary on the state of baseball in the 1890s. The concept could be linked to the terrible impact of the depression, although it is interesting that fan turnout was high in 1894, when unemployment had risen to historic highs. A better explanation might be found in the way the business side of baseball was being handled. The owners had clearly made a mistake when they adopted the 12-team concept. They refused to recognize this, despite the fact that every season, five to six teams had no realistic chance to compete for the pennant. It was difficult to maintain fan interest when teams at the bottom of the league finished far out of first place.

In 1898, St. Louis finished 63½ games behind the pennant winning Beaneaters. The next season, the gap between the first-place team and last place Cleveland Spiders was 84 games. Cleveland also finished 35 games behind the eleventh place Washington team. Along with the dominance of the Orioles and Beaneaters, this lack of competition was fatal to the 12-team concept. As the decade of the 1890s wore on, attendance began to show a steady decline. From a high of more than 3 million in 1889, attendance leveled off at about 1,850,000 in the mid-1890s and, even as the depression began to end in the late 1890s, never approached the record level.

It is possible that some of the blame cannot be placed on baseball; rather, it was the result of competition from new sports. The 1890s saw the beginning of bicycle mania with the adoption of an easy-to-control two-wheeler with rubber tires and a chain gear that made riding fast and easy. Bike riding swept the nation, as reflected in the hugely popular song "Daisy, Daisy," about a beau proposing to his girl. College football also became a big-time sport in the 1890s. Dominated by the Ivy League schools, Walter Camp of Yale formalized the football rules with concepts like the four-down system, while establishing the key position of the quarterback. In a stroke of promotional genius Camp also started the idea of an All-American team, a notion other sports would eventually adopt.

Football was a brutal game despite its Ivy League connection but remained popular among college students. The Yale–Harvard game in 1893 drew more than 50,000 fans—a figure baseball would not match for a single game until the 1920s. Golf and tennis, both largely upper-class sports, were also beginning to gain popularity with the middle classes. While sports were considered manly occupations, it is interesting to note that women began playing tennis and golf in the 1890s. With John L. Sullivan's defeat by Jim Corbett in 1892, boxing lost much of its appeal. Corbett was a clever defensive fighter, but fans preferred the rough knockout power of their heavyweight champ. None of the other divisions in boxing won a broad following until the emergence of middleweight Stanley Ketchell in 1908. No heavyweight proved popular with fans until Jim Jeffries a decade later, and he never approached Sullivan's popularity. It wasn't until the emergence of Jack Dempsey after World War I that boxing had a charismatic heavyweight champion. The sport stultified until the 1920s.

The baseball magnates also were abusing their powers. They moved players from team to team as they saw fit. Moreover, there was no incentive to reward players for outstanding performances, of which there were many in the 1890s. When three leagues operated in 1890, there were approximately 360 players on the major-league roster. Now, in the 12-team league, with rosters set at 13, only half that number could play. This meant the owners had a large pool of talent to draw on if they wished, and that pool helped keep salaries low.

At the same time baseball was struggling economically, the game on the field was being played at an exceptionally high level. The professionalization of baseball play had progressed in the 1880s, but the 1890s would see it approach something approximating the modern game. The establishment of the final distance for the pitcher's mound undoubtedly was the biggest factor, but the general level of play grew smoother and steadier. The explanation could be as simple as the fact that the game had been played professionally for almost four decades, and the various aspects of baseball play had been refined. For example, it was now rare for an outfielder to drop a fly ball. Catchers were moving closer to the batter, which allowed pitchers to judge the strike zone more accurately. The quality of equipment—gloves, bats, and even uniforms—made the game easier to play. And finally, the quality of athlete playing baseball in the 1890s reached high levels.

In the 1890s, the game produced some of its first great superstars, who would compare with the best players in the modern era. With the pitcher's mound now established at its current distance and the other changes that came into baseball, it is easier to compare baseball of the 1890s with the so-called modern game. At least a dozen of the best players from the 1890s are in the Hall of Fame, a sure sign that the baseball establishment recognized their talents. Such players as catcher Buck Ewing, shortstop Honus Wagner, second baseman Napoleon Lajoie, outfielders Willie Keeler and Ed Delahanty, and pitchers Cy Young and Kid Nichols debuted in the 1890s and set the standard for their positions for the future.

Everything in the game changed with the setting of the pitching distance at 60 feet, six inches. In 1892, the last year of the old distance, the National League batting average was .245 and the league ERA was 3.28. One year later, with the new rule, the league batting average rose to .280 and the ERA to 4.66. There were six 30-game winners in 1892, followed by four one year later. In 1893, 12 men had a higher batting average than the batting champ one year earlier. Offense dominated from 1893 onward, as pitchers learned to adjust to the new mound distance.

Baseball in the Gay Nineties was played with unusual roughness. The Baltimore Orioles are associated with this brand of play, usually blamed on the many Irish American players on the team, personified by third baseman and future manager John McGraw. Despite the attention given to the Orioles, the Boston Beaneaters were probably the best team in the National League in the 1890s. Both were superb teams, combining great pitching, solid hitting, and sturdy defense. They specialized in what was called "inside baseball": lots of bunting, hit-and-run plays, stealing bases, moving the runner, and so forth. They also resorted to various forms of trickery: substituting soft baseballs when the opposition was at bat, tripping runners, and blocking bases when the umpire was distracted.

Tommy McCarthy of Boston is often credited with inventing the hit-and-run play. What did distinguish the Orioles was their umpire baiting, trick plays, rough language, and generally unruly behavior. Some commentators believe the Orioles' roughhouse version of baseball helped drive fans away from the game. The badgering of the umpire reached new levels in the 1890s, with umpires being attacked by fans—often encouraged by the players—having their shoes stepped on by players in spikes, and so on. The National League tried to order reforms, but those efforts were halfhearted. The fact of the matter is, that type of play was the nature of the game in the 1890s. Connie Mack, who had a reputation for being a gentleman, once observed of the great Orioles team of the 1890s that there were no gentlemen on that squad. Despite that, five of them reached the Hall of Fame. The men who ran baseball did not police the game, but instead concentrated on business matters and manipulating their clubs for their financial benefit.[5]

There were serious disputes among the magnates who ran baseball in the 1890s. One of the most unpopular was Andrew Freedman, a Jewish business-man from New York. Freedman, through good political connections, purchased controlling interest in the New York Giants and proceeded to run the club like his personal fief. Foreshadowing George Steinbrenner by 70 years, he hired and fired a dozen managers in the near-decade he ran the Giants. Freedman wanted to set up a baseball trust, modeled on the concept then popular in American big business. This would control player movement, level wages, and change the ownership of failing franchises. Freedman's aggressiveness and ruthlessness turned off his fellow owners, and they eventually bought him out.

By the end of the decade, it was clear something had to be done. The 12-team concept wasn't working. It was becoming clear that fans were being turned off by the way baseball was being played. More importantly, for the magnates who ran the game, the economic situation looked grim. After the 1899 season, the magnates talked about a number of possible solutions. They thought they might revive the two-league structure, which had proven profitable in the 1880s. A new American Association was discussed but found few backers because it would improve the bargaining position of the players by making more jobs available.

Dissatisfied with the 12-team league, the magnates decided to close down four franchises, pay off their owners, and return to the old eight-team structure of the National League. It seemed like a good decision, especially as the own-ers of two of the teams, Baltimore and Cleveland, were paid off and two oth-ers, Washington and Louisville, had proven flops throughout the 1890s. The magnates were proud that they had taken the correct, hardheaded decision and looked forward to better times. But they had completely misread the situation. The depression was over, prosperity was returning to the country, and there were many cities interested in major-league-quality baseball. It was only a matter of time before someone took advantage of the changing situation.

ENTER BAN JOHNSON

In the chaos following the controversy concerning the Players League and the breakup of the American Association, some of what we would call minor leagues were in trouble. One of the more important of these, the Western League, with teams in solid cities in the Midwest, had been an important developer of talent for the National League and American Association. In 1894, the Western League owners appointed a new president, Byron "Ban" Johnson.[6]

Johnson was an example of the upwardly mobile, middle-class business types who came to power in the United States in the years following the Civil War. Born in 1863, his father a school administrator, Johnson attended Marietta College and then studied law at the University of Cincinnati. He drifted into journalism and became a sports editor for the *Cincinnati Commercial Gazette*, with a special interest in baseball. A big man, weighing 300 pounds, clean shaven, with his hair parted in the middle like so many men in the 1890s, Johnson was a decisive individual with strong ideas of how baseball should be managed. He took over the Western League in 1894, turning it into a model organization. He stressed clean baseball, banned umpire baiting, and battled gambling and the other curses of baseball in the Gay Nineties. He earned a reputation as a good administrator and was highly regarded by the National League owners for running a successful league. During his tenure as president of the Western League, he formed friendships with baseball players with ambitions beyond playing, for example, Charles Comiskey and Connie Mack.

In 1899, when the National League decided to reduce its size, the magnates spoke to Johnson about taking over a new American Association. Johnson wasn't interested. He had bigger plans. As the quality of the Western League improved, Johnson began to think of applying for major-league status. As a first step, he gave the Western League a new name, the American League. It was an inspired choice given the mood of a nation that had just won a "Splendid Little War" against Spain and was about to enter a new age of surging imperial expansion.

Johnson took advantage of the four clubs dropped by the National League in 1900, to place teams in Chicago and Cleveland, and began laying the plans for expanding into the east to create a more balanced structure for his new league. By signing some of the players freed by the shrinking of the National League, he improved the quality of play in his new league. In 1901, he decided to challenge the National League by demanding recognition as an equal major league. When the National League refused to even discuss matters with him, Johnson said he would not recognize the National Agreement and declared war, saying that within a short period of time the "American League will be the principle (baseball) organization of the country."[7]

Johnson was in a strong position. He had secured financial backing and placed teams in eastern cities to provide a stronger position and balance for the American League. The new league had teams in Boston, Philadelphia, Baltimore, and Washington in the east to join Chicago, Cleveland, Detroit, and Milwaukee in the west. In Philadelphia, he brought together Connie Mack with A. J. Reach and Ben Shibe, wealthy sporting goods manufacturers, to run the club there. He moved Charles Comiskey to Chicago to take over a new White Stockings franchise and arranged solid backing for the teams in Cleveland and Boston. He was blocked from placing a team in New York because the National League Giants had powerful friends in Tammany Hall who denied him a playing field. Johnson's position was strong even without New York because the population of his team's cities totaled 6.9 million, just 600,000 less than the National League total.

Johnson was aided in his war with the National League when a new players' association was created in 1900. The Protective Association of Professional Base Ball Players was modeled after the Brotherhood of the past but presented a more moderate program of reforms. The organization did get the magnates' attention when a representative of Samuel Gompers's American Federation of Labor advised them on tactics. The existence of a players' association strengthened Johnson when war broke out between the two leagues in 1901. He gave the signal to raid National League rosters by offering long-term contracts to players who were unsigned, guaranteeing larger salaries, and promising not to trade players without their consent. Although figures vary, one source estimates that of the 182 players in the American League during the 1901 season, 111 were former National Leaguers. The *Sporting News* reported that 74 of the 111 had jumped from the National League to Johnson's new organization. Some National League players threatened to jump to the American League as a way to negotiate better contracts with their teams. The National League owners were furious but were powerless to stop Johnson.[8]

As important as anything Johnson did was the high quality of the talented players he lured to his league. They included some of the National League's greatest players and such future Hall of Famers as Napoleon Lajoie, Clark Griffith, Cy Young, Jimmy Collins, Ed Delahanty, and John McGraw. It is estimated that their salaries doubled. Lajoie, for example, signed for $4,000 to play with Connie Mack, $1,600 more than the Phillies were paying. McGraw took over Baltimore as a playing manager at $11,000 a year for three years. To make matters worse for the National League, Johnson's new league did well at the box office. It drew 1.7 million to 1.9 million for the Senior Circuit, indicating it was here to stay.

The 1902 campaign proved even worse for the National League. The owners resorted to lawsuits, arguing that players who jumped to the American League had breached their contracts. In most cases, they lost on the grounds that the players' contracts lacked mutuality under the law. In Pennsylvania, they won the case against Mack for taking Lajoie and another player, Elmer Flick, from the Phillies. That issue became moot when Lajoie was sent to Cleveland, where he signed a three-year, $25,000 contract. To avoid legal problems, he didn't play when Cleveland took the field in Philadelphia.

The 1902 campaign was a booming success for the new league, now often referred to as the Junior Circuit. The Athletics, christened Mack's "White Elephants" by John McGraw, were a huge success in the City of Brotherly Love. Mack embraced McGraw's slur and turned it into a symbol for the team. They easily won the pennant in the American League behind the pitching of an unknown lefthander, Rube Waddell, who won 23 games in little more than a half-season. Pittsburgh won the National League pennant, but any talk of battle between the two best teams in baseball was rejected. That idea would come later.

The real shock of the season was the ease with which the American League outdrew the Nationals by more than a half-million fans. Mack's A's outdrew the Phillies 420,000 to 112,000, a huge humiliation for the National League. In every city with two teams—St. Louis, Chicago, Philadelphia, and Boston—the American League outdrew the National League. Three American League teams drew more fans than the top-performing National League New York Giants. American League players topped their National League counterparts in batting average, home runs, runs batted in, triples, and doubles. Any doubt that the American League was here to stay was banished. After the season ended, the National League sued for peace.

The two leagues agreed on a unified structure for baseball. After rejecting a National League suggestion to return to the failed 12-team concept, it was decided to form a commission to be made up of the presidents of the two leagues, plus a third party chosen by them. This National Commission would be the ruling body of baseball for 20 years. Due to his powerful personality and grasp of what was necessary for baseball to prosper, Ban Johnson dominated the National Commission until the Black Sox Scandal created the office of Commissioner of Baseball. Each party recognized the sanctity of their contracts, the reserve clause would be honored, and complicated issues of territorial rights would be negotiated. For the team owners, the end of the war meant salaries would return to normal and the bidding for players would stop. A by-product of the peace treaty was the creation of an American League team in New York. The Baltimore franchise was moved to New York so that the new league would have an outlet in America's biggest city.

The National Commission, in reality Johnson, worked efficiently to quash rumors of gambling and the fixing of games, and restored a sense of order to baseball. After 20 years of franchise shifts, league wars, and players' strikes, a decade of baseball prosperity and stability followed. Other than an occasional rumor of a fixed game, the biggest issue facing baseball in the first decade of the new century was the problem of alcoholism among the players. Many came from backgrounds where drinking was acceptable behavior, notably the Germans and Irish, who still constituted a large number of major leaguers in the first two decades of the twentieth century.

Every team had its heavy drinking cohort. The most tragic case of alcoholism was the death of Ed Delahanty. A .346 hitter in a 16-year career, and thought by most contemporary observers to be one of the best pure hitters in baseball, Delahanty was a heavy abuser of alcohol. In July 1903, he was put off a train at Niagara Falls and fell to his death. Rube Waddell, the great left-handed pitcher for Connie Mack's A's, was what we would call a functioning alcoholic. He would often sneak out of the ballpark to a local bar and trade baseballs for drinks. He drank too much, squandered all his money, and died at 37. Pittsburgh tried to get Honus Wagner to give up drinking beer and withheld money from one of its pitchers, Howie Camnitz, to slow his drinking. Connie Mack admitted he had to suspend four or five of the players on his 1913 team for alcohol-related problems. In general, however, the matter of drinking was laughed off in those days and would not be taken seriously by Major League Baseball for decades.[9]

THE DEADBALL ERA

Baseball in the opening years of the twentieth century has been characterized as the Deadball Era for good reason. The combination of the new pitching distance and a softer, rubber-centered baseball meant defense tended to dominate. Only twice between 1903 and 1910 was the ERA in the majors more than three runs per game. Pitching truly dominated. There were eight 30-game winners in those years, and a number of teams posted season ERAs of less than 2.00.

The greatest pitcher of the era was undoubtedly Christy Mathewson of the New York Giants. At 6-foot-1, he was big for his time, a powerful right-hander who had mastered almost pinpoint control, once hurling 68 consecutive innings without a walk. He was the idol of New York, the nerve center of the country at the time, and a Frank Merriwell-like hero to young people. He won 373 games during his career, including 30 or more four times and 20 or more for 12 straight years. Mathewson had many rivals: Rube Waddell, whose 349 strikeouts in a season was an amazing feat given that batters did not swing hard in the Deadball Era; Ed Walsh, who won 40 games in one season; and Jack Chesbro, who set the all-time record for most victories in a season, with 41, were typical of the hurlers of that era. Pitchers were expected to complete the games they started. There were no relief specialists, pitchers who would come in to save a game. The total of complete games by pitchers would be shocking by modern standards. For example, it was common for pitchers to complete 30 games in a season. In 1902, Vic Willis of Pittsburgh completed 41 of his games, while Cy Young of Boston also finished 41 that season. In the year he won 41 games, Chesbro completed 48.

Offense in the Deadball Era consisted of a lot of bunting and hit-and-run plays, and the use of the stolen base to offset the dominance of pitching. League batting averages in the first years of the century tended to stay in the .240 range, with few home runs. Batters choked up on the bat and tried to slash at the ball. Fly balls tended to be easy outs, with outfielders now all wearing gloves and playing shallow. Almost all the home runs hit in these years were the inside-the-park type—line drives that carried past the outfielder and rolled to the fences of the ballparks, almost all of which had deep foul lines and huge center fields. Home runs were rare. In 1908, the American League leader, Sam Crawford, hit seven. It was rare for the home run champ to top double figures. The famous "Hitless Wonders," the Chicago White Sox of 1906, World Series winners against a vaunted crosstown Cubs squad that won 116 games, hit exactly seven home runs that season.

Baseball was not without its great hitters in the Deadball Era. Honus Wagner, Sam Crawford, and Napoleon Lajoie would rank among the greatest players in baseball history. John McGraw, no mean judge of baseball talent, called Wagner the greatest player of all time, greater than Babe Ruth. Wagner compiled a lifetime batting average of .329 and won eight batting titles. A superb defensive shortstop, Wagner, despite incredibly bowed legs, could outrun most of his contemporaries, stealing 722 bases during his career. Lajoie was the greatest second baseman of his time, hitting .339 for his career, including a high mark of .422 in 1901. When he managed Cleveland, they were known as the "Naps" in his honor. Sam Crawford is the least known of that generation of great hitters, but playing alongside Ty Cobb, he compiled some remarkable offensive statistics: 2,964 hits and an all-time record of 312 triples.

The greatest player of the era and the man who personified Deadball baseball was, of course, Ty Cobb. Born in Georgia in 1886, and nicknamed the "Georgia Peach," Cobb was a man obsessed with success. Scarred as a young man when his mother killed his father by accident, he directed his energies toward being the best player in baseball. A loner, he played with a fine-tuned recklessness, running the bases with abandon, spiking fielders, taunting pitchers, and occasionally engaging in fights with his own teammates. He had an unusual batting stance. He hung his head over the plate, as if taunting pitchers to throw at him, and spread his hands wide apart on the bat. He would slide his hands up to punch at the ball and down to slash at the pitch. "When I played ball," he wrote in the best Social Darwinist tradition of his time, "I didn't play for fun. . . . It's no pink tea, and mollycoddles had better stay out. It's a contest and everything that implies, a struggle for supremacy, a survival of the fittest."[10]

Cobb's figures speak for themselves: He has the highest lifetime batting average in baseball history, .366, and more than 4,000 hits, along with almost 900 stolen bases. He was never popular in the way Mathewson was, an idol and a hero, but he was someone fans came to see, and he defined baseball in the Deadball Era.[11]

With all its problems in the past, baseball thrived in the Deadball Era. Attendance for the first decade of the new century exceeded 50 million, by far the best figure in the history of the sport. Teams such as Connie Mack's A's drew well, often topping the 400,000 mark for the 1902 season. The New York Giants, in an exciting pennant race in 1908, set an attendance record of 800,000, a figure that would not be topped until the Babe Ruth era, during his time with the New York Yankees team of the 1920s. With the country sharing in prosperity for the decade following the depression of the 1890s, baseball prospered. Wages rose slowly during those years, and the work week outside of the agricultural sector began to dip to about 44 to 48 hours. More money in the hands of the working class and a shorter work week, along with the popularity of Major League Baseball, helps explain the prosperity of the game.

Baseball's income was basically derived from ticket sales, to which was added the sale of refreshments, scorecards, and advertising on the ballpark fences. A sign of baseball's hold on the public was the huge success of the song "Take Me Out to the Ball Game," which appeared in 1908, and is still sung today in many ballparks. An interesting sidenote on the song is how it reflects the popularity of baseball with women. The person singing the song is a young girl begging her beau to take her to the ball game. Women were seen at baseball games—especially after Johnson insisted that the game be cleaned up—but they were still a rarity. The fan base was overwhelmingly male; almost exclusively white; and from the photographs of the time, mostly middle class. With games starting at 3:00 or 3:30 in the afternoon, it was still difficult for the working classes to attend games, except on Saturday. Sunday baseball was still rare. An examination of photos taken during the first 20 years of the century indicates a proliferation of caps and hats on the men in the crowds. The majority would be wearing suits, not working-class jackets.

One of baseball's most imaginative actions following the peace treaty of 1903 was the resurrection of the idea of a playoff. In 1903, the pennant winners in each league, the Pirates and the Beaneaters, agreed to play a best-of-nine series to determine the best team in baseball. Labeled the World Series, the idea was championed by the growing sports press as a great way of showing off the new game.

The Pirates had easily won the National League title for the third year in a row. They had a good team, led by Honus Wagner, who won the batting title with a .355 average. Their pitching was solid, and they led the National League with 34 home runs. In the American League, Boston easily defeated Connie Mack's A's by 14.5 games. Boston was led by Cy Young, who won 28 games, and had a balanced offensive lineup, notably featuring the league home run and RBI leader, Buck Freeman. The National League was expected to win handily over the upstart Americans, but in one of the first of many surprises in baseball history, after Pittsburgh took a three-to-one lead in the series, Boston swept the next four games, with 20-game winner Bill Dinneen winning two of the games, one of which was a 3–0 shutout in Game 8.

The World Series was an artistic and financial success. The winning players' share was $1,180 each, while the losing Pirates actually received more because their owner, Barney Dreyfuss, turned over his share of profits to them. The World Series money was approximately half of an average player's regular salary. Not bad for two weeks' work. The owners also did well. Gross receipts worked out to $50,000, and that figure gradually rose throughout the decade. In 1912, the gross figure was $490,000, with the winning players receiving $4,000 and the losers $2,600. Those figures guaranteed that the World Series idea would not go away, even though in 1904 John McGraw refused to play against an American League champion on the grounds that the National League was the only true major league. He faced a storm of protest from fans and sportswriters, accusing him of acting like a "spoiled baby." His own players were unhappy with him, as they had their eyes on World Series money.[12]

Beginning the next season, in 1905, the World Series idea was revived and would emerge as the greatest single sporting event in the nation until overtaken in the 1970s by the Super Bowl concept. The second World Series, between the A's and the Giants, led by two iconic managers in Connie Mack and John McGraw, ended any doubts about the popularity of the event. Mack and McGraw set the model for future baseball managers. Both were brilliant baseball minds, but their differing personalities largely determined how they viewed the game.

McGraw played a no-holds-barred version of baseball, with intimidation one of his hallmarks. Inspired by his days with the old Baltimore Orioles of the 1890s, he loved to hit-and-run, steal bases, and play for one run in hopes of getting more. Umpires were to be constantly challenged, oftentimes with the most brutal of language. Mack was the personification of the gentleman in baseball. Known as the "Tall Tactician," he wore a suit instead of a uniform but ran his team with an iron will. He preferred intelligent players. Thus his affection for college graduates. His teams were built around a balance of solid hitting and great pitching.

The 1905 Series went five games, and each contest was a shutout. Christy Mathewson hurled three of them, the last of them a clincher, making him the first pitcher to win three games in the World Series. There was controversy concerning this series. Waddell, the A's best pitcher, hurt his arm and claimed he suffered from rheumatism in his shoulder. Mack had his suspicions and never forgave Waddell, dealing him to St. Louis two years later. Despite his tremendous talent, Mack said, "I couldn't stand him any longer."[13] This series had everyone talking about baseball, even into what came to be called the "Hot Stove League" during the winter months. It was the kind of thing that made baseball so successful. In the first decade of World Series play, the so-called Junior League won six, including four in row. It was clear that the two leagues were now equal in quality.

A close examination of the two leagues at this time would show the American League with a slight edge in terms of developing new talent. Among future Hall of Fame players who began playing in the American League between 1901 and 1910 were Ty Cobb, Tris Speaker, Walter Johnson, Eddie Collins, Chief Bender, Eddie Plank, and Frank "Home Run" Baker. Aside from Mathewson and Wagner, who began his career in the 1890s, the Senior Circuit could not boast such an impressive group.

The new decade also saw an influx of college players to the majors. Baseball was now played on college campuses, and the best college players began to seek a major-league career despite the sport's reputation for roughness. Baseball provided a good living. Salaries were commensurate with what a lawyer or doctor made, and by the 1900s baseball also conveyed fame and prestige. Many players used their major-league experience to secure college coaching jobs when their careers were over. Connie Mack, in particular, had a fondness for college types because they were easier to teach and presented few problems. His best pitchers in the first years of the century were college men: Eddie Plank from Gettysburg, Jack Coombs of Colby College, and Chief Bender from Carlisle. Mack also signed future Hall of Famer Eddie Collins in 1906, fresh off the campus of Columbia.[14]

By 1908, baseball had cemented its hold on the American public, helped by the popularity of a new generation of players and events like the World Series. The game was followed year-round in the press, and even the new movie industry filmed baseball games. The generation of rough-and-tumble owners had given way to sounder businessmen like Shibe, Comiskey, and Dreyfuss, who knew how to nurture baseball's growing popularity. The bad, old days of the 1890s were over.

Questions for Consideration

1. How did the depression of the 1890s affect professional baseball? What was baseball's response, and was it successful?
2. Why did the 12-team format of the National League prove a failure?
3. Discuss Ban Johnson's role in creating the American League. Why was the new league a success?
4. What was the response of the National League to the challenge of the American League to their dominance?
5. Discuss some of the factors that help explain baseball's popularity during the early years of the twentieth century.

6. What is the argument of Riess's essay on race and ethnicity in baseball in the early years of the twentieth century (see pp. 72–85)? Do you find his case convincing? Give your reasons.
7. Compare John McGraw and Connie Mack as managers. How were they different, and why were successful?
8. What does the creation of the modern World Series idea tell us about the state of baseball in the early years of the twentieth century?

Notes

1. For an analysis of these changes and other major modifications in baseball, see Peter Morris, *A Game of Inches: The Stories behind the Innovations That Shaped Baseball* (Chicago: Ivan R. Dee, 2006).

2. Harold Seymour, *Baseball: The Early Years* (New York: Oxford University Press, 1960), especially chapters 21 and 22, which discuss the financial aspects of the emergence of the 12-team National League, particularly its impact on players' salaries.

3. Seymour, *Baseball*.

4. Leonard Koppett, *Koppett's Concise History of Major League Baseball* (Philadelphia: Temple University Press, 1998).

5. For the rough play of the 1890s, see Bill James, *The New Bill James Historical Baseball Abstract* (New York: Free Press, 2001), 52–57.

6. Eugene Murdock, *Ban Johnson: Czar of Baseball* (Westport, CT: Praeger, 1982) is the best overview of Johnson's career.

7. Geoffrey Ward, *Baseball: An Illustrated History* (New York: Alfred A. Knopf, 2001), 65.

8. Seymour, *Baseball*.

9. Harold Seymour, *Baseball: The Golden Age* (New York: Oxford University Press, 1971).

10. Quoted in Benjamin Rader, *American Sports: From the Age of Folk Games to the Age of Televised Sports*, 5th ed. (Englewood Cliffs, NJ: Prentice Hall, 1990), 159.

11. Roger Abrams, *The First World Series and the Baseball Fanatics of 1903* (Boston: Northeastern University Press, 2003) provides the best overview of baseball's first modern World Series.

12. Norman Macht, *Connie Mack and the Early Years of Baseball* (Lincoln: University of Nebraska Press, 2007), 347.

13. Harvey Frommer, *Baseball's Greatest Managers* (Guilford, CT: Lyons Press, 2017), 441.

14 Connie Mack, *My 66 Years in the Big Leagues* (Philadelphia: Universal Press, 1950), 32.

RACE AND ETHNICITY IN AMERICAN BASEBALL: 1900–1919

Steven A. Riess

Conventional wisdom has long held that professional baseball has been an excellent source of upward social mobility for the ambitious, hardworking athlete. Baseball was said to recruit its players on a democratic basis, regardless of ethnicity or other factors. Like the entertainment industry, boxing, crime, politics, or even the church, baseball was viewed as an excellent opportunity for impoverished, uneducated youths who had no social contacts to help them get started in a career. A test of that conventional wisdom is to see whether or not baseball has indeed been a source of mobility for the downtrodden in the cities by examining the ethnicity of major-league ballplayers in the first two decades of the twentieth century.

By the turn of the century, professional baseball was becoming a well-paying, high-prestige occupation. Wages averaged $2,000 at a time when the average worker earned under $700 a year and was higher than the pay of many professionals. Rookies usually earned $1,200, although one Harvard man began at $4,000. By 1910, several players and managers were earning salaries in excess of $10,000. In addition, a successful player could make more money by using his fame to get endorsements and to obtain easy offseason work. The high wages and the lifestyle of the professional ballplayer attracted a large number of middle-class sons to the occupation. The improved social status of the sport was reflected by the players' education: One-fourth of the major leaguers had attended college compared to under 5 percent of other men their age. Ballplayers were also beginning to be welcomed at the finest hotels, to travel in polite society, and to marry respectable, well-educated, middle-class girls.

Baseball attracted its recruits from its young fans. Fans who attended baseball games were supposedly from all social and economic groups. But in reality, most

Steven A. Riess, "Race and Ethnicity in American Baseball: 1900–1919," *Journal of Ethnic Studies* 4, no. 4 (Winter 1977): 39–55. Reprinted with the kind permission of the author.

spectators were white-collar men who had the time to go to the ballparks since games were played in the middle of the afternoon, usually Monday through Saturday. Nonmanual workers could put in a full day at the office, ride the streetcar or trolley to the ball field, enjoy a two-hour game, and still get home in time for dinner. Blue-collar fans were much more restricted. The average unskilled man worked 55 hours a week, which meant that he could not see a game unless he took off from work. Sunday was his only day off, but Sunday baseball was widely prohibited in 1900. In addition, the 10 cents for carfare and 50 cents for a ticket became quite expensive to a man earning less than $2 a day. The fans would become much more democratic after World War I, when workers' wages rose substantially at the same time that working hours dropped, and when Sunday baseball was played in the large eastern cities.

Harold Seymour has asserted, on the basis of limited evidence, that most working-class fans in the nineteenth century were either of native descent or second-generation Irish and Germans who bought cheap bleacher seats. These fans probably had jobs with unusual working hours, e.g., bakers; had short working days, such as construction workers; or had their day off during the week, as would policemen or firemen. Club owners tried to interest German Americans in their sport by placing advertisements in German-language newspapers, and by providing beer and Sunday games in heavily German cities like St. Louis and Cincinnati. Irishmen who frequented games were thought to be merchants, off-duty policemen, bartenders, porters, clerks, or expressmen. Irish interest in the national pastime was so great that certain sections of some ballparks appeared to be exclusively patronized by them, such as "Burkeville" at the Polo Grounds, or the "Kerry Patch" at St. Louis Sportsman's Park.

These working-class spectators assimilated into the dominant American culture and had actively participated in baseball rituals since childhood. Blue-collar fans were prominent mainly in western towns, which had Sunday baseball. These fans often took their young sons to the ballpark as a kind of ritual passage into boyhood. They seldom brought their wives, whose place was in the kitchen. James T. Farrell recalled in *My Baseball Diary* what baseball's influence was like on a growing poor Irish boy:

> Obviously, because I was born on the South Side of Chicago, I became a White Sox fan. Since baseball took such a strong hold upon me, it permeated my boyish thoughts and dreams. It became a consuming enthusiasm, a part of my dream or fantasy world. The conversations about baseball which I sometimes heard at home, the nostalgic recollections of players who have passed out of active play, the talk of players' names in an almost legendary way, all this was part of an oral tradition of baseball passed on to me, mainly in the home, during the early years of this century. It was a treat to a

little boy to be taken to a ball game and also to sit while his elders talked of the game. Along with this, my elders approved of my interest in baseball and encouraged me. . . . Baseball was a means of an awakening for me, an emergence from babyhood into the period of being a little boy.

Baseball was one of the few topics of conversation men could intelligently and confidently discuss with other men or with their own children. It provided a common experience which helped transcend differences among people.

New immigrants from Austria-Hungary, Italy, and Russia did not become baseball fans. They were primarily concerned with the problems of earning a living and sustaining their traditions in the new world, not in assimilating the normative behavior patterns of the new society. They worked at the arduous and poorest-paying jobs, and had little time left over for diversions. What leisure time they had was spent at ethnic clubs or ethnic taverns meeting and talking with others of similar backgrounds. Occasionally a newcomer might try to Americanize himself by learning about such American institutions as baseball and boxing. In Abraham Cahan's short novel *Yekl, A Tale of the New York Ghetto*, Jake the tailor is ridiculed by his fellow workers for devoting so much attention to a child's game.

Little attention was paid to baseball or to other American sports in the foreign-language newspapers, which were interested in their ethnic group's welfare in the United States and in their homeland. When a sports item did appear in these newspapers, it involved ethnic pride. In Chicago, where people of foreign parentage comprised nearly 78 percent of the population in 1890, the Czech press often printed the results of the Bohemian-sponsored amateur baseball leagues. The Czechs took pride in their young men who became professional baseball players, and the editors of *Denni Hlasatel* looked to the day when every major-league club would have at least one Czech on its roster. A newspaper helping its readers acculturate might occasionally try to introduce them to baseball. Abraham Cahan's *Jewish Daily Forward* (New York) printed an article in 1907 entitled, "The Fundamentals of Baseball Explained to Non-Sports," which was accompanied by a diagram of the Polo Grounds.

Despite the lack of interest shown by the new immigrants, professional baseball actively sought ballplayers from these ethnic groups. Chicago teams recruited Slavic players in order to attract the interest of the large Czech and Polish communities there. Most Slavic major leaguers spent at least part of their careers in Chicago. In New York, the Giants made notable efforts to discover Jewish athletes who would attract the attention of middle-class Jews moving into the Washington Heights neighborhood where the Polo Grounds was located. In 1916, they signed Benny Kauff, the star of the Federal League, who, it turned out, was of Slavic origin. Seven years later, the Giants signed Moses Solomon, but he failed to make the team.

Although the immigrants were not interested in the national pastime, their sons took up baseball, learning to play it in school and on city streets. Youngsters memorized the statistical accomplishments of their heroes and debated the comparable prowess of their idols. The cost of a ball game was usually too great for a ghetto youth, but if his interest was keen enough, he might get in without paying. On occasions, professional teams distributed free tickets to youth groups like the YMCA, the Boy Scouts, or settlement houses. But there were other ways: finding baseballs hit out of the park, clearing trash in the stands before game time, sneaking into the park, watching the game through a knothole in the fence, or just waiting at the ticket entrance in hopes that a spectator might have an extra pasteboard, or a ballplayer would give away an unneeded pass. In the 1890s, Morris Raphael Cohen would walk from his home to the nearby Brooklyn baseball park, then located in Brownsville, and watch a game through a hole in the fence. Young Harry Golden was able to attend ball games during summer in the early 1900s because of the job he shared with friends delivering pretzels to the Polo Grounds for a quarter plus carfare. On the day when he brought the pretzels, he would arrive at 10 o'clock and lounge in the clubhouse until the game started, running errands for the New York Giants players. After the game he returned home to the Lower East Side in time to sell his evening newspapers to the workers on their way home.

Black Americans viewed baseball quite differently from the new immigrants from Eastern and Southern Europe. Blacks were familiar with baseball and enjoyed attending ball games. But they were barred from participating in professional baseball. Black athletes had been professional ballplayers in the nineteenth century, and the Walker brothers had even played in the major leagues in 1884, for Toledo, but racial prejudice forced the blacks out of organized baseball in the 1890s. As a result, blacks formed their own semiprofessional teams.

Black fans attended professional and semiprofessional games in all parts of the country. In northern cities they would sit wherever they pleased but usually were restricted to the bleachers because of the expense of other locations. Southern franchises made special arrangements to segregate their black supporters by providing them with a separate entrance and their own seating area. However, it is unlikely that many blacks went to professional ball games because of the cost. The average black New Yorker in 1900, working as a servant or laborer, earned $4 to $6 a week.

Most black baseball fans attended the semiprofessional games played by black teams. The best black clubs toured the country, playing both black and white teams. Sometimes their opposition included major-league stars. These games were also popular with white fans, and on occasion, the white spectators outnumbered blacks. Home games were generally scheduled on Sundays in readily accessible fields: New York's Harlem Oval, which seated 2,600 and was located at 142nd Street and Lenox Avenue; Chicago's Schorling Park, which held

4,000 and was situated at 39th and Shields on the perimeter of the black belt. The New York promoters had to circumvent the penal codes, which prohibited Sunday baseball by selling programs instead of tickets. A bleacher seat cost a quarter and a grandstand seat 50 cents. Leading black teams like the Leland Giants, the Chicago American Giants, the Lincoln Giants, and the Philadelphia Giants were so popular that they played a number of games each year at the larger major-league parks. In 1911, four Black teams played a doubleheader at the Polo Grounds, which attracted 13,000, even though fans were charged the same high prices demanded by the New York Giants at their home games.

The Ethnic Background of Baseball Players

In the nineteenth century, most of the professional baseball players were either native-born Americans or of Irish or German descent. This continued during the first decades of the twentieth century. The single change in ethnic composition was the increasing percentage of native white American athletes entering the sport as it became respectable and well-paying. Over 90 percent of the professional players in the early 1900s belonged to these groups. Although young men of recent immigrant stock, mainly Russian Jews and Italians, achieved fame and even dominance in boxing, only a handful succeeded in professional baseball.

Baseball was a good source of social mobility for Irishmen. Irish Americans generally had difficulty improving their lot. While many nineteenth-century German immigrants arrived in America with a trade or capital to purchase a farm, Irish newcomers arrived unprepared for their new environment except that they could speak English. Irishmen had little alternative but to take the lowest-paying jobs requiring muscle power. A recent study of social mobility in Boston indicates that in 1890, just 10 percent of the Irish Americans did worse in advancing themselves than other white ethnic groups. For instance, of the second-generation Irish Bostonians born in the period 1860–1879, 38 percent were white-collar, while of the Yankees and second-generation British and Western Europeans, over 50 percent were white-collar. The Boston Irish's lack of success was exemplified by the concentration of blue-collar Irishmen in the least-skilled jobs. Irishmen completely dominated the boxing ring in the last half of the nineteenth century. One-half of the 16 world champions in the 1890s were of Irish extraction. This dominance declined somewhat in the early 1900s; yet, eight of the 26 champions crowned between 1900 and 1910 were Irish.

Baseball was a popular sport in the northeastern cities where the Irish immigrants settled, and many second-generation Irish played baseball, usually on teams sponsored by saloons or political clubs. The most proficient players were recruited to play professionally, and some eventually made the major leagues. Their example encouraged other Irish youths to seek a career in professional baseball.

Their parents encouraged baseball as a career. This attitude differed markedly from the attitudes of nineteenth-century middle-class parents who abhorred the idea of their sons becoming professional ballplayers.

The Irish dominance of baseball was reflected in the claim of one expert that approximately one-third of the major leaguers in the early 1890s were of Irish extraction. While many had names which were apparently of Irish origin, to characterize them all as Irish is a mistake. Many of them were probably of Scotch-Irish descent. Nevertheless, the public saw baseball as Irish dominated. Some observers were asserting by the 1910s that Irish domination had ended, replaced by native white Americans who were attracted to the then-national pastime by its improving pay and prestige. Grantland Rice disagreed with those journalists who found the Irish influence declining. Irishmen filled 11 of the 16 managerial posts in the American and National leagues in 1915.

In the twentieth century, the number of major-league players of German and Irish origins were approximately equal, and together they outnumbered the native-born players, who were the largest single group. Germans were the largest immigrant group in the nineteenth century, and they quickly assimilated into the mainstream of American society. German migrants were much more geographically mobile than the Irish and did not remain in their ports of entry, but moved into the heartland. They were also much more socially mobile. In Boston, 27 percent of German newcomers held white-collar jobs in 1890, compared to 10 percent of the Irish. Many German migrants arrived with skills acquired in the old country or with money to purchase farms. The class difference between first-generation Germans and Irish continued into the second generation, with 52 percent of the Germans in white-collar jobs, compared to 38 percent of the Irish. However, vertical mobility rates between second-generation Germans and Irish of the same social class were nearly identical.

Despite the relative success of the German migrants, their sons and grandsons were strongly attracted to professional baseball as a career. Middle-class sons found it a good way to maintain their status, and lower-class Germans saw in baseball a chance to improve their social rank. The same thoughts probably went through the minds of Irish and native American youths of similar class backgrounds.

In terms of recruitment patterns, there was some difference between Germans and Irish. There appear to have been more college-educated Irishmen than Germans in the major leagues, but the evidence is too sketchy to be certain. Poor youths with athletic skills could obtain financial compensation for participating in college sports. But whether or not poor Irishmen were more likely than indigent Germans to take this route to success is something we just don't know and which requires further research.

Although baseball presented itself as a democratic sport, which was an important factor in assimilating immigrants, only a handful of the major leaguers were new immigrants from Eastern or Southern Europe. An examination of the ethnic background of rookies in selected years indicates that in the period 1901–1906, there were five Bohemian, two Jewish, and no Italian first-year men. In 1910, there were no rookies from any of these groups, and in 1920, there was one Bohemian and two Italians out of 133. Veterans resented their presence. They were worried these newcomers might take their jobs, force down salary levels, and destroy the prestige of their occupation. Many fans apparently wanted to see the sport remain distinctly American and jeered and belittled players of recent immigrant stock. Contemporary explanations for the absence of the new ethnics occasionally had racist overtones, such as the *New York Tribune's* suggestion that these newcomers lacked the courage necessary to stand firmly in the batter's box and take a strong swing at the ball.

The immigrants whose absence was probably most discussed were the Jews. Although by 1900 they already comprised a sizeable percentage of the population in cities like New York and Chicago, there were few Jews in professional baseball. This trend has continued to the present day. The first Jewish major leaguers were Nick Bertonstock and Lip Pike, who played in the NAPBBP in 1871, but in the next 70 years they were succeeded by some 55 others. Jewish absence was particularly noteworthy since many baseball owners and officials were Jewish. Louis Kramer was founder of the American Association and its president in 1891. Nathan Menderson was president of the Cincinnati Reds from 1882 to 1890. In the next 20 years other baseball magnates of Jewish descent included Barney Dreyfuss of the Pittsburgh Pirates, Andrew Freedman of the Giants, Julius Fleischmann of the Reds, and Judge Harry Goldman, and the brothers Moses and Sidney Frank, of the Baltimore Orioles. Baseball was viewed as a low-prestige enterprise, and the old business elite shunned it for more respectable investments. Their absence provided opportunities for Jews and other non-WASPs to make money and gain status. The experience of these club owners was similar to that of the Jewish furriers, jewelers, and nickelodeon operators who built up the film industry.

Mass Jewish migration to America from Russia and Austria-Hungary began in the 1880s and lasted until the start of World War I. These immigrants were far better prepared for city life in the United States than peasant newcomers from Poland and Italy; many of the Jewish newcomers had already been exposed to urban society in Europe, and they brought with them more skills, a tradition for entrepreneurship, and a profound respect for education. Jewish newcomers were quite successful. By 1910, one-fourth of the Jews in Boston had white-collar jobs, a success story similar to that of the British immigrants of the previous generations. Most Jewish nonmanual workers were peddlers earning small incomes, but it was a job which entailed risk taking and developed business skills which would be important for the group's future. Italian immigrants, by comparison, did more poorly than their Jewish contemporaries. Just 12 percent of the Italian immigrant generation held white-collar jobs, a record similar to the Irish immigrants of the late nineteenth century.

Ambitious second-generation Jews who lacked the capital or initiative to start a small business, or who were poorly educated, might seek other avenues of social mobility in crime, entertainment, or professional athletics, particularly boxing. These were many of the same avenues for advancement that prior downtrodden groups like the Irish had taken. Boxing was a natural occupation for ghetto youngsters to enter since it was related to their day-to-day experiences. It was a functional skill, important for boys to learn if they wanted to survive in the urban jungle. Jewish boys coming home from school were often set upon by roving gangs of Irish or Italian toughs, and it was necessary that they learn to defend themselves. This street fight training prepared youngsters for careers as policemen, criminals, or boxers.

Jewish parents vigorously opposed the pugilistic ambitions of their sons, but family qualms often gave way to the paycheck which boxers brought home to help support the family. At first only a handful of Jews fought in the ring, but once a few like Leach Cross, a man who fought to pay his way through dental school, and Abe Attell, the world lightweight champion, achieved widespread fame, they became models for the younger to emulate. They were regarded as race heroes defending the honor of the Jewish people and proving to the world that the Jewish male was not weak and cowardly. Three of the 19 American world champions in the 1910s were Jewish, equal to the number of Irish and German champions. In the next decade, 17.5 percent of the champions were Jewish, placing them third behind the Italians and Irish. They were second to the Italians in the 1930s, with 14.3 percent.

Contemporary sportswriters were puzzled by the dearth of Jews in professional baseball while they were so prominent in boxing. In 1903, Barry McCormick noted in the *St. Louis Republic*, "He [the Jew] is athletic enough, and the great number of Jewish boxers show that he is adept at one kind of sport at least." However, Mc-Cormick could only identify two Jews, Barney Pelty and Harry Kane, in the major leagues. Baseball did not fit well into the Jewish immigrants' experience. Jews living in the crowded Lower East Side of New York had little opportunity to play baseball and become sufficiently proficient. Space was at a premium, with the population density reaching 500,000 per square mile. Furthermore, young Jews had little leisure time to spend playing baseball because they either worked full-time or attended school and worked afterwards. Most of their spare time came at night when it was too late to play baseball and possible to go to a settlement house or a gymnasium to learn the fundamentals of boxing.

The few Jewish major leaguers encountered discrimination. Several altered their names to hide their ethnic backgrounds and protect themselves against unfair treatment. Seven major leaguers with the surname Cohen changed it to such nondescript names as Kane, Bohne, and Ewing. Johnny Kling and Jacob Henry Azt, who were thought to be Jewish, but were actually German, received considerable abuse from colleagues who believed they were Jewish.

Baseball magnates in Chicago and New York, where there were large Jewish populations, wanted to hire Jewish ballplayers because they would attract their fellow Jews to the ballpark. The New York Giants made special efforts in the late 1910s to recruit a Jewish star since the surrounding Washington Heights neighborhood was rapidly becoming a Jewish community. When the Federal League folded before the start of the 1916 season, Giants owner Harry Hempstead signed a number of its best players, including the league's star, Benny Kauff, who was widely believed to be Jewish, although he was actually Slavic. In 1923, a local Jewish youth, Moses Solomon, put in a brief appearance with the Giants. Three years later, the team purchased a highly regarded minor leaguer named Andy Cohen to replace the great Rogers Hornsby, who had just been traded to Boston. Cohen was publicized by the New York press as a ghetto youth making good. However, they were far off the mark, because Cohen had been born in Baltimore, raised in Waco, Texas, and educated at the University of Alabama, hardly a Lower East Side environment. Cohen never fulfilled the Giants' high expectations and lasted just three years in the majors.

The majority of Jewish ballplayers did not come from New York, but from towns in the hinterlands. Harry Kane was born in Hamburg, Arkansas, and others from towns like Atlanta, Farmington, Missouri, and Middleport, Ohio. These athletes were far removed from the ghettoized Jewish influences and probably assimilated more quickly into the mainstream American culture, which approved of baseball, than did Jews raised in Brownsville or the Lower East Side, where the sport was widely castigated as a children's game played by men in short pants. Moreover, there was space to play baseball and more opportunities to become proficient at it in communities that were less crowded than New York's Jewish neighborhoods.

Besides the Jews, the other major, new immigrant groups were the Italians and Slavs, who began migrating to the United states en masse in the 1880s, settling primarily in northeastern and Midwestern cities. They came without skills or capital and had to take the lowest-skilled, poorest-paying jobs. The first-generation Italians and Slavs did not display the same entrepreneurial bent as their Jewish contemporaries, nor did they have the same respect for education. They took their children out of school at early ages and put them to work in factories and mines to help supplement the family income. Consequently, second-generation Italians and Slavs were not as well prepared as their Jewish peers to move up into white-collar jobs.

Opportunities were available to the poor, unlettered second-generation Italians and Slavs in such well-paying but low-prestige occupations as crime, entertainment, and boxing, positions which the respectable middle class shunned. In their poverty-stricken communities, the only people who ever had fat bankrolls were generally either criminals or pugilists, and they became role models to the youngsters who idolized them. Many Slavic and Italian young men became boxers, taking advantage of the skills they learned in the streets. They received training at settlement houses, private gymnasiums, and church-sponsored athletic facilities. The first Polish world champion boxer was Stanley Ketchell in 1907, and Pete Herman, the first Italian champion, was crowned in 1917. Italians became very prominent in professional boxing, and between 1920 and 1955, there were more Italian boxing champions than from any other ethnic group.

However, in the first third of the century, few Italians or Slavs entered professional baseball. The first Polish batting champion was Al Simmons in 1930, and the first Italian was Ernie Lombardi in 1938. Like the Jewish immigrants, these newcomers lived in crowded tenement communities where there was limited space available for parks, which made it difficult for their sons to play baseball. Also, most of their leisure time came after dark, when it was too late to play baseball.

The most successful of the new immigrant groups in professional baseball were the Czechs. Bohemian immigrants in Chicago and the industrial towns of Pennsylvania and Ohio founded athletic clubs so they could continue playing their traditional sports. These clubs often sponsored baseball leagues since the national pastime was popular among the second generation, and it was a good way to keep Czech youngsters tied to their heritage. Many watched the Bohemian teams compete on Sundays, and the results were reported in the Czech press and occasionally even in the big-city dailies. Bohemian amateur clubs in Chicago contributed several players to the major leagues in the 1910s.

The underrepresentation of Italian and Slavic players continued until the latter part of the 1930s. In 1929, for example, only four regulars among the five major-league teams in New York and Chicago were of recent immigrant stock, and two of them were Jewish. As late as 1935, *Who's Who in the National League* indicated that there were just four Italians and two Slavs on the combined rosters of the Brooklyn Dodgers, the New York Giants, and the Chicago Cubs.

American Indians were far more prominent and successful in professional baseball than the new immigrants in the first two decades of the century. The first Indian major leaguer was Lou Sockalexis, who played for Cleveland from 1897 to 1899, and was followed by about 30 other players of Indian descent in the next 20 years. Indian major leaguers were given a disproportionate amount of attention in the press because their presence was so surprising and out of the ordinary, and because certain of the Indian ballplayers like Chief Meyers and Chief Bender happened to be outstanding performers. Baseball's propagandists publicized the Indian backgrounds of these major leaguers as proof of the sport's democratic recruitment policies.

Indians were attracted to professional baseball because they believed it was an occupation free from racial prejudice, where talent alone would determine their ultimate success. As Chief Bender noted,

> The reason I went into baseball as a profession was that when I left
> school [Dartmouth], baseball offered me the best opportunity both
> for money and advancement that I could see. I adopted it because
> I played baseball better than I could do anything else, because the
> life and the game appealed to me, and because there was so little
> of racial prejudice in the game. . . . There has been scarcely a trace
> of sentiment against me on account of birth. I have been treated the
> same as the other men.

Cubans were another ethnic group prominent in baseball during the Progressive Era. Although the Cuban Esteban Bellan played in the NAPBBP in 1871, the island was not really exploited as a source of ballplayers until the 1910s. Baseball was a popular sport in Cuba, and visiting Cuban teams toured the Northeast in the early 1900s playing semipro games. In the meantime, a different major-league club visited Cuba each year to play exhibition games against local stalwarts. Major-league players and managers, particularly Clark Griffith of the Reds, were impressed by the quality of baseball they saw there, and in 1911, Griffith began signing Cubans to major-league contracts. By 1915, there were at least five Cubans in the majors and 11 more in the minors.

The matter of race was a big problem in recruiting Cubans. Unlike the U.S., little, if any, racial prejudice existed in Cuba, and blacks and whites were given equal opportunities there. Many star players were black, but professional scouts could not sign them because of racial barriers in the United States. American magnates were careful to point out that the Cubans they did sign were white Spaniards ("Castilians"), well-to-do, and from superior family backgrounds. Veteran American players were not happy with the Cuban invasion, fearing they would take jobs away from them and cause a drop in prevailing salaries by accepting lower wages. However, the veteran players did not have much to fear from Cubans, or even Indians, for that matter, since only a handful became professional athletes, and fewer still made the major leagues. Indeed, these two groups together comprised less than 2 percent of the major leaguers from 1900 to 1920.

Asians and blacks were completely excluded from professional baseball even though the sport claimed to select its players solely on the basis of talent. Their absence reflected American racial prejudices. Except for Hawaiians, few Asians played baseball. A major crisis did occur in 1915, when an Oriental of great promise was discovered by Frank Chance, manager of the Los Angeles team in the Pacific Coast League. Chance wanted to sign him to a contract but feared the wrath of his ballplayers and the antipathy of West Coast fans.

The exclusion of blacks was far more significant because they presented a real threat to white baseball players. About 30 blacks had actually played in organized baseball in the nineteenth century before the racial barriers were drawn shut. The first black professional ballplayer was John W. "Bud" Fowler, who played for New

Castle, Pennsylvania, in 1872. Twelve years later, Moses Fleetwood Walker, a former student at Oberlin and Michigan, became the first Afro-American in the major leagues when he signed to play with Toledo of the American Association.

The fate of the pioneer black players was not a happy tale, for they were poorly treated by both their teammates and the fans. In 1889, *Sporting News* surveyed the dismal situation, noting that "race prejudice exists in professional baseball ranks to a marked degree, and the unfortunate son of Africa who makes his living as a member of a team of white professionals has a rocky road to travel." White players refused to socialize with their black teammates and tried to force them out of the sport. Negroes were given poor coaching, sliding runners tried to spike them, and pitchers tried to hit them. Spectators were equally ill-disposed to black athletes, insulting them and threatening their lives. Late in the 1884 season, Toledo's manager received a letter from Richmond a few weeks before a scheduled three game series there:

> We the undersigned do hereby warn you not to put up Walker the
> Negro catcher the evenings that you play in Richmond, as we could
> mention the names of 75 determined men who have sworn to mob
> Walker if he comes on the grounds in a suit. We hope you will listen to
> our words of warning, so that there will be no trouble; but if you do not
> there certainly will be. We only write this to prevent much bloodshed,
> as you alone can prevent.

After 1898, there were no black players in organized baseball. An unwritten policy developed among baseball magnates who agreed not to sign any blacks. The principal challenge to that pact was aborted during spring training in 1901, when Giants manager John J. McGraw tried to pass off the black star Charles Grant as an Indian. However, Charles Comiskey recognized Grant. A minor challenge to the racist policies arose in 1910, when a new association known as the United States League was established outside the jurisdiction of organized baseball with franchises in Baltimore, Brooklyn, Boston, Newark, Patterson, Philadelphia, Providence, and Trenton. The league promised to hire any able athlete regardless of race or background, and it was reported that three of the first 100 players signed by the circuit were black. However, this experiment in biracial athletics was short-lived, for the league collapsed almost immediately after the start of its season.

Excluded from organized baseball, blacks organized their own semiprofessional teams and leagues. The quality of play among the best clubs was high. Black teams often played all star aggregates of white major leaguers on Sundays during the summer or in the fall after their season ended. White players and managers were occasionally quoted in newspapers, praising the abilities of the black players they competed against at home and in Cuba. A *St. Louis Post-Dispatch* reporter stated that the black ballplayers were actually superior to their white counterparts:

> It is in baseball that the descendant of Ham is at his athletic best. Less removed from the anthropoid ape, he gets down on ground balls better, springs higher for liners, has a stronger and surer grip, and gets in and out of a base on all fours in a way that makes the higher product of evolution look like a bush leaguer.

He predicted that whites would eventually be superseded in baseball, as they had been in boxing.

Most of the black semiprofessionals came from the South. They worked as railroad porters, waiters, or government employees and played baseball on the weekends. A few had college experience. The best athletes made baseball a full-time job. They played for teams like the Chicago Giants, who played baseball 12 months a year, touring the Northeast or Midwest in the summer, and then playing in a California winter league or at a Florida hotel, where they entertained the guests. The touring teams played up to 200 games a year, traveling by modest means, staying at whatever hotels would admit them, and getting paid on an irregular basis. One black magnate estimated that the average black player in the early 1900s was paid $466 for the season, compared to $571 for minor leaguers and $2,000 for major leaguers. The leading historian of black baseball estimates that the typical black ballplayer in the 1910s was paid $40 to $75 a month, while stars received $105. The highest reported salary was paid to the great John Henry Lloyd, who earned $250 a month in 1917. The athletes who played baseball on a full-time basis received compensation comparable to that of black letter carriers or school teachers. Some of the stars were better paid than school principals. Nevertheless, black ballplayers were not highly regarded by the black middle class, which considered them unrespectable and irresponsible, and they were barred from better black homes.

Most profits from black baseball ended up in white hands. Nearly all the black clubs were owned by white men, and the semiprofessional teams scheduled their games through a white booking agency, which forced the few black owners to accede to disadvantageous terms if they wished to get any games. Nat Strong, head of the agency, had a great deal of power and prevented teams that refused to do business on his terms from getting ball games. In 1909, he led the fight to oust cafe proprietor John W. Connors, then the only Afro-American owner of a black New York baseball club, out of the sport. Connors had refused to accept Strong's stipulations granting him a fixed guarantee rather than the typical and more profitable terms, which called for a percentage of the gate.

After World War I, an effort was initiated to wrestle control of black baseball away from white domination. The movement was led by Rube Foster, a former star pitcher, who had become the owner of his own semiprofessional club. Foster felt that since the players and two-thirds of the spectators at Negro games were black, the profits from the ball games should stay in black hands. In 1920, he organized the Negro National Baseball League with franchises in eight cities, all owned and operated by blacks. Foster further hoped that this black association could create ancillary jobs for blacks as scouts, umpires, clerks, secretaries, and other occupations needed to support a baseball enterprise.

Black ballplayers hoped the day was not too distant when they would be welcomed into organized baseball and paid the high salaries of major leaguers. These athletes pinned their hopes on the success of Cubans and Indians in the major leagues, for the blacks hoped their presence indicated a liberalized attitude toward men of color, foreshadowing their own admission into professional baseball. The advancement of light-skinned Cubans was watched with particular interest by players and by journalists like Lester Walton, sports editor of the *New York Age*, one of the principal black newspapers of the day. Walton wrote at the end of the 1911 season:

> With the admission of Cubans of a darker hue in the two big leagues it would then be easy for colored players who are citizens of this country to get into fast company. Until the public gets accustomed to seeing Negroes on big-league teams, the colored players should keep their mouths shut and pass for Cubans.

The dreams of these black ballplayers were not fulfilled for another generation, until after World War II, when Jackie Robinson was chosen by Branch Rickey to break the color barrier. In 1963, the proportion of black Americans in the big leagues reached 10 percent, approximately their share of the national population. By 1972, their percentage had nearly doubled to 18.9. Another 8.7 percent were black Latins. Yet there are relatively few black fringe players, there are few black executives, and only one black manager, Frank Robinson. Aaron Rosenblatt has demonstrated rather convincingly that a black player has to hit about 20 points higher than a white benchwarmer to remain on the squad.

The historic experience of blacks in baseball was in no way similar to that of the white immigrants. Second- and third-generation Germans and Irish were prominent on major-league rosters from the earliest days of professional baseball, and while the new immigrants were poorly represented until World War II, they had an equal chance to become major leaguers once they were assimilated. Even Cubans and Indians were accepted in organized baseball. But baseball's democratic ideology did not extend to black Americans, who were completely excluded from professional baseball because of racial prejudices. This semiofficial policy existed, although experts acknowledged the quality of the best black ballplayers. Unlike the foreign-born immigrants who had to learn about various American institutions like baseball, blacks constituted a readily available but unused source of talent for professional baseball during the Progressive Era.

TAKE ME OUT TO THE BALL GAME

Jack Norworth

Katie Casey was base ball mad.
Had the fever and had it bad;
Just to root for the home town crew,
Ev'ry sou Katie blew.
On a Saturday, her young beau
Called to see if she'd like to go,
To see a show but Miss Kate said,
"No, I'll tell you what you can do."

"Take me out to the ball game,
Take me out with the crowd.
Buy me some peanuts and cracker jack,
I don't care if I never get back,
Let me root, root, root for the home team,
If they don't win it's a shame.
For it's one, two, three strikes, you're out,
At the old ball game."

Katie Casey saw all the games,
Knew the players by their first names;
Told the umpire he was wrong,
All along good and strong.
When the score was just two to two,
Katie Casey knew what to do,
Just to cheer up the boys she knew,
She made the gang sing this song:

Jack Norworth, "Take Me Out to the Ball Game," Albert Von Tilzer, York Music Company, 1908.

"Take me out to the ball game,
Take me out with the crowd.
Buy me some peanuts and cracker jack,
I don't care if I never get back,
Let me root, root, root for the home team,
If they don't win it's a shame.
For it's one, two, three strikes, you're out,
At the old ball game."

CHAPTER 4

Baseball's Silver Age, 1909–1919

A Sign of Baseball Growth

Baseball prospered in the decade and half a following the peace agreement of 1903, with the game entering what baseball historian David Voigt called its "Silver Age." Baseball had seemingly solved most of its pressing problems, and the game benefited from the expanding wealth of the nation. National wealth increased by more than $100 billion in the first two decades of the century. Attendance continued to grow. In the second decade of the century, the attendance growth slowed, but the final figure for the decade was 56 million, slightly more than a 10 percent increase from the first decade. No club, however, topped the Giants' attendance record of almost 800,000, set in 1908.

Overall, the American League continued to outperform the National League. Between 1901 and 1919, the American League attracted more spectators in 18 of the 19 seasons. In some years, the margin was striking. In 1907, for instance, it attracted three-quarters of a million more fans than the National League. There is no clear reason why this was the case. Exciting pennant races were about equally distributed between the two leagues. A possible explanation is that the players entering the American League were better than their National League counterparts.

Baseball was much better administered now than it had been in the past. A new generation of owners entered baseball in the teens, replacing some of the buccaneers who had run baseball for years. Jacob Ruppert purchased the Yankees and began the process of turning the franchise into one of baseball's powerhouses. Charles Weeghman got the Cubs as part of the Federal League settlement, and he eventually sold the team to chewing gum magnate William Wrigley. Charles Stoneham, a stockbroker who some believed was a banker for

New York numbers writers, bought the Giants. William Baker took over the Phillies. Along with owners like Ben Shibe, Charles Ebbetts, and Barney Dreyfuss, the game was in safer—if at times more ruthless—hands than when it was being guided by some of the reckless characters who ran baseball in the 1890s.

Baseball continued to benefit from the lack of a real challenger for athletic talent. Football remained a college game, popular with its alumni, but it had no great national following. Football also had a bad reputation for violence and serious injuries. In 1905–1906, Harvard and Columbia discussed giving up the sport because of the injuries incurred. Golf and tennis were still in their infancy. In an interesting commentary on the times, Teddy Roosevelt advised President William Howard Taft that it would be fatal to allow himself to be seen golfing.[1] As a result, young males with athletic skills flocked to baseball to the extent that baseball had a virtual monopoly on such talent, a monopoly that would last for another six decades. This factor enabled baseball to renew itself every generation or so.

The progress of baseball paralleled the rapid changes taking place in the country. America's population increased by approximately 25 million in the first two decades of the century, with the greatest growth taking place in the urban areas, where professional baseball was played and the money to support the game was found. At least until the outbreak of World War I, immigration accounted for a considerable part of this increase, with the majority of migrants coming from Eastern Europe, including Jews, Poles, and Russians. Southern Europe, especially Italy, also contributed to this increase. Unlike the Germans and Irish, who quickly adopted baseball as part of their process of Americanization, however, none of these ethic groups made an impact on the sport until the 1930s. It took time for these groups to see in baseball a vehicle for assimilation and a way of showing that they were true Americans. A careful look through the roster of any of the teams in the majors in the teens would rarely turn up a Polish, Italian, or Jewish name. The Irish still played a major role in baseball. In 1911, six of the managers in the American League were Irish; two in the National League were.

Signs of baseball's prosperity and its hold on the imagination of the public were reflected in the great ballpark-building boom of 1909 to 1923. Part of the City Beautiful movement associated with the Progressives, they were an expression of the confidence of the time. Until 1909, other than Baker Bowl, home of the Philadelphia Phillies, the existing ballparks were constructed of wood, which meant they were subject to fire damage. Rebuilding was not difficult, and a ballpark could be constructed in a matter of weeks or months. Reflecting the prosperity of baseball, construction of new ballparks began in 1909, only now using brick, stone, reinforced concrete, and steel as building materials.

During the next five years, 10 ballparks were newly built or thoroughly remodeled along modern lines. The first, and the pacesetter for those that followed, was Shibe Park. Named after the owner, Ben Shibe, it was built in

1908–1909, for slightly less than $500,000 for land and construction. Located at 20th Street and Lehigh Avenue, in what was a middle-class neighborhood in north Philadelphia, it was easily reached by trolley or train. This was crucial for the new ballparks. They had to be placed where they could take advantage of the growth of public transportation, which was transforming the cities in those years. Shibe Park was well located. The Pennsylvania and Reading railroads ran nearby, and there were major trolley lines on Lehigh Avenue and the main north–south thoroughfare, Broad Street, which was just five streets away. What made Shibe Park so exceptional was its neo-classical style and the main entrance tower, which contained the executive offices, just like any other big business. The covered grandstand sat 10,000, while another 12,000 sat in the bleachers that ran along the first- and third-base lines. There was even a garage under the stands for those wealthy fans who drove to the game, one of the first signs that the automobile, then a rarity in American life, would have an intimate connection with baseball.[2]

Other ballparks followed rapidly. Four months after Shibe Park opened, Barney Dreyfuss christened his new ballpark in Pittsburgh, named Forbes Field after one of the heroes of the Seven Years' War, which saw the founding of the city. Never one to be outdone, Dreyfuss topped Shibe Park in amenities. His grandstand was triple-decked, with elevators and ramps to take fans to their seats. Moreover, it supplied boxes with telephones for busy executives needing to conduct business. He also charged $1.25 for a box seat and $1 for reserved seating, more than other ballparks at the time. Dreyfuss believed it would have the effect of drawing a better-off fan. He also showed foresight and imagination by building his new ballpark a 10-minute trolley ride from the downtown business district. He guessed correctly that Pittsburgh would expand and the trolley would bring the customer to him.

Shibe and Dreyfuss set off a building boom in baseball. In 1910, Charles Comiskey followed suit with a new park on the South Side of Chicago, not far from the infamous stockyards. The park, named after him, cost $550,000 to build, with the land costs adding another $150,000, making it the most expensive of the early ballparks. Built to imitate the Roman Coliseum, it had a red brick façade and featured a plot of Irish sod brought from Ireland. It was also the largest of the new parks, at 362 feet down the foul lines and 420 feet to center. Home runs would be rare.

The last of the innovative ballparks, Ebbets Field opened in 1913. Built on a plot with the revealing name of Pigtown, Charles Ebbets carefully bought up the land through a dummy corporation. The cost of the new ballpark eventually totaled $900,000, as Ebbets wanted a structure more modern than any other built. He shrewdly recognized the potential of the area in which he built it, believing the neighborhood was on the upswing. For him, the most important factor in spending all that money was the fact that nine trolley lines passed through the area, making it easy to reach.[3]

The ballpark-building boom lasted until 1916, with new parks opening in Boston (one for the Braves and one for the Red Sox), Washington, St. Louis, Detroit, and Cincinnati. The Chicago Cubs inherited the future Wrigley Field from the collapsing Federal League in 1916. All the teams in the major leagues now had modern ballfields, except for the Phillies and the New York American League team, who moved from their decrepit Hilltop Park to the Polo Grounds in 1913. They became known as the Yankees and would eventually construct the last and most modern of the great ballparks built during this era, Yankee Stadium, in 1923.

The building boom was a testament to the success baseball had become by the middle of the second decade of the century. Like the modern apartment buildings and early skyscrapers, the Flatiron and Woolworth buildings, subways, and elevated lines, they reflected the growing prosperity of the country and the faith in the future of the nation.

Another clear sign of the prosperity of the game was the increasing value of the baseball franchises. The New York American League franchise had been transferred from Baltimore for $18,000 in 1903. A dozen years later, the New York franchise was sold for between $400,000 and $500,000. An equally remarkable sale occurred when the New York Giants changed hands in 1919. John Brush, who paid $125,000 for the Giants in 1903, sold them to Charles Stoneham for $1 million. Even the lowly Braves, junior partners to the more popular Red Sox, went from a value of $75,000 in 1907, to $300,000 six years later. Just about every team in the majors turned a profit during the first years of the new major-league structure. McGraw's successful Giants earned $500,000 between 1906 and 1910. Comiskey estimated a profit of $150,000 in 1912.[4] According to one economic analysis of baseball during the second decade of the century, the average value of a baseball franchise was $585,000.[5]

The owners were always looking for new ways to make money. They sold advertising space on the outfield walls and in the scorecards that fans could buy at the games. Concessions, which were controlled for years by a company founded by Harry Stevens in the 1880s, began to bring in big money, especially when the hot dog caught on as the iconic baseball food.[6] Popcorn and Cracker Jacks (which became associated with baseball in the public mind), along with beer in some ballparks, and soda and ice cream, were also sold during the games and brought in decent sums for most teams. Growing fan interest in baseball also was reflected in the founding during the teens of such new sports publications as the popular *Baseball Magazine* and *Who's Who in Baseball*. In 1913, another sign of baseball's popularity was Western Union's willingness to pay each team $17,000 for the rights to telegraph their games. Important games like the World

Series were sent by telegraph to businesses in cities, where they were shown on electrical boards for fans to watch.

THE CHALLENGE OF THE FEDERAL LEAGUE

One consequence of baseball's prosperity and popularity during these years was another attempt to form a third major league. In 1913, a group of successful businessmen led by James Gilmore, a wealthy stationer from Chicago; Phil Ball, who ran a successful ice house business in St. Louis; and the Ward Brothers of New York, whose Tip Top Bread company was one of the biggest bakeries in the nation, met to plan a new league. They were joined by Harry Sinclair of the Sinclair Oil Company, an aggressive businessman cut from the same cloth as John D. Rockefeller and Andrew Carnegie. He would later be implicated in the Teapot Dome Scandal that helped destroy the presidency of Warren Harding.[7]

Modeling their strategy on Ban Johnson's success in establishing a new league in 1900, the businessmen decided to directly challenge the monopoly that the American and National leagues claimed for professional baseball. They believed there was room for a third league and found it easy to line up a group of financiers for teams in cities that once had a major-league team or in the past had supported Major League Baseball. They also knew baseball salaries had been kept artificially low by the reserve clause and believed for that reason that they would be able to tap into the pool of aggrieved players.

When the Federal League requested recognition as a major league, they were turned down on the grounds that there was no need for a third league and there weren't enough players to fill their rosters. The Federal League declared war and began raiding the major leagues. They believed they had a good chance of succeeding, just as Ban Johnson had a decade earlier. Just to make sure the National and American leagues understood how serious they were, the Federal League brought an antitrust suit against the two major leagues.

There were sound grounds for believing in their future, as a new attempt at a players' union had emerged in 1910. Led by a former player, Dave Fultz, who had gone to law school, a new organization called the Base Ball Players' Fraternity began to sign up members in growing numbers. Fultz claimed with considerable exaggeration that by 1912 he had more than 1,200 major leaguers and minor leaguers enrolled in his organization. The Fraternity's demands were similar to those of past attempts at organization: higher pay, some kind of pension program, modification of the reserve system, and so on. Just as the Fraternity peaked in strength, the Federal League was born. The Fraternity would have leverage to use against the established leagues.[8]

For the 1914 season, Federal League teams were established in Chicago, Pittsburgh, St. Louis, Indianapolis, Baltimore, Buffalo, and Kansas City. Of the successful major-league cities, Philadelphia, New York, and Boston were missing. Brooklyn also was granted a franchise. These sites were similar in their makeup to what Johnson started with in 1900, so there was optimism that the league would succeed. There is evidence that some of the investors had ulterior motives—they wanted to use the Federal League to force their way into the major-league franchises.

Enlisting players was easy. There was a great deal of anger in major-league circles about the way players were treated. In 1911, one of the best pitchers in the American League, Addie Joss, had died suddenly of meningitis. His family was left with nothing. Ban Johnson quickly arranged an all-star game that raised almost $13,000 for his wife and children. This didn't satisfy the players and only highlighted how tenuous their situation was. When the Federal League came along with lucrative offers, it found a receptive audience among the disgruntled players.

The Federal League was able to recruit a talented group of major leaguers by not only offering more money, but also promising to modify the reserve clause and even pay players a share of any money if they were sold to another team. They offered some of the best players unheard-of salaries. Ty Cobb was guaranteed a five-year contract worth $75,000, an unprecedented sum in those days. Cobb was tempted because he had been engaging in a salary dispute with Detroit, which they had resolved by paying him $15,000, soon to rise to $20,000. He decided to stay with his old team. To keep Walter Johnson, then the premier pitcher in the majors, Washington doubled his salary and gave him a $6,000 bonus for signing with them instead of jumping to the Federal League.[9]

Just about every player increased his bargaining position. By one estimate, baseball salaries doubled due to competition from the Federal League from $3,200 to $6,200 in two years. For some idea of what this means, compare the uproar caused by Henry Ford in 1914, when he raised pay for his workers from $2.25 to $5 a day, or $1,500 a year. At that time, the average baseball salary was five times as high as a result of the Federal League.

The Federal League got off to a good start. Among the major-league players they signed was shortstop Joe Tinker of the famous Cubs infield of Tinker, second baseman Johnny Evers, and first baseman Frank Chance. (This was the infield that inspired writer Franklin P. Adams to pen his iconic verse "Baseball's Sad Lexicon." "These are the saddest of possible words, Tinker to Evers to Chance . . . Making a Giant hit into a double, Words that are heavy with nothing but trouble, Tinker to Evers to Chance.")

Tinker became manager of the Chicago Whales and, by his joining the new league, served to lure other players. Harold Seymour estimates that 81 major leaguers played in the Federal League during the two years of its existence. Among them were a handful of talented major leaguers. Examples include baseball's premier defensive first baseman, Hal Chase; Benny Kauff, who led the Federal League in batting in two consecutive seasons; and George Stovall, who jumped from the St. Louis Browns to take over as player-manager of the Kansas City team.

For two years, the three leagues engaged in a ruinous competition. Every team lost money. Attendance in the National and American leagues suffered a precipitous decline as a result of the Federal League challenge. For comparison, American League attendance declined by more than 1 million from 1913, the last season before the Federal League challenge. For the National League, the figure was 400,000 less. To make matters worse, players' salaries had increased to unparalleled levels. Taking a group of 20 top players as an example, in 1913 they were paid a total of $76,000. After two years of Federal League bidding, they had doubled that total. The National and American league owners couldn't afford this kind of destructive competition. One of the first to react was Connie Mack. After the 1914 season, he began selling off the members of the great A's dynasty he had built during the past five years, the team that won four pennants and three World Series.

It was also becoming clear to the Federal League owners that they couldn't continue the war. After the end of the 1915 season, some of the Federal League owners, led by Gilmore and Harry Sinclair, hatched a plot to make the best deal from folding their league. They threatened to move a team to New York for the 1916 season and continue raiding the two major leagues. Actually, they wanted to be bought out at the best price available. Their bluff worked. The Federal League closed, and two of their owners were allowed to buy into the majors: Weeghman got the Cubs and moved them into the ballpark he had built for his Federal League team, the later-named iconic Wrigley Field. Phil Ball took over the St. Louis Browns, which had been losing money for years. Other Federal League owners were bought off, except for those controlling the Baltimore franchise. The Baltimore owners were offered $50,000, which they rejected. Instead, they launched an antitrust suit against the major leagues, claiming they were victims of a conspiracy hatched by the major-league owners. Baltimore won the case, and the jury granted an award of $80,000, which under the provisions of the Sherman Antitrust Act, was tripled to $249,000 according to the existing antitrust laws. The case was appealed to the U.S. Court of Appeals in Washington, which reversed the verdict on the grounds that baseball was not a form of interstate commerce and thus not subject to antitrust laws. Baltimore appealed, and the case eventually was heard by the Supreme Court, where a decision was reached that determined the legal status of baseball for the next 70 years.[10]

The Federal League challenge was the most serious organizational threat Major League Baseball faced in its young history. Its failure indicates that the National and American leagues had put their business on a sound basis. They were fortunate in one sense: The Federal League challenge had come in 1914, when the U.S. economy was in recession. The losses sustained by all sides could not continue. The solution for baseball's problem was the kind that big business had traditionally followed: consolidation and absorb your opponents. It worked for baseball owners, but not for the players.

The owners agreed there would be no reprisals directed against any of the players who jumped to the Federal League. Aside from Benny Kauff, winner of two batting titles in the Federal League, there was little interest in buying the contracts of the jumpers, certainly nothing comparable to what had happened in the war between the American and National leagues earlier in the century. Salaries gradually drifted back to levels reached before the Federal League wars. Fultz's Fraternity, which had taken a moderate stance during the war, soon lost members and dissolved.

THE STATE OF BASEBALL IN THE TEENS

The decade of the teens saw the continuation of American League domination. In the 10 World Series of the decade, the American League won eight; the Nationals won two, one of which was the controversial Black Sox series of 1919. A partial explanation for this domination is the creation of two iconic baseball dynasties in the American League: Connie Mack's great A's teams of 1910–1914, and a series of fine Red Sox teams that won four World Series.

Mack's team was built around a talented group of pitchers and his famous $100,000 infield, which featured two Hall of Fame players, Eddie Collins and Frank "Home Run" Baker. The A's were the first American League team to win 100 games, in 1910. During the next four years, they averaged 98 victories. A's pitchers won 20 games seven times from 1910 to 1914. The pitching staff was led by future Hall of Famers Chief Bender, Eddie Plank, and a talented right-hander named Jack Coombs. The A's won three World Series, getting revenge against McGraw's Giants by beating them handily in 1911 and 1913. The only World Series Mack's team lost was a defeat at the hands of the so-called Miracle Braves of 1914. In one of the most surprising upsets in baseball history, a Braves team in last place in July came on to not only win the pennant, but also sweep the highly favored A's in four-consecutive games.

With the Federal League challenge looming, Mack took the opportunity to begin to unload his stars for ready cash. He believed success had undermined their thirst for victory. Collins went to the White Sox and helped them win two pennants. Baker was sold to the Yankees, where he anchored third base in the late teens. Plank signed on with the Federal League and had one good season left. Bender was old, and his career went downhill after 1914. In all, Mack pocketed $180,000 through their sale—enough to pay off his bills and begin the long process of building another pennant contender.

The Red Sox teams of the teens won the World Series of 1912, against a favored John McGraw Giants team. The Red Sox won 105 games that season (an American League record) and produced one of the best outfields in baseball history: Duffy Lewis, Harry Hooper, and Tris Speaker, the latter two being Hall of Famers. The pitching staff was led by Smoky Joe Wood, who won 34 games against just five defeats. Interestingly, Wood hurt his arm the next year and continued in baseball as an outfielder with a career batting average of .283. Beginning in 1915, the Red Sox won three of the next four World Series and were now led on the mound by an exciting, young, hard-throwing pitcher, Babe Ruth.

The A's and Red Sox completely dominated American League play in the teens. The only other team to win a pennant and a World Series was Comiskey's White Sox in 1917. Comiskey was building a solid team that would peak in 1919, the year of the Black Sox Scandal. In the National League, pennant race winners were better balanced. McGraw's Giants won four, the Phillies won in 1915, Brooklyn in 1916, the Cubs in 1918, and Cincinnati in 1919. Only the Braves in 1914 and Cincinnati in 1919 won a world title, the latter tainted by scandal. Truly, the American League had become dominant, just as Ban Johnson predicted.

It is difficult to explain this imbalance. It is clear the American League produced a better talent pool than the National's in the teens. Why this is the case is not clear. It could be better scouting of talent. Connie Mack had a number of friends who did informal scouting for him, but then so did John McGraw. It is possible that the cleaner brand of baseball Ban Johnson insisted on for his league attracted a higher-quality player. It is interesting that there were more college-type players in the American League than the National. Whatever the reason, the American was the superior league in the teens.

Bill James, in his analysis of baseball decade by decade, lists the all-stars of the teen years, a total of eight position players and four pitchers. The position players were from the American League, as were two of the four pitchers. Among the dominant American League stars of the teens was Ty Cobb, who came into his own during those years. Between 1910 and 1919, Cobb won every batting title, except for 1916, when he was beaten out by another great player, Tris Speaker. Often regarded as the greatest player in the game after Cobb, Speaker compiled a lifetime batting average of .344, had 3,500 hits, and holds the record for most doubles in a career (793). Five times he hit better than .380. Other American League greats who emerged in the teens included

Shoeless Joe Jackson, a lifetime .356 hitter, and George Sisler, who twice hit better than .400. The teens also saw the arrival of perhaps the greatest figure in baseball history, Babe Ruth. The National League did not produce any batting stars of that caliber.

Perhaps the purest talent to enter the so-called Senior Circuit during those years was a pitcher, Grover Cleveland Alexander. Known as "Old Pete" because he pitched until he was 43, Alexander broke in with the Phillies in 1911, setting a rookie record by winning 28 games. He strung together three consecutive 30-win seasons in which his combined ERA was just 1.53. Alexander suffered from epilepsy and was a chronic alcoholic from World War I onward. His 373 wins ties him with Christy Mathewson for most victories for a National League pitcher.

Overall, the quality of play in both leagues showed continued improvement and professionalism. The improvement in equipment partially explains this phenomenon. Roger Bresnahan is credited with adopting the shin guards worn by cricket players beginning in 1907. Strangely enough, few catchers followed his lead because it was considered less than manly. Johnny Kling of the Cubs said he would wear shin guards "as soon as I can muster up nerve enough."[11] Bresnahan also improved the catcher's mask by adding soft padding inside to better absorb the shock from foul balls. Such protective devices enabled catchers to stay in the game longer. Catchers rarely caught 100 games at this time because of various injuries, mostly from foul balls. In 1904, only one catcher in the majors was behind the plate for 100 games. Ten years later, no catcher in the National League went to bat 400 times, while just one in the American League reached that figure. These changes enabled the catcher to move closer to the batter and thus form a better target for the pitcher. The catcher would also have a better chance of throwing out base stealers.

Just about every batter had his bats made for him to suit his style of batting. The thick-handled bats of the past were giving way to narrower-handle models, although the weight was rarely more than 34 ounces. Babe Ruth supposedly swung a bat that weighed 40 ounces. Players began ordering their own model bats, with ash being the overwhelming choice of wood for good contact and drive. Hillerich bats were among the most popular under the name "Louisville Slugger" model.

One of the most important developments was in the improvement of gloves. Gloves grew bigger, which made for better defense. In 1919, pitcher Bill Doak invented a revolutionary glove for fielding. He placed a web between the thumb and first finger of the glove, giving it two pockets, one in the glove itself and a second in the webbing. Players soon became adept at catching the ball in the web, which took pressure off their hands. Partly as a result, the number of errors declined sharply. In 1901, National League teams committed 2,500 errors. By 1920, that figure declined by 1,000.[12]

In general, the baseball in use throughout this period remained the rubber center one produced by Reach and Spalding. Battered and dirty, scarred by the pitcher, spit on with tobacco, rubbed with slippery elm, the ball truly earned the name the "Deadball Era." Balls were left in play until they were virtually dead and umpires rarely added new balls during the game. Foul balls hit into the stands had to be returned to the field. Only gradually did the teams carry more baseballs than a couple for a game. In 1911, without warning and for reasons we don't know, the major leagues experimented with a cork centered ball. It was much livelier and the results were quickly apparent. League batting average in the American League rose from a typical "Deadball Era" .243 to an unheard of .273. Cobb and Shoeless Joe Jackson both topped the .400 mark that season. Four years later with the older version of the baseball in use batting averages were back to their past levels in the 240s.

The result of all these gradual changes was to make the game faster and to require a high degree of professionalism on the part of the players in the majors. Like all institutions, baseball stressed constant improvement as a way of attracting new fans.

BASEBALL AND THE GREAT WAR

Major League Baseball didn't have a "Good War" during World War I. In the past, military conflicts had caused trouble for baseball. The game nearly shut down during the Civil War. The Spanish-American War was over so quickly in 1898 that the baseball season wasn't affected. The timing of World War I created particular problems. It came when Major League Baseball was confronted by the Federal League. With that issue resolved, baseball quickly returned to normal in 1916 but that season was not a particularly happy one. Attendance bounced back, although not approaching the high levels of 1908 or 1909. The season itself was lifeless. Other than another batting title for Ty Cobb and another 30 game winning season for Grover Cleveland Alexander there were no outstanding statistical highlights. The World Series returned to normal and Boston won easily over Brooklyn, winning four of the five games. Babe Ruth won his first game and began a string of 29 scoreless innings in the World Series. He also went 0 for 5 at the plate.

Before the next season began, baseball was confronted with a major problem—what to do with the nation now at war. War against the Central Powers was declared on April 6 just as the 1917 season was about to get underway. In World War II when a draft would be initiated in 1941, some players, like Bob Feller and Hank Greenberg, had already joined the military even before America's entry into the war after Pearl Harbor. Nothing like that happened on the eve of World War I. Soon after America's entry into the war, a "work or fight" order was issued by the American government which would cover males in their twenties.[13] Baseball would not receive special treatment.

In 1917, baseball was not affected significantly by the draft. Only a handful of players were called up, starting with Hank Gowdy, a highly regarded catcher with the Boston Braves. The war engendered intense patriotic feelings directed against Germany. Suddenly, all things German lost their popularity—German shepherds became scarce and the name sauerkraut was changed to Liberty cabbage. Courses teaching the German language in school were banned in some parts of the country. Baseball didn't lag far behind in demonstrating its patriotic feelings. To show their patriotism, teams carried out military drills using bats instead of rifles. Ban Johnson even offered a prize of $500 for the best-drilled team.

The 1917 season was another uneventful one. Attendance did not recover to the highs of the past, and once again nothing outstanding happened during the season. The World Series went off as normal, with Charles Comiskey's White Sox defeating John McGraw's Giants handily, four games to two.

With the draft role averaging about 200,000 per month by the end of 1917, it was clear that baseball had to consider the war's impact on the sport's future. There was growing criticism of athletes being "slackers" and not doing their part in the war effort, and that sports in general was a nonessential activity. There was little sympathy when baseball officials sounded out the government about the future. Some of the owners wanted to suspend the 1918 season, but Ban Johnson argued they should play out the schedule. In 1918, baseball players began to be drafted in large numbers. Other players opted for essential war industries, like working in shipyards, steel mills, or the mines. Many of them were accused of not really doing war work, but playing baseball for the company team, a charge that was often correct.

For the 1918 season, the owners, fearful of government pressure to shut down the game, decided to shorten the season to 140 games instead of 154 and play the World Series right after Labor Day. They were right to act, because the secretary of war, Newton Baker, decided to toughen up the regulations regarding the "work or fight" rule. Suddenly, baseball began to lose players. Eventually, 124 American and National league players served in the armed forces. One former major leaguer, Eddie Grant, who had played for the New York Giants, was killed in action in 1918 in the battles around the Meuse-Argonne in October. A handful of others were injured, of whom the most serious was former pitching great Christy Mathewson, who was gassed in a training accident. He never recovered from his attack and died in 1925, just 45 years old.

The 1918 season was a disaster for baseball. Attendance dropped to all-time lows as fan interest lagged. Players were angered when they found they would only be paid through August since the September schedule was wiped out. The

World Series turned out to be a major letdown. The World Series teams discovered that prize money would now go to all the teams in the first division and that revenue devoted to their share would be the lowest since 1903.

The Series itself was a rather lifeless one. The Red Sox won once again, beating a good Cubs team, four games to two. Babe Ruth's scoreless innings streak ended, but foreshadowing his future as a batter, he drove in two runs with a triple and led the Red Sox in RBIs.

The real story of the Series came before Game 4. The players on both teams threatened to strike if they weren't guaranteed more money. The game was delayed an hour. Ban Johnson implored the players not to strike, as it would be unfair to the 20,000 fans in the stands and cast doubt on the teams' patriotism. The players finally agreed to play without getting a guarantee of more money. When the Series ended, they found out they had been cheated once again. The players' share would be $1,100 for the winning Red Sox and just $670 for the losing Cubs, the lowest pay in the brief history of the World Series. Still angry after the collapse of the Federal League, which had seen their salaries reach unheard-of levels, they felt betrayed once again.[14]

These actions left the players outraged. The sense that the owners had mistreated them and other players since the Federal League war created an angry and unhappy group of major leaguers. It is important to keep this atmosphere in mind when thinking about the origin of the Black Sox Scandal the next season. The players were convinced they had been cheated by the owners and, even worse, that they were taken for granted. It is easy to see how some would want revenge by throwing games or, in this case, throwing the World Series.

After the World Series, the owners had to consider what to do for the next season if the war continued. While it is not absolutely clear what action they would have taken, it appears they were going to close down Major League Baseball for the duration of the war. The argument for this was their belief that there wouldn't be a sufficient base of players available in the third year of the war to field 16 teams. Baseball was relieved of that worry when the Germans surrendered on November 11. The United States and baseball had escaped another crisis.

Question for Consideration

1. According to the Riess essay, did baseball provide an outlet for upward mobility? Do you find his argument convincing? Give your reasons.
2. What happened to the great A's dynasty created by Connie Mack between 1909 and 1914? What does this tell you about the nature of baseball at that time?

3. Discuss the reasons behind the ballpark construction boom between 1909 and 1916. What does this development have to say about baseball?

4. Why did the Federal League fail? Why was it unable to duplicate the success of Ban Johnson's American League development earlier in the century?

5. Why did baseball struggle economically between 1910 and 1918? What was the nature of some of the problems baseball faced in those years?

6. Discuss some of the legal issues involved in the dissolution of the Federal League. Was the resolution of the crisis reasonable?

7. How did baseball deal with the problems created by U.S. involvement in World War I?

Notes

1. Harold Seymour, *Baseball: The Golden Age* (New York: Oxford University Press, 1971).

2. Bruce Kuklick, *To Every Thing a Season: Shibe Park and Urban Philadelphia* (Princeton, NJ: Princeton University Press, 1991) has a thorough analysis of the building of Shibe Park, especially in chapter 1. For the details and background of Shibe Park, see Rich Wescott, *Philadelphia's Old Ballparks* (Philadelphia: Temple University Press, 1996).

3. For the new ballparks see, Philip J. Lowry, *Green Cathedrals* (New York: Walker & Company, 2006).

4. Seymour, *Baseball*.

5. Michael Haupert, "The Economic History of Major League Baseball," *EH.net Encyclopedia*, https://eh.net/encyclopedia/the-economic-history-of-major-league-baseball/ (accessed May 6, 2018).

6. Michael Gershman, *Diamonds: The Evolution of the Ballpark* (Boston: Mariner Books, 1993).

7. Gary Hailey, "Anatomy of a Murder: The Federal League and the Courts," *National Pastime: A Review of Baseball History* 4 (Spring 1985): 62–73.

8. Seymour, *Baseball*.

9. Seymour, *Baseball*.

10. For an overview of the Federal League's impact on baseball, see Robert F. Burk, *Never Just a Game: Players, Owners, and American Baseball to 1920* (Chapel Hill: University of North Carolina Press, 1994).

11. Peter Morris, *A Game of Inches: The Stories behind the Innovations That Shaped Baseball* (Chicago: Ivan R. Dee, 2006), 441.

12. For the development of equipment, see Morris, *A Game of Inches*, especially chapter 9.

13. Seymour, *Baseball*.

14. Seymour, *Baseball*.

ANATOMY OF A MURDER: THE FEDERAL LEAGUE AND THE COURTS

Gary Hailey

The Federal League War

Late nineteenth-century professional baseball was plagued by wars between the established National League and a succession of upstart leagues. The American Association war of 1882, the Players League war of 1890, the American League war of 1900—all these bitter conflicts resulted in huge losses for almost everyone involved, not to mention widespread public disenchantment with the professional game.

More than two decades of strife ended in 1903, when the National League and the American League signed a peace treaty. American League president Ban Johnson testified at the *Federal Baseball* trial that the purpose of the peace treaty was to restore "normal conditions" to professional baseball. . . .

Later that year, the two major leagues and several minor leagues adopted the "National Agreement," which provided for mutual respect for player contracts, reserve lists, and territorial rights. It also established a "National Commission," consisting of the major-league presidents and a third man selected by them, to rule the sport.

Peace—or, to put it another way, the lack of competition between the two leagues—brought prosperity. Attendance and profits reached unprecedented heights, and the World Series added greatly to the public interest in the pennant races. That prosperity attracted the attention of potential rivals. In 1913, several wealthy businessmen organized the Federal League of Professional Baseball Clubs. Prior to the start of the 1914 season, Federal League president James Gilmore asked

Gary Hailey, "Anatomy of a Murder: The Federal League and the Courts," *National Pastime: A Review of Baseball History* 4 (Spring 1985): 62–73. Edited with permission from the Society of American Baseball Research with special thanks to Celia Tan.

Ban Johnson if O.B. would allow the Federal League to operate under the National Agreement as a third major league. Johnson told Gilmore that, "there was not room for three major leagues."

The Federal League owners declared war. They quickly erected brand-new stadiums in the league's eight cities—Baltimore, Brooklyn, Buffalo, Chicago, Indianapolis, Kansas City, Pittsburgh, and St. Louis. They also declared that the reserve clause in O.B.'s standard player contract was unenforceable and began to sign up players under reserve by existing major and minor league clubs. . . .

The Reserve Clause

Much of the National Agreement and many of the rules and regulations issued by the National Commission dealt with the right of reservation, which National Commission chairman and Cincinnati Reds president August "Garry" Herrmann described as "absolutely necessary" to O.B. For example, Article 8, Section 1 of the National Agreement provided that: "[N]o nonreserve contract shall be entered into by any club operating under the National Agreement until permission to do so has first been obtained." Article 6, Section 1 of that document stated that no club could "negotiate for the purchase or lease of the property"—that is, players—"of another club without first securing the consent of such club." "In consideration of the compensation paid to the [player] by the [team], the [player] agrees and obligates himself to contract with and continue in the service of [the team] for the succeeding season at a salary to be determined by the parties of such contract."

The Blacklist

Other rules of O.B. were intended to discourage players under reserve from jumping to "outlaw" organizations that were not parties to the National Agreement, such as the Federal League. Articles 22 and 23 provided that any player who signed a contract or even entered into negotiations with an outlaw team "shall be declared ineligible" for at least three years. Any National Agreement team that signed an ineligible player could be drummed out of O.B. Any player who even appeared in an exhibition game with an ineligible player was himself subject to blacklisting. . . .

Johnson Fights Back

Johnson made his opinions known. In a March 5, 1914, interview with a New York *Evening Sun* writer, Johnson "declared war" on the Federal League.

> There can be no peace until the Federal League has been exter-
> minated. . . . [W]e will fight these pirates to the finish. There will be
> no quarter.
>
> Yes, I've heard that peacemakers are at work, but they are wasting
> their time. The American League will tolerate no such interference.
>
> This Federal League movement is taken too seriously, why, the
> whole thing is a joke. They are holding a meeting once a week to
> keep from falling to pieces. Quote me as saying that the Federals
> have no money in Buffalo, Indianapolis, and Pittsburgh. They have
> no ballparks in any of their cities, except an amateur field in Kansas
> City and a ramshackle affair in Pittsburgh.

The Johnson interview appeared in print the day before 50-odd major leaguers returned to New York on the *Lusitania* after an around-the-world trip. According to the plaintiff, Johnson's tough talk was intended to frighten those players away from the Federal League, as well as to destroy the new circuit's credibility with the public.

The 1914 Season

In spite of organized baseball's opposition, the Federal League opened the 1914 season confident of success. Opening Day attendance was high, with Baltimore's home opener attracting a standing-room-only crowd of 19,000.

The 1914 pennant race was a close one: Indianapolis, led by outfielder Benny Kauff (who hit .370, stole 75 bases, and scored 120 runs) and pitcher Cy Falkenberg (a 25-game winner with a 2.22 ERA and nine shutouts), edged Chicago by one and a half games, with Baltimore a close third. Still, total Federal League attendance did not approach that of either the American or National league. The Chicago Feder-als led the league in attendance but drew fewer fans than the sixth-place White Sox. The established leagues suffered as well; AL attendance fell from 3.5 million in 1913 to 2.75 million in 1914.

The players were not complaining about the competition between the rival leagues. The Federal League eventually signed 81 major leaguers and 140 minor leaguers to contracts, nearly all of them at much higher salaries. Other players used the threat of jumping to get more money from teams in O.B. Several players—includ-ing Ray Caldwell, Walter Johnson, "Reindeer Bill" Killefer, and Ivy Wingo—signed con-tracts with Federal League teams but were persuaded to jump back to their former clubs. Caldwell made $2,400 in 1913, but the Yankees gave him a four-year contract paying $8,000 annually to bring him back into the fold. Killefer's and Wingo's salaries also more than doubled, while Johnson's went from $7,000 to $12,500.

Several times, disputes over who had rights to a player ended up in court. Or-ganized baseball did not take legal action against players who were reserved but not under contract, but it did go to court to restrain players who had signed contracts for the 1914 season from jumping leagues. Early that season, pitchers Dave Davenport and George "Chief" Johnson, and outfielder Armando Marsans of the Cincinnati Reds, jumped to Federal League clubs. A Missouri federal judge granted the Reds' request for an injunction against Marsans, but a court in Illinois refused to issue a similar injunction against Johnson because the contract lacked "mutuality." On similar grounds, a New York court denied a White Sox request for a court order to prevent first baseman Hal Chase from jumping to the Buffalo Federals.

On January 5, 1915, the Federal League took the legal offensive by filing an antitrust suit against organized baseball. The Chicago federal judge assigned to hear the case was none other than Kenesaw Mountain Landis, who had the reputation of being a committed trustbuster. The trial of that case ended on January 22, and the Federal League hoped for a quick decision from Judge Landis. But the future commissioner seemed to be in no hurry to act. In March, Brooklyn Federals owner R. B. Ward approached Ban Johnson and again asked O.B. to allow its rival to become a party to the National Agreement.

1915: The War Continues

The Federal League opened the 1915 season with high hopes. Over 27,000 fans were on hand for Opening Day in Newark, where oilman Harry Sinclair had moved the Indianapolis franchise. But attendance fell off rapidly, and the losses began to mount. By the end of the league's second season, Brooklyn's Ward had lost $800,000; the Kansas City and Buffalo clubs were insolvent. Baltimore lost $35,000 in 1914, and almost $30,000 in 1915.

"It Was One Big Bluff"

Gilmore approached Sinclair and Ward with an audacious plan. First, they rented a suite of Manhattan offices and purchased an option to buy some vacant land at 143rd Street and Lenox Avenue. They then asked Corry Comstock, a New York City engineer and architect who was also the vice president of the Pittsburgh Federal club, to draw up plans for a grandiose, 55,000-seat stadium. Gilmore then announced to the press that the Federal League planned to "invade" New York in 1916.

The purpose of all this? According to Gilmore, "It was one big bluff," a trick to force O.B. into "coming around and making some kind of offer." Gilmore's machinations certainly fooled the Baltimore club. While he was trying to bluff O.B. into buying out the Federal League, Baltimore officials were naively making preparations for the 1916 season. Colonel Stuart S. Janney, a prominent Baltimore attorney who held stock in the team and served as its lawyer, testified that the club's directors and stockholders had not expected to turn a profit overnight and were prepared to supply whatever additional financing was necessary for the 1916 season.

These preparations were encouraged by a series of letters Gilmore wrote to club officials in the fall of 1915, all of which contained some implication that the Federal League would be alive and well enough to operate in 1916. In an October 13 letter, Gilmore wrote: "I hope that your club is signing up some good talent for the coming year. I had wonderful faith in Baltimore as a major-league city and know if you can get a fighting team there and keep it in the race, you will draw wonderful crowds and easily pay expenses. . . ."

Peace Talks

Baltimore officials did hear rumors that some Federal League owners were negotiating a settlement. At a November 9 league meeting in Indianapolis, Baltimore president Rasin asked Gilmore, Weeghman, and Sinclair point-blank if there was any truth in newspaper reports to that effect. All three denied that they were in communication with organized baseball, but Rasin suspected at the time that their denials "might not be frank." In early December, Rasin saw more "newspaper talk" that O.B. and the Federal League were about to cut a deal. When he called Gilmore, Gilmore again assured him that there was no truth to the rumors.

On December 12, Gilmore ran into three National League officials in the lobby of New York City's Biltmore Hotel. One of them asked Gilmore to "come around and take this matter up" at the National League owners' meeting scheduled for the next day. Gilmore turned down the invitation. "Absolutely nothing going," he said. "We have gone too far and made too much progress on our New York invasion."

The next day, the same men called Gilmore and asked him to "come over and fix this thing up." Gilmore—hoping to hook his adversaries a little more firmly before reeling them in—feigned disinterest. "I told you the other day I would not have anything to do with it," he said, "and I will not talk about it."

Gilmore then turned to Harry Sinclair and said, in a voice loud enough for his caller to hear, "Harry, these people want [us] to come over and talk to them. Do you want to go?" Also intending the caller to hear him, Sinclair replied, "We might as well go and hear what they have to say." The two of them went to National League president Tener's office to discuss the situation.

Gilmore, Sinclair, and the National League representatives came to a tentative peace agreement. First, the N.L. agreed to make all blacklisted Federal League players eligible to play in O.B. and to let the Federal League owners sell their players' contracts to the highest bidder. Next, the N.L. owners offered to buy the Brooklyn Federals' park for $400,000, subject to the American League owners agreeing to kick in half of that sum. They also promised to approve the sale of the Chicago Cubs to Chicago Federals owner Charles E. Weeghman and put up $50,000 of the purchase price. The N.L. owners then agreed to buy out the Pittsburgh Federals for $50,000. Sinclair was a close friend of St. Louis Federals owner Phil Ball, and he assured the conferees that Ball would be satisfied if he could buy either the Cardinals or the Browns. The Buffalo and Kansas City clubs were no longer members in good standing of the Federal League—their owners had run out of money before the season ended, and the other teams had provided funds to pay their players in order to keep the league's financial problems a secret—so there was little need to worry about them. There was apparently no discussion concerning the Newark franchise, even though owner Sinclair was present.

That left only the Baltimore club. Gilmore testified that he asked for $200,000 for Baltimore's owners but was laughed at. He later told Sinclair that he thought it was wise "to start high." The meeting then broke up.

On December 16, 1915, Rasin received a telegram from Gilmore: "You and Hanlon be at Biltmore in morning. Important." Rasin, Hanlon, and Janney took a midnight train to New York and went to Gilmore's apartment at the Biltmore Hotel on the morning of December 17. Gilmore explained that he had summoned them to New York to tell them that the 1916 Federal League season was "all off." Gilmore then told the stunned Baltimore officials about the tentative peace agreement of the 13th.

Janney and Rasin asked why Gilmore and the others had agreed to sell out, but Gilmore did not reply. They then asked what arrangements had been made concerning the Baltimore club's interests. None, said Gilmore; however, he was sure that Baltimore would be "taken care of" before the settlement was made final.

Later, Sinclair, Weeghman, and representatives of other Federal League teams joined the meeting. They told the Baltimoreans that the opportunity to make peace had arisen suddenly and unexpectedly, and no one then present in New York felt he had the authority to speak for Baltimore; however, like Gilmore, they were all sure that the National Commission would give due consideration to Baltimore's claims.

The Baltimore officials were in no mood to take Gilmore's advice and "accept the situation philosophically." According to Janney, the discussion "grew rather bitter." When Sinclair defended his and his allies' actions, "quite a dispute arose" between him and Janney; "his words and mine," Janney testified, "were not always of the smoothest." Janney argued that the Federal League clubs should get some share of the proceeds of any agreement to dissolve the circuit, but Sinclair said he "would have none of that."

Gilmore and his allies hoped to finalize the December 13 agreement at a meeting with American and National league club owners that evening at the Waldorf-Astoria Hotel. According to Gilmore, Comstock, and Ward, Rasin moved that a committee of three—Gilmore, Sinclair, and Weeghman—be authorized to represent all the Federal League clubs at that meeting. Rasin denied that he made such a motion.

The Waldorf Meeting

The Waldorf meeting was called to order by National Commission president August Herrmann at 9:10 P.M., Friday, December 17, 1915. [. . .] The conferees quickly ratified those parts of the tentative peace agreement of December 13 that provided that the National League would put up $50,000 toward Weeghman's purchase of the Cubs; that organized baseball would pay R. B. Ward's heirs $20,000 a year for 20 years in exchange for the Brooklyn Federals' stadium; that organized baseball would pay $50,000 to the owners of the Pittsburgh Federals; and that all Federal League players would be eligible to return to O.B. . . .

At about the time the meeting was beginning, a *Baltimore Sun* reporter went to the Biltmore to tell Janney that it looked as if Baltimore might be able to get a National League team. Janney hurried to the Waldorf, where Rasin also told him that Baltimore had a good chance of landing an established franchise if they asked for one. . . .

Janney was right to call further discussion futile. Under both American and National league rules, the transfer of any franchise to Baltimore would require the unanimous consent of the league owners. From the statements of the owners at the meeting, it is clear that any motion to give Baltimore an existing team—Janney and Rasin had thought the Cardinals might be available—would have been met not with unanimous consent, but unanimous refusal.

The two sides agreed that a detailed settlement, including something for Baltimore, should be worked out by the National Commission and a Federal League committee of three. Gilmore proposed that himself, Sinclair, and Weeghman serve as that committee, and neither Janney nor Rasin objected.

There was then some discussion of the Federal League's pending antitrust suit against organized baseball, which Judge Landis still had not decided. National League counsel John C. Toole felt that the suit should be withdrawn before any more negotiating was done. The owners of the Baltimore team responded that Toole was putting the "horse before the cart." They argued that composition of any committee to decide the issue of compensation should be resolved first, then the lawsuit withdrawn.

When the meeting was adjourned, Toole telegraphed organized baseball's Chicago attorney. . . . The Federal League was dead, but Gilmore and his allies weren't shedding any tears over its demise. Fearful that the league was doomed anyway, they decided to cut their losses rather than fight to the finish. Organized baseball was happy to offer the Federal League a generous settlement. After all, there was still a chance that Judge Landis would issue a damaging verdict in the Federal League's antitrust action. The rival league's New York bluff also raised the specter of even more bitter competition for players and fans, with plenty of red ink to go around.

Ban Johnson would have preferred not to call a truce. The Federal League's threat to put a team in New York may have fooled the National League, but the American League knew better: It had considered building a new stadium in the Lenox Avenue property years earlier but found that it was absolutely impractical to locate a park there. . . .

The National Commission and the Federal League committee signed a peace treaty in Cincinnati on December 22. Before the agreement was concluded, Gilmore called Rasin to ask if Baltimore would accept $75,000, but Baltimore said no. Another meeting to discuss Baltimore's claims was held in Cincinnati on January 5, 1916, but no settlement was reached. A day or two later, Baltimore filed a complaint with the U.S. Department of Justice, but Assistant Attorney General Todd announced on January 11 that he had no reason to believe that organized baseball had violated the antitrust laws.

The War Moves to the Courtroom

On January 27, the Baltimore stockholders voted to authorize the club's directors to spend up to $50,000 on "litigation in such form as they deem advisable" to protect the stockholders' interests. They eventually filed suit in Washington on September 20, 1917.

After a year and a half of legal skirmishing, a jury was sworn in on March 25, 1919. The testimony summarized above was presented, the judge gave his instructions, and the jury retired to deliberate on April 12. Given the judge's instructions to the jury—which, in essence, told the jury that O.B. had in fact violated the federal antitrust laws, and that the Baltimore club was entitled to recover for any damages it suffered as a result—the verdict came as no surprise. The jury found in favor of the plaintiff and assessed damages at $80,000. The antitrust laws provide that guilty defendants pay three times the amount of the actual damages plus attorneys' fees, so the final judgement was for $254,000.

Organized baseball's lawyers immediately appealed to the U.S. Court of Appeals for the District of Columbia. They attacked the trial court's decision on a number of legal grounds but focused most of their attention on a single key issue: By far the most important question presented by the assignments of error is whether professional baseball is interstate commerce.

In his memoirs, George Wharton Pepper, O.B.'s top lawyer, described his appeal strategy:

> I raised at every opportunity the objection that a spontaneous output of human activity is not in its nature commerce, that therefore organized baseball cannot be interstate commerce; and that, it not being commerce among the states, the federal statue could have no application. . . . I argued with much earnestness the proposition that personal effort not related to production is not a subject of commerce; that the attempt to secure all the skilled service needed for professional baseball is not an attempt to monopolize commerce or any part of it; and that organized baseball, not being commerce, and therefore not interstate commerce, does not come within the scope of the prohibitions of the Sherman [Antitrust] Act. . . .

On December 6, 1920, the Court of Appeals issued its decision, which was written by its chief justice, Constantine J. Smyth. Chief Justice Smyth first stated that interstate commerce "require[s] the transfer of something, whether it be persons, commodities, or intelligence" from one state to another. But, Smyth wrote,

> A game of baseball is not susceptible of being transferred. . . . Not until [the players] come into contact with their opponents on the baseball field and the contest opens does the game come into existence. It is local in its beginning and in its end. Nothing is transferred in the process to those who patronize it. . . . It didn't really matter that baseball players traveled across state lines, or that the players carried their bats, balls, gloves, and uniforms across state lines with them. . . .
>
> The transportation in interstate commerce of the players and the paraphernalia used by them was but an incident to the main purpose of the appellants, namely the production of the game. It was for it they were in business—not for the purpose of transferring players, balls, and uniforms. The production of the game was the dominant thing in their activities. . . . So, here, baseball is not commerce, though some of its incidents may be.

Chief Justice Smyth then cited with approval cases holding that those who produce theatrical exhibitions, practice medicine, or launder clothes are not engaged in commerce.

The Baltimore club tried to persuade the United States Supreme Court to reinstate the original verdict in its favor. But Justice Oliver Wendell Holmes, writing for a unanimous Court, upheld the decision of the Court of Appeals.

> Exhibitions of base ball . . . are purely state affairs. It is true that, in order to attain for these exhibitions the great popularity that they have achieved, competitions must be arranged between clubs from different cities and states. But the fact that in order to give the exhibitions the league must induce free persons to cross state lines and must arrange and pay for their doing so is not enough to change the character of the business. . . . [T]he transport is a mere incident, not the essential thing. That to which it is incident, the exhibition, although made for money, would not be called trade or commerce in the commonly accepted use of those words. As it is put by the defendants, personal effort, not related to production, is not a subject of commerce.

The Supreme Court's decision was issued on May 29, 1922—almost seven years after the Baltimore Federals played their last game.

Given the legal doctrines of the day, the *Federal Baseball* case was correctly decided. The courts of that era applied the federal antitrust laws only to businesses that were primarily engaged in the production, sale, or transportation of tangible goods.

It is popularly believed that organized baseball was given immunity from the antitrust laws because baseball was a sport, not a business. That belief has grown out of a passage in the Court of Appeals opinion:

> If a game of baseball, before a concourse of people who pay for the privilege of witnessing it, is trade or commerce, then the college teams who play football where an admission is charged, engage in an act of trade or commerce. But the act is not trade or commerce; it is sport. The fact that [organized baseball] produce[s] baseball games as a source of profit, large or small, cannot change the character of the games. They are still sport, not trade.

But a close reading of that language and the rest of Chief Justice Smyth's opinion shows that the key to the decision was not the fact that baseball was a sport. The more crucial fact was that baseball—as well as the practice of law or medicine, the production of a grand opera, and the other nonsporting activities cited in the opinion—was not commerce.

Antitrust doctrines have changed radically since *Federal Baseball* was decided in 1922. The cases that the Supreme Court relied upon in holding that baseball wasn't interstate commerce have long ago been overruled. By 1960, the Supreme Court had held that doctors, theatrical productions, boxing promoters, and even the National Football League were subject to the federal antitrust laws.

But baseball has somehow retained its uniquely privileged status. In 1953 and again in 1972, in the celebrated Curt Flood case, the Supreme Court affirmed the holding of *Federal Baseball.* Justice Blackmun, in *Flood vs. Kuhn,* noted that base-ball's antitrust immunity was "an anomaly" and "an aberration." But, he noted,

> Remedial legislation had been introduced repeatedly in Congress, but none has ever been enacted. The Court, accordingly, has concluded that Congress as yet has had no intention to subject baseball's reserve system to the reach of the antitrust statutes. . . . If there is any inconsistency or illogic in all this, it is an inconsistency and illogic of long standing that is to be remedied by the Congress and not by this Court.

Is the *Federal Baseball* ruling of any consequence today? After all, the players' union has managed to decimate the reserve clause through collective bargaining, Free agency, arbitration, limits on trades without consent—no longer is the major-league player, in Curt Flood's words, "a piece of property to be bought and sold irrespective of [his] wishes."

Surely then *Federal Baseball*—a case decided over 60 years ago, long before television, jet airplanes, free agents, and night baseball—would finally be laid to rest. Of course, that was what Curt Flood's lawyers thought would happen in 1972. *Federal Baseball* may be an anomaly and an aberration—but it may also outlive us all.

CHAPTER 5

The Roaring Twenties and Baseball's Golden Age, 1920–1930

Postwar Troubles

The 1920s, like the 1880s and the 1950s, has often been characterized as baseball's "Golden Age." Of the three decades with that designation, the 1920s most deserves it. This decade witnessed one of the greatest popular explosions of interest in baseball history. Attendance rose from 56 million in the previous decade to an unheard-of figure of 93 million in the 1920s, percentage-wise the biggest increase decade to decade in baseball history. The 1920s also saw the emergence of the single most popular and, in many ways, the most significant player in baseball history, Babe Ruth.

In a decade of bigger-than-life national heroes—Charles Lindbergh, Jack Dempsey, Red Grange—Ruth easily overshadows them all. The 1920s also was the decade when Judge Kenesaw Mountain Landis emerged in the public mind as the conscience of baseball, the incorruptible arbiter of all that was good in the game, the man who saved baseball from the Black Sox Scandal. Finally, largely, if not exclusively, because of Ruth, the very nature of baseball changed. From the Deadball Era during the first 20 years of Major League Baseball, with its low scores and lack of power, baseball shifted to the modern power game. The home run, a rarity in the past, suddenly became the defining feature of baseball. For that reason, it could be said that baseball as we understand it today was born in the decade of the Roaring Twenties.

To some extent, developments in baseball after World War I mirrored what was happening in the nation. A brief recession in late 1919 caught the nation off guard. The recession was complicated by the rapid demobilizing of the military after the war. Baseball's owners had expected the war to continue for another year and responded by deciding to shorten the coming season as a way of lessening expected losses. This turned out to be a shortsighted decision, as baseball boomed during the 1919 season. With the war over, fans flocked to the game, smashing past attendance records.

At a more important level, when the war ended suddenly in November 1918, baseball faced serious structural problems. For some time, there had been a cold war developing between the owners and Ban Johnson, who had dominated the sport since the inception of the National Agreement in 1903. The three-man National Commission had worked well for a decade or so, but then, with new ownership entering baseball, men who owed nothing to Johnson, problems began to emerge.

The first significant challenge to Johnson's authority came in a complicated case. The Pittsburgh club believed they had won the rights to George Sisler, a superbly talented pitcher and hitter, when he signed a contract with the Pirates. Sisler, however, never played minor league baseball and instead went to college. In 1915, after college, he offered his services to the highest bidder, arguing he was underage when approached by the Pirates, and, more importantly, he had never signed any contract. He was declared a free agent by the National Commission and thus able to negotiate with anyone. St. Louis outbid the Pirates, and the Pirates owner, the influential Barney Dreyfuss, was furious and blamed the National Commission for not stepping in and awarding Sisler to Pittsburgh. He never forgave Johnson or the other members of the commission.[1]

At the same time, some of the new owners believed that the three-man commission, which Johnson had controlled, had lost its usefulness. Johnson, who could be heavy-handed, found his power waning with the new generation of owners who entered baseball in the late teens. Men like Jacob Ruppert and William Wrigley of the Cubs believed Johnson had shown his limitations when the players threatened a strike during the 1918 World Series. The owners recognized that it was the players who called off the strike and that Johnson had handled the matter badly. In December 1918, the owners created a committee to reorganize the National Commission. They decided that what the commission needed was an independent authority, even someone from outside baseball. This is where Judge Landis's name first appeared in connection with baseball administration. He was remembered for his sympathetic handling of one of the first challenges during the Federal League war when he sat on a controversial case until it was settled outside of court.

In 1919, Johnson's position further deteriorated when he tried to intervene in two player transactions. He unsuccessfully tried to ban a player the White Sox wanted, turning Charles Comiskey into an enemy. Then, in July 1919, one of the best young arms in the American League, Carl Mays of Boston, jumped the team. The Yankees signed him, and when Johnson voided the trade, Ruppert, the Yankees owner, went to court and got an injunction banning Johnson from interfering in the Mays signing. Johnson's days were numbered. The infighting in baseball in 1919, and leading into the 1920 season, portended a major shake-up of the sports administrative structure.

Baseball wasn't the only institution in turmoil in 1919. That year witnessed similar disarray in the nation. A wave of strikes spread throughout the country, with a record-setting 4 million days lost to labor unrest. Just about every industry was affected by the labor agitation. There were strikes in such major industries as steel and coal. Even odd occupations were caught up in the strike mania. Actors on Broadway struck, as did the police in Boston. The latter strike served to launch the career of an obscure governor of Massachusetts, Calvin Coolidge. Coolidge ordered the strike ended with a statement that caught the public's attention: "There is no right to strike against the public safety, anytime, anywhere."[2] Those words won him the vice presidential nomination on the Republican ticket, led by the eventual winner of the 1920 presidential election, Warren Harding.

Labor unrest shattered the nation's nerves. Unemployment, which was virtually nonexistent during the war, suddenly shot up, reaching 11 percent by 1921, swelled by the ranks of returning servicemen. The turmoil was intensified by a series of anarchist attacks unlike anything in the past. There were bombings, including attacks on members of President Woodrow Wilson's cabinet and prominent industrialists. A bomb exploded on Wall Street outside the office of the House of Morgan in 1920, killing 38 people and wounding 200 others. Many people believed revolution was in the air, and the United States was caught up in a Red Scare that tore the nation apart for two years.[3]

THE BLACK SOX SCANDAL AND ITS CONSEQUENCES

In the midst of this turmoil, the 1919 season took place. Some teams set attendance records, while baseball returned to normal—or what seemed to be normal. In the National League, Cincinnati won its first pennant, beating back challenges from John McGraw's Giants and the 1918 champs, the Chicago Cubs. In the American League, there was a three-way race among the White Sox, Cleveland, and the suddenly surging New York Yankees that went down to the wire, with Chicago winning the pennant by 3.5 games over the Indians. Sportswriters believed the White Sox were the best team in the majors. Chicago possessed two outstanding pitchers, Eddie Cicotte and Lefty Williams, who won 50 games between them, and an offensive that featured stars like Shoeless Joe Jackson, third baseman Buck Weaver, and future Hall of Famer Eddie Collins at second.

Perhaps the most surprising development of the 1919 season was the amazing home run performance put on by 24-year-old Babe Ruth of the Boston Red

Sox. Ruth had been one of the best left-handed pitchers in the American League, twice winning 20 games and leading the league in ERA and shutouts once. In 1918, while starting 19 games and pitching 166 innings, he was the coleader in home runs, with 11. The next season, his manager, Ed Barrow, who would later become general manager of the great Yankees teams of the 1930s, moved him to the outfield. In 1919, Ruth established a new record by hitting 29 home runs, a figure no one had come close to in the Deadball Era. He also led the league in runs batted in and runs scored. His days as a pitcher were over. Ruth's home run record that season was considered a freak. Still, most attention in baseball was directed toward the coming World Series.

The belief in sporting circles was that the White Sox, being clearly superior in most categories, would easily dispatch Cincinnati. While this belief was popular, it was a mistake to dismiss Cincinnati. They had won more games during the season than the White Sox and had a first-class pitching staff with an ERA three-quarters of a run lower than Chicago. Cincinnati's winning percentage was the second highest in modern National League history. They were managed by Pat Moran, who had won the 1915 National League title with the Phillies and was regarded as second only to John McGraw in leadership skills. Despite this, they went into the World Series as clear underdogs.

Shortly before the Series, the odds started to drop, with word spreading that the wise money (read gamblers) were shifting to Cincinnati. Rumors of a fix floated around, but this had often been the case in the past. After all, gambling had been a part of baseball since its origin and was certainly a major part of the professional game.

The outline of the Black Sox World Series is fairly clear. Some of the White Sox players were disgruntled at the way they were treated by the team owner, Charles Comiskey. Despite having one of the best teams in baseball and setting an attendance record for the White Sox in 1919, Comiskey was notoriously cheap. He paid his players as little as possible. Joe Jackson, a lifetime .350 hitter, was making $6,000 at a time when Ty Cobb was being paid $20,000. Comiskey's best pitcher, Eddie Cicotte, was making less than $10,000, despite winning 29 games in 1919. The White Sox team also was divided into cliques, with many of the players resenting second baseman Eddie Collins, who had signed a lucrative contract when Comiskey bought him from the A's.

A group of players led by first baseman Chick Gandil and Cicotte approached gamblers and offered to throw the World Series for $100,000. The gamblers did not have the cash to finance the deal and turned to Arnold Rothstein, known as the "Big Bankroll" and one of the leading bookmakers in the nation, for the cash. Rothstein, acting through other gamblers, including Sport Sullivan of Boston and Abe Attell, a former lightweight boxing champ, provided some up-front money. Eventually, eight White Sox players were in on the deal, among them Joe Jackson, Cicotte, Lefty Williams, and Happy Felsch, a highly regarded outfielder.

The Series was scheduled for the best-of-nine instead of the traditional best-of-seven to give the owners an opportunity to make some extra money after the abbreviated 1918 campaign. Cicotte was hit hard in the first game of the Series, and Williams lost Game 2. At this point, some of the baseball writers began to grow suspicious that the rumors floating about a fix were real. By the opening day of the Series, the odds had shifted from favoring the White Sox to even money. Christy Mathewson, covering the Series for a newspaper syndicate, believed that something was going on, as did a number of newspapermen writing about the Series. Chicago won Game 3 behind a pitcher, Dickie Kerr, who wasn't in on the conspiracy. Cicotte and Williams then proceeded to lose the next two games. Now everyone was suspicious. We know the players had not been paid what they were promised, so the White Sox won the next two games, with Cicotte winning one of them. In Game 8, Williams lost for the third time. Rumors persisted that he and his family had been threatened if he didn't lose the game.

To deal with these rumors after the Series, Comiskey made a public offer of $20,000 to anyone who could substantiate the charge that the games had been thrown. It was a public relations move, because we know he believed the games were thrown but wanted to protect his best players for the future. Cicotte, Williams, and Jackson, in particular, were important to him because they constituted the heart of the team.

Talk that the World Series was crooked persisted into the next season. Then, in September 1920, in the midst of a heated American League pennant race, which the White Sox had a chance to win, it surfaced that the Phillies had been approached to throw a game against the Cubs. To investigate that incident and other charges of crooked baseball, a grand jury was impaneled in Chicago. A few days later, a bigger story erupted in the headlines when a sportswriter for a Philadelphia paper wrote a front-page article based on inside information from one of the gamblers involved in the World Series bribery. The headline caused a sensation: "Gamblers Promised White Sox $100,000 to Lose." Cicotte and Jackson confessed to taking bribes and eventually named the other six Black Sox players involved.

Before the 1921 season opened, the eight Black Sox players went on trial for conspiracy to defraud the public by taking bribes to throw baseball games. They were found innocent because their confessions had disappeared. The incident had a peculiar smell about it, given Chicago's reputation for shady politics. It looked as if Comiskey had saved his team and perhaps the scandal would fade from memory. But at this point a new figure entered the fray.[4]

JUDGE KENESAW MOUNTAIN LANDIS

The rumors of baseball games being fixed, the squabbling among the team owners, the growing dislike of Ban Johnson, and the breakup of the National Commission led to growing support for an independent outsider taking over as some kind of overseer of baseball. The idea gained momentum even before the Black Sox Scandal. Approaches were made to a number of prominent Americans, including former president William Howard Taft, then teaching law at Yale. Among other names mentioned were William Gibbs McAdoo, former secretary of the treasury under Woodrow Wilson, and even the most famous person in the United States at the time, General John J. Pershing. None of them were interested.

The one name that kept popping up was that of federal judge Kenesaw Mountain Landis. Landis was a fanatical baseball fan—he was known to suspend trials so that he could attend ball games—and he had won the affection of the baseball establishment by showing strong support for baseball during the turmoil related to the Federal League challenge to Major League Baseball.

In November 1920, with all the bad news about baseball circulating, especially the breakup of the National Commission and the talk of players throwing games at the behest of gamblers, the owners offered the job of commissioner to Judge Landis. Knowing how badly they needed him, he insisted on strict terms. He was to be the sole arbiter of disputes in baseball, the owners were not to criticize his decisions, and the presidents of the two leagues were reduced to figureheads. Johnson protested but found he was powerless. He hung on as president of the American League for a few years, drinking heavily before he retired in 1927. Landis was to be paid $50,000 a year. Originally, baseball paid him $42,500 while he kept his judicial position, with a salary of $7,500. When he was forced to surrender his judgeship, baseball made good on the $7,500 he lost.

Landis was 54 when he became commissioner of baseball. He was named after a battle his father took part in during the Civil War. Landis attended high school but never graduated and then got his law degree from YMCA Law School in Cincinnati. He practiced law without making much of a mark until he was chosen to manage Republican Frank Lowden's campaign for governor of Illinois. Although Lowden lost, Landis was rewarded for services rendered by an appointment to the federal bench by President Theodore Roosevelt.

Landis was a typical product of the Progressive Era, someone who believed that good government was good politics and someone was needed to look after the welfare of the ordinary person. Landis gloried in the role of judge and often as jury also. He won national attention when he compelled John D. Rockefeller to testify in his court and then fined Standard Oil $29 million for trying to gain control of the oil industry. The fine was never paid and Landis's ruling was overturned, a frequent happening with his legal decisions. When the RMS *Lusitania* was torpedoed, he issued a legal summons ordering the Kaiser to appear in his court to answer charges of war crimes. Needless to say, the Kaiser passed up the trip to Chicago.

These incidents were typical of Landis. He was often arbitrary in his judgments. Opinionated, self-righteous, dramatic with a shock of wild white hair, Landis fit the image of a man of rectitude. He solidified his image the day after the Black Sox players were found innocent. Calling in the press, Landis gave them a statement that included the words that indicated what kind of commissioner he was going to be: "Regardless of the verdict of juries, no player that throws a game, no player that sits in conference with a bunch of crooked players and gamblers, where the ways and means of throwing games are discussed, and does not promptly tell his club about it will ever play professional baseball."[5] Landis would run baseball the way he saw fit. All eight Black Sox players were banned, including Buck Weaver, who only knew of the bribes but took no action.

During the next decade, Landis solidified his position, banning players involved in gambling incidents and asserting his power. Historian Bill James provided a list of 22 players he claimed were banned for violating what Landis called the integrity of the game. Among those banned were Benny Kauff, the batting champion of the Federal League; Heinie Zimmerman, National League batting champ in 1912; and outfielder Lee Magee, who played for a number of teams.[6] Landis also recognized that the best future for baseball was to keep the sport out of the courts. He was not afraid to criticize owners or players. He forced John McGraw to give up ownership of a race course and gambling casino in Havana, Cuba. Even baseball's new hero, Babe Ruth, had to bow to his authority.

After the 1921 World Series, Ruth led a barnstorming tour, which was counter to baseball's rules at the time. For doing so, he was banned for the opening weeks of the 1922 season and denied his World Series money. Later, when popular singer Bing Crosby tried to buy the Pittsburgh Pirates, Landis rejected the deal because Crosby owned racehorses. When William Cox, the owner of the Phillies, was found to have bet on his own team, Landis forced him to sell. He was the lord high commissioner of baseball and never let anyone forget it. He liked to intervene on behalf of players, telling them to come to him if they had problems.

When he discovered that the Cleveland Indians were holding up Tommy Henrich's promotion to the majors, Landis made him a free agent. Henrich sold his services to the Yankees for $25,000. He freed a number of Cardinals farmhands, blaming the Cardinals organization for hoarding them in the minors. By one estimate, he freed more than 200 players during his 24-year tenure as commissioner. The owners soon discovered they had created a monster.[7] Landis cultivated the press and built a reputation for honesty. When his contract came up for renewal, the owners, who would have gladly gotten rid of him, found he was too popular. He was commissioner for life, dying in office in 1944, a few days after signing yet another seven-year contract.

Landis, with the lavish backing of the sporting press, became the face of baseball after the Black Sox Scandal. His decisiveness in dealing with the scandal and related sordid baseball issues helped win the confidence of the public and the belief—not always correct—that baseball had been purified. Landis had his faults, and his judgment was often benighted. He hated night baseball, believed the farm system concept would ruin baseball, was regarded by many as a racist, and didn't like the idea of broadcasting baseball games. Despite these black marks, he projected an aura of rectitude to baseball when it most badly needed it.[8]

BASEBALL'S ANTITRUST EXEMPTION

While Landis was solidifying his position as commissioner, another contentious issue, this one legal, was working its way to resolution. The case brought by Baltimore against Major League Baseball arising out of the collapse of the Federal League finally had reached the Supreme Court. Many baseball authorities believed the sport would be found guilty of unfair trade practices, as defined by the Sherman Antitrust Act. Baseball initially had been found guilty on those grounds in a District of Columbia court, but that judgment had been overturned by the Court of Appeals. The case now sat with the Supreme Court. Major League Baseball hired distinguished lawyer George Wharton Pepper to argue the case for them. Pepper was one of the best-known lawyers in the nation, the very definition of a "Philadelphia lawyer," someone with a talent for winning difficult cases. Pepper argued that baseball was a special case and that it was "not in its nature commerce." He also insisted that, despite crossing state boundaries, baseball exhibitions essentially were local events and thus not counter to the Sherman Act.[9]

The Supreme Court, on May 22, 1922, issued a unanimous ruling written by the most distinguished member on the court, Oliver Wendell Holmes. Holmes reaffirmed the decision of the District of Columbia court. He wrote that while baseball was indeed a business that sought a profit, it was not "trade or commerce" in a legal sense because "personal effort, not related to production, is not a subject of commerce."[10] Baseball did not constitute interstate commerce because the movement of the teams across state lines was incidental to the business, and no product was involved. Baseball's owners were relieved. They had expected the worst.

While Holmes's decision has been ridiculed as irrational, there are a couple of points to keep in mind. The decision was unanimous, a sure sign that Holmes was speaking for the other judges. Among those justices who concurred was Louis Brandeis, one of the most original legal thinkers of his time. It is also worth noting that later, on two separate occasions, the court had an opportunity to reverse Holmes and they passed it up. According to some legal commentators, this seemly contradictory decision made sense given the legal philosophy that prevailed at the time. Holmes's reasoning, according to one distinguished jurist, was "consistent with Progressive Era jurisprudence regarding the treatment of 'incidental' interstate transportation."[11]

Holmes's decision, which survived intact for 70 years, is as important to the development of baseball as was Landis's tenure as commissioner. It gave baseball protection from antitrust violations, enabling the owners to run the game as they wished. It also weakened the position of the players economically, leaving them at the whim of the owners. This can clearly be seen when analysis of players' salaries in the booming 1920s is examined. While players definitely improved their financial position, salaries didn't rise to match the enormous profits baseball generated during the decade. Other than Ruth and Ty Cobb, no player in the majors was making more than $20,000 by 1924, five years into baseball's booming attendance increase. Walter Johnson, after a decade and a half as one of the leading pitchers in the majors, was paid $12,000 that season, the same salary he received when he turned down an offer from the Federal League a decade earlier. He was finally raised to $20,000 the next year. That same year, 1924, the major-league teams generated revenues of $10 million, while paying out $3.6 million in players, managers, and coaches salaries. The profit for that season, not a particularly exciting one, was $4.6 million.[12]

THE TRANSFORMATION OF BASEBALL

One of the things that made the 1920s so significant in baseball history is that it witnessed the shift of the game away from pitching to put the emphasis on hitting—and a particular kind of hitting, the home run. Pitching had dominated baseball since the pitcher's mound was moved to 60 feet, six inches in 1893. Along with a dead ball, trick pitches (especially the spitball), and more reliable fielding, hitting was deemphasized. The way the game was played up to the 1920s was to use sacrifice bunts, hit-and-run plays, and the stolen base to play for one run. The batters tended to choke up on the bat and try to slap the ball between fielders. Fly balls were to be avoided because, given the professionalism of the major leaguers, they became easy outs.

Ballparks were large with huge outfield distances. Shibe Park and the Polo Grounds, for instance, had center-field fences 500 feet deep. Instead of lifting high fly balls, the batter tried either to place his hits or hit line drives that couldn't be handled easily with the gloves available at the time. Home run totals were low. Tommy Leach led the National League in 1902 with six homers, all of them inside-the-park types. In fact, most home runs hit before the age of Babe Ruth were of the inside-the-park variety. Leach, for instance, hit 61 home runs in his career, and 49 were inside the park. Frank Baker of the A's earned the nickname "Home Run" Baker because he hit two home runs out of the ballpark in the 1911 World Series, an event regarded as remarkable.

The nature of the baseball game changed almost overnight. In 1918, the home run champ in the National League hit a total of eight, while in the American League the leading total was 11. The A's led the American League that season with 22 homers. The total number hit in both leagues was 237. Things began to slowly rise the next season. What caught everyone's attention was the fact that Babe Ruth, now playing every day, broke the home run record by hitting 29. Some indication of how remarkable that figure was can be gained by noting that the rest of his Red Sox teammates hit just four homers. The total number of home runs for both leagues doubled to 475. There is some indication that a livelier baseball was tried out in 1919, although the evidence is sketchy.

In 1920, everything changed dramatically. We know that a new baseball was being used, one similar to the cork-centered ball tried in 1911, when numerous hitting records were established. Moreover, umpires were instructed to use more baseballs, especially if the ball was scuffed badly. Trick pitches were banned, although those pitchers who used the spitball were allowed to use it for the rest of their careers. In 1920, baseball had its first fatality when Ray Chapman was hit in the head by a dirty, stained ball and died. This confirmed baseball's decision to use fresh balls in games.

No one was ready for what happened next. Ruth had been sold to the New York Yankees in the biggest transaction in baseball history to that point. The deal was for $125,000, plus a loan from Jake Ruppert of the Yankees to the Boston owner, Harry Frazee, of $325,000. Frazee, who dabbled in Broadway shows, was short of cash and was selling off the best Boston players. When he was finished, the Red Sox, once one of the best teams in the majors, would drop into the second division for the next generation. A team that won four pennants and four World Series in the teens would not win another pennant until 1946, and another World Series until 2004. Frazee's temerity in selling Ruth gave rise to a belief—at least among Red Sox faithful—that Boston fell into the doldrums because of what they called the "Curse of the Bambino."

In 1920, Babe Ruth topped his record total of 29 home runs by the end of June. He went on to hit 54 that season, forever changing how the game would be played. That season, Ruth shattered every slugging record in baseball history. He batted .388, leading the league in not only home runs, but also runs scored and runs batted in. His nearest competitor in home runs had 19. Ruth's slugging percentage was .847, a record that lasted for 81 years. To put things in perspective, Ruth personally hit more home runs that season than every team in the American League and all but one, the Phillies, in the National League. He single-handedly changed baseball forever.

Ruth's batting approach was different from past batters. He didn't choke up on the bat and try to punch at the ball. Swinging from the end of the bat, he uppercut the ball, launching long, majestic fly balls that, with the new baseball, easily reached the stands. Other batters noticed and slowly began to copy his style. Ruth's timing was perfect. The pitchers had lost their edge with the banning of the trick pitches, and Ruth was the right man to come along and take advantage of the new situation. Plus, this approach suited him temperamentally. He was a big man, at more than 6-foot-2, with a huge upper body, long slender legs, and large hands. He took a mighty swing, corkscrewing his body around, and the ball literally jumped off his bat. His personality was as big as his home runs. An outgoing and fun-loving man, it was said he played like a big kid, and the fans loved him.

Attendance had risen after the war, but in 1920, it reached new levels. The Yankees, long a tenant in the Polo Grounds, drew 1.2 million fans, the first team in baseball to top the million mark. The Yankees' attendance averaged 1 million a season during the decade. McGraw was embarrassed and ended their lease on the Polo Grounds. The Giants, despite their success in the early part of the decade, never drew 1 million fans, something that bothered McGraw. Being kicked out of the Polo Grounds didn't matter to Ruppert because he had made plans to build a new ballpark, something different from anything baseball had ever seen. Yankee Stadium opened in 1923. It was triple decked, making it the biggest and most modern of the new ballparks. Seating 60,000, it became the standard for new ballparks for 50 years. Designed for left-handed hitters, with the right-field stands just 295 feet down the line, appropriately Ruth hit the first homer there. The baseball establishment were not fools. They noticed what Ruth did for the Yankees and saw how fans flocked to see the Babe hit one.

Hitting reached new highs in 1920, with both leagues consistently averaging between .280 and .290. The number of runs per game rose from 7.75 in 1919, to 10.25 six years later. For baseball, the success of offense was found in the crowds that flocked to the games. Almost every team set attendance records during the decade. The Yankees topped 1 million a number of times, as did the Tigers and Cubs. Baseball's owners knew they had stumbled onto a good thing and did everything to encourage offense.

A case can be made that Ruth saved baseball after the Black Sox Scandal and was far more important for the future of the sport than Judge Landis. Ruth's success spawned imitators. Power hitting became part of every team's makeup. During the 1920s, five men topped the 40-homer mark, a figure deemed impossible before Ruth showed the way. With the increase in power, stolen bases, once one of the keys to success, virtually disappeared. It wasn't that there were no longer any fast runners, but rather it was considered risky to try to steal when you could wait around for someone to hit a home run. Teams now were built around power, and those teams that hit the most home runs were the most successful in the 1920s.[13]

In the American League, the 1920s belonged to the New York Yankees, largely because of Ruth. Later, he was joined by such talented hitters as Lou Gehrig, Bob Meusel, and Earle Combs to form what was known as "Murderers Row." Led by this group, the Yankees won six pennants and three World Series during the decade. By the early 1920s, they had easily outstripped the Giants as the most popular team in baseball. Having lost the 1921 and 1922 World Series to the Giants, they beat them handily in 1923, which marked the passing of the torch to Yankee domination of New York City baseball. Never again did the Giants beat the Yankees in a World Series. Beginning with the 1922 Series, it became commonplace for these games to be sold out, a sign that baseball had caught the imagination of the nation.

The Yankees slugging dynasty was replaced by Connie Mack's second great club, which dominated baseball between 1929 and 1931. Like the Yankees, the A's featured a fearsome hitting lineup that included future Hall of Fame players Jimmie Foxx, Al Simmons, and Mickey Cochrane. This A's team also featured one of the most dominant pitchers of the era in the person of another Hall of Famer, Lefty Grove.

The National League had been slower to adopt the long-ball approach to baseball but eventually did so. John McGraw's last great teams, the 1921–1924 squads, had no one to match Ruth's power numbers but as a team consistently hit in the .290 range during those years. The St. Louis Cardinals of the decade were led by the greatest right-handed hitter in baseball history, Rogers Hornsby. Hornsby led the National League in batting for six consecutive seasons, during which he batted better than .400 three times. From 1921 to 1925, his average was better than .400. He also was a power hitter with a total of 300 homers in his career. He led the Cardinals to a World Series victory over the Yankees in 1926.

Other dominant teams in the 1920s, Washington, Pittsburgh, and the Cubs, featured solid hitting lineups, although they lacked the home run punch of the Yankees. It was clear that pitching was no longer dominant. During the decade there was only one 30-game winner, a figure topped eight times in the previous decade. Earned run averages for both leagues rose sharply during the 1920s, from 2.91 in 1919, for the National League, to 4.71 a decade later. The figure for the American League was comparable. The long-ball era was here to stay.

Aside from the growing influence of power hitting, the decade of the 1920s was not a particularly creative one. It didn't need to be. Baseball was prospering as never before. Every team in the major leagues turned a profit during the 1920s, except the Phillies. In a couple of areas, baseball experimented with concepts that would later become associated with the sport, for example, radio broadcasting of games. Radio was in its infancy but rapidly gaining in popularity. In 1921, a radio station in Pittsburgh, KDKA, broadcast a Phillies–Pirates game. That same year, the World Series was broadcast, but it wasn't done live. Reporters in the studio using telegraph reports recreated the games. The next year, the Series was broadcast live, with two famous sports figures doing the games. Graham McNamee would go on to become the first true sports announcer. He was joined in 1922 by the most celebrated of the sportswriters, Grantland Rice. Rice served as the first "color man," while McNamee did the play-by-play.

Radio broadcasting didn't catch on in the 1920s, although Chicago, under William Wrigley's direction operating through WGN, broadcast Cubs games throughout the Midwest. It would not be until the late 1930s that radio broadcasting became a major feature of baseball.[14]

The one creative example for baseball in the 1920s was the emergence of the first attempt at organizing a league for African Americans. African Americans had been playing baseball since the beginning of the sport. They played at every level of professional baseball, including the highest leagues in the years after the Civil War. As the nation resegregated in the 1880s, they were gradually frozen out of organized baseball. The response of the African American community was to organize their own teams and play one another. It appears that after the 1880s they rarely played against white professionals despite the belief of many white players that they were good enough to play in the major leagues. While playing conditions were often poor and they received little recognition from the white press, what evidence we have indicates the quality of play was high. Most historians of nineteenth- and early twentieth-century baseball believe many of the best African American players could have made a major-league roster.

Frank Grant, who had a distinguished career with Buffalo of the International League and later played with one of the most popular of the African American teams, the Cuban Giants, was regarded as an outstanding baseball talent. Bud Fowler was believed to be one of the hardest-throwing pitchers in the 1880s. Fowler's contemporaries, the Walker brothers, Moses and Welday, could have made any major-league roster but for the racial prejudice of the times. In the early 20th century, Oscar Charleston, Rube Foster, and perhaps Sol White were of major-league quality. Perhaps the greatest African American player of the era was John Henry Lloyd, a shortstop often called the black Honus Wagner. Wagner himself described Lloyd as the greatest player he had ever seen, even greater than Babe Ruth.[15]

Before the 1920s, most African American baseball was not league-oriented. Rather, leagues and teams came and went. Black baseball was mostly barnstorming. As an occupation, it was a well-paying one for African Americans. They could earn anywhere from $50 to $250 a month at a time when most well-paying occupations were closed to them. Moreover, they played year-round. In the winter, they could travel to the Caribbean, where they were not only paid well, but also guaranteed an income for 12 months of baseball.

The first serious attempt to try to duplicate the success of Major League Baseball came in 1920. Andrew "Rube" Foster, a talented pitcher with various African American teams early in the century, was the driving force behind setting up the first true Negro League. He had administrative experience since he ran a number of teams and was involved in booking barnstorming trips. In 1920, Foster met with leading figures in African American baseball circles and organized the Negro National League. He was taking advantage of the large migration of African Americans north during the decade of the teens, inspired by the need for labor during World War I. Modeled on the existing major-league structure, he placed teams in those cities that had large African American populations and where baseball had proven successful: Chicago, Kansas City, New York, and Philadelphia.

Foster's idea was to emulate Major League Baseball. He wanted to get rid of contract jumping, establish a clear schedule, and perhaps set up the kind of pennant races that characterized white baseball. He even had an idea for a World Series. What Foster was doing was characteristic of African American society at the time of rigid segregation: He was creating a parallel world for African Americans so that, in this case, they could play the national game the way the whites did.

The Negro National League lasted for a decade. Foster ran things and made most of the decisions until his health broke down in 1926. He was president of the league but instead of a salary took 5 percent of the gate for every Negro National League game. Foster saw that his league was run professionally. Salaries ran as high $2,000 a season, while the lowest-paid player was guaranteed $750 a year.

Despite his best efforts, the Negro National League suffered from the same problems that had plagued white baseball in its early years. Players still jumped their contracts and joined barnstorming African American teams if the money was better. After Foster's death, the league gradually broke up, but he had left a mark. The idea of a Negro League to absorb the African American talent in baseball was given a huge boost by Foster's failed league. He showed that there was a fan base and that, in the right circumstances, a Negro League could prosper. His failure would give rise to and inspire the great Negro League baseball of the 1930s and 1940s. Those leagues would prove the training ground for the first generation of African American players who integrated baseball in the 1940s and 1950s.[16]

Baseball's experience in the 1920s was overwhelmingly positive once the success of the game helped everyone forget about the Black Sox Scandal. For this, credit has to be given to Babe Ruth, Judge Landis, and the excitement the long ball brought to baseball. The game was doing well, much like the nation, when the bottom fell out in the fall of 1929.

Questions for Consideration

1. How does the state of baseball after World War I mirror or reflect conditions in the United States at that time?
2. Both Babe Ruth and Judge Landis have been credited with saving baseball after the Black Sox Scandal. Assess the impact each man had on baseball. Was one more responsible for baseball's success than the other?
3. What were the issues involved in the Black Sox Scandal? Why did it pose such a danger for Major League Baseball?
4. Describe the legal resolution of baseball's antitrust exemption. What was its significance for baseball?
5. Discuss the development of the first Negro National League. In what ways did it parallel similar developments in early professional baseball?
6. Is labeling the 1920s "Baseball's Golden Age" justified? If so, why?
7. What are some of the reasons for the dramatic increase in offense in the 1920s? What was Babe Ruth's role in this development? Were there other factors at work?
8. The 1926–1928 Yankees and the 1929–1931 Athletics have been called two of baseball's greatest teams. Compare and contrast them. Which one was better in your estimation? Give your reasons.
9. Compare Babe Ruth and Ty Cobb as representatives of their baseball eras.

Notes

1. Harold Seymour, *Baseball: The Golden Age* (New York: Oxford University Press, 1971).

2. Robert F. Burk, *Much More Than a Game: Players, Owners, and American Baseball since 1921* (Chapel Hill: University of North Carolina Press, 2001), 9.

3. There is an excellent discussion of this period in David A. Shannon, *Between the Wars: America, 1919–1941* (Boston: Houghton Mifflin, 1965).

4. Eliot Asinof, *Eight Men Out* (Chicago: Henry Holt, 1963) remains the classic study of the Black Sox Scandal. There is also a fine analysis in Seymour, *Baseball*, chapter 15.

5. Asinof, *Eight Men Out*, 273.

6. Bill James, *The New Bill James Historical Baseball Abstract* (New York: Free Press, 2001).

7. David Pietrusza, *Judge and Jury: The Life and Times of Judge Kenesaw Mountain Landis* (South Bend, IN: Diamond Communications, 1998) is the best overview of Landis's career.

8. Pietrusza, *Judge and Jury*.

9. For an overview of the Supreme Court decision, see G. Edward White, *Creating the National Pastime: Baseball Transforms Itself, 1903–1953* (Princeton, NJ: Princeton University Press, 1996).

10. Burk, *Much More Than a Game*, 9.

11. Samuel A. Alito Jr., "The Origins of the Baseball Antitrust Exemption: *Federal Baseball Club of Baltimore, Inc. v. National League of Professional Baseball Players*," *Baseball Research Journal* 38, no. 2 (Fall 2009): 86.

12. Burk, *Much More Than a Game*.

13. The best biography of the Babe is Robert Creamer, *Babe: The Legend Comes to Life* (New York: Simon & Schuster, 1992).

14. Curt Smith. *Voices of the Game*, (South Bend, IN: Diamond Communications, 1992) gives an overview of early baseball broadcasts. White, *Creating the National Pastime*, 206–211.

15. Benjamin Rader, *Baseball: A History of America's Game* (Urbana: University of Illinois Press, 2008).

16. Robert Peterson, *Only the Ball Was White: A History of Legendary Black Players and All-Black Professional Teams* (New York: Oxford University Press, 1992) is one of the best introductions to the history of the Negro Leagues. For Rube Foster, see Gerald Brennan, "Foster, Andrew Rube," in David L. Porter, ed., *Biographical Dictionary of American Sports: Baseball*, 3 vols. (Westport, CT: Greenwood Press).

THE BABE ON BALANCE

Marshall Smelser

Babe Ruth's success depended on his constitution and his temperament, but it also owed much to the accident of timing. If he had come to New York before the First World War he would have played with a weakly financed team much less able and popular than the Giants. He came to New York when the Yankees had rich, ambitious owners who were able to make the most of the interest he stirred. The result was a rising zest for public spectacles, and Ruth rose with the flood, in just the right place. From 1920 to 1932, there was a stormy excitement over baseball unknown before or since. The only rival idols of baseball heroes were college football players and, occasionally, boxers. A career like Ruth's is no longer possible. Today, baseball has the lively competition of professional football, hockey, golf, and basketball, which split the popular interest. Imagine concentrating the popular feeling for the darlings of basketball, hockey, and football entirely on baseball heroes, and mostly on Babe Ruth. That's the way it was in the 1920s. Where Ruth stood was the center of the world of games. As the most cursory reading of the 1920s sports pages shows, his feat of hitting 54 home runs in 1920 was deliriously exciting.

No one was more persistently popular, not even Lindbergh. The press used hundreds of tons of extra newsprint to tell of Lindbergh, but the story ran out in a few years. Babe Ruth's story went on and on. He met an elementary need of the crowd. Every hero must have his human flaw which he shares with his followers. In Ruth, it was hedonism, as exaggerated in folklore and fable. If he had been nothing more than an exceptional batter, he would have been respected, but he attracted more than respect. The public love of Ruth approached idolatry, and his reputed carnality was necessary to the folk-hero pattern. As Waite Hoyt said, he was "the kind of bad boy it was easy to forgive." He fit the public image of what a highly

Marshall Smelser, "The Babe on Balance," *American Scholar* 44, no. 2 (Spring 1975): 299–304.

paid ballplayer *ought* to be, and, if he didn't really fit, the people wished to believe any legend that would shape the image. (They still do.) The combination of great skill on the field and a shared flaw off the field made him the most admired and theatrical man in the game.

He made money. Salaries, plus a bonus in the early 20s, and a percentage of club exhibition games paid him about a million dollars. World Series shares and barnstorming profits made him perhaps another half-million. Many kinds of what we might call celebrity income also brought in about a half-million. In real purchasing power, the only athletic heroes who have done better are a few heavyweight boxing champions and Pele, the Brazilian soccer player.

It is hard to think of him as doing anything else with his life. If he could have started earlier in golf, say as a caddie, he might have made as much as $25,000 a year, which was a high annual income for a golf professional in his time. With his nearly perfect physical coordination, he could no doubt have become a mechanically excellent pianist, but he showed no artistic tastes. Boxing had no money ceiling at the time, but the company and the game itself were dangerous, and he did not have the kind of killer spirit necessary. Football was not then profitable; it had to be baseball.

People like to think he would have played even better if he were playing today, but the only advantage today's batters have is that American League fences, according to a calculation suggested by Cleveland Amory, are closer, on the average, by about 24 feet. This advantage is offset by all-night flying, less regular hours, the creation of the specialized relief pitcher, and the inferiority of the lighting for night games. Furthermore, Ruth didn't have to compete with blacks.

Ruth's last photographs have made him seem a freak carved out of rubber with no ability except to hit the ball a long way. Red Smith said what most expert witnesses felt: "The truth is that he was the complete ballplayer, certainly one of the greatest and maybe the one best of all time." Ruth seems almost to have been tailored to the game. We can list very few serious rivals for the adjective "best." Smith's word "complete" is the key word. Ruth could have been in the big leagues a long time at every position except second base, shortstop, and third base, positions in which left-handed throwers are handicapped. For example, only two pitchers in the Hall of Fame (Whitey Ford and Lefty Grove) have better won–lost percentages than Ruth's. His many-sidedness was so dazzling that if it were supported only by oral tradition, apart from baseball's great heap of numbers called statistics, young people would snicker at the Ruth stories of their elders. Every art form has its greatest practitioner. Every art form also has able men who say there is *one* way to perform (the one way changes from time to time) and set down the rules. In each case the greatest practitioner first excelled according to the rules, then threw them away and soared higher. Ruth pitched conventionally, and as peer of the best, in 1915, 1916, and

1917, but found one position too confining. He went on to prove he could do almost everything else better than almost everybody else. The collaboration of Ed Barrow and Babe Ruth in converting a pitcher to a master of the whole game was the most influential single act in baseball history since the decision to pitch overhand instead of underhand.

To rate one player as the best is, of course, to place a high value on opinion. True, the pitching strategy of Ruth's day differed from todays, and for the worse. But we can fairly contrast him with his contemporaries. After 1919, while in his prime, he was incomparable. There is no doubt at all that he was the best in his own time.

Ty Cobb's name naturally comes to mind, but Ruth could have done anything Cobb did, if he chose to do it, except steal as many bases. Branch Rickey, perhaps baseball's only true intellectual, saw Ruth as "a rational conservative in play as compared to Cobb." Cobb would often risk games in order to shine, but Ruth never. Ruth's risks were risks to snatch victory. We don't dwell much on Ruth as a man thinking, but thinking is not some kind of juggler's trick or a special exercise of the consciously literate. A man thinking is a man completely attending to something he is doing. In the ball game (although almost nowhere else) Ruth qualified as Homo sapiens.

He was, even more, an instinctive player. The leaping spirit of life that animated Ruth's play can solve many a game puzzle which reason is too slow to solve.

Hercules, the Greek patron of athletes, was usually pictured as a man carrying a club. Whether civilized man is man the tool-user, or man the timekeeper, or man the fuel-burner (as anthropologists debate), the oldest graphic symbol of civilization is said to be the club-carrying man. That is what Ruth was. Despite his pitching and fielding records, we remember him as the man with the club, primitive but successful, the fundamental man who was victor over everything. Like Hercules, he satisfied the feeling of the people of his time that there was practically nothing a man couldn't do if he was strong enough and had a big enough stick.

There is an old saw that says, "You can't win 'em all." Babe Ruth at bat seemed to be asking, "Why not?"

The explosive popularity of Babe Ruth in 1919 and 1920 marked the division between quite different styles of play. The characteristic elements of the earlier style were the bunt, the hit-and-run play, and the stolen base. In 1911, the total of stolen bases in both leagues was 3,394; in 1951, it was 863. The new idea was to clutter the bases with runners who waited for a long hit to bring them home in a group. But not only batting and running changed. Pitchers had to work more carefully, pitching to alleged weaknesses, preferring to walk batters than to chance the home run.

The earlier game was consciously dedicated to the nineteenth-century god Science. To bunt, to steal, to hit-and-run were explicitly called "scientific" baseball in the first decade of this century, by which time the religion of Science had trickled down to the popular culture. Babe Ruth, the iconoclast, showed the fans they need not believe in the old god—that baseball was for fun, not for a moral duty.

Ruth and those who tried to play as he played prompted changes in the rules, equipment, and strategy. If one Ruth could fill a park, wouldn't 16 Ruths fill 16 parks? The ball became livelier, and the pitcher was forbidden to spit on it. Even welterweight infielders now had bats with heavy barrels and thin handles. The successors of those pitchers who were kings of diamonds from 1900 to 1920 faced the painful fact that slight .220 hitters could wreck winning games in late innings by swinging for the fences.

The change was not universally welcomed. For those who liked baseball as a game played with a sphere and a cylinder, blending the sport of gymnastics with geometry, it made the game much too dependent on strength. The new game has also somewhat lowered the standard of outfield play, since almost none of the annual 3,000 home runs require any response on the field. But the people, by buying tickets in greater proportion, showed they liked what had happened. It is still true that an advertised duel between two leading pitchers may sell an extra 10,000 tickets. Nevertheless, a 1–0 loss for the home team, pitched by a pair of journeymen, will please the crowd less than a 16–15 win.

You can't keep Ty Cobb's name out of this kind of discussion. It is only fair to the intelligent, flexible, and neurotic Cobb to say that if he had first appeared in 1925 instead of 1905, he would have been as great a player, but a different kind.

As it was, the earlier game was the Cobb game; the later was the Ruth game. Cobb hit roughly as many home runs as Ruth stole bases, which is the simple formula of the game. Their value to their teams, on the scoreboard, was about equal. Cobb was worth 170 runs per season; Ruth 167 (based on runs scored, plus runs batted in, minus home runs, divided by seasons of play). But Cobb did his work coldly and craftily, while Ruth played loosely and joyously, and the happy big bang sold a lot more tickets than Cobb's foxiness did. Ruth was the first man who seemed capable of breaking up the ball game every day he played. "Did he hit one today?" became a national household question.

We often read that Babe Ruth "saved baseball" at the time of the 1919 Black Sox Scandal (exposed in 1920) by reviving interest in the game. That is not quite accurate. His 29 home runs of 1919 and his 54 of 1920 eclipsed the scandal, blocked it out of the minds of the *Volk*, so that the miscreants got about a tenth of the attention they would had in, say, 1910. What he did for baseball was to enliven it so that the trend of attendance was reversed. From 1910 to 1918, baseball attendance did not increase as rapidly as the population. From 1919 to 1930, attendance increased at a much greater rate than did the population. Until we know some other cause we may credit the Ruth game with turning the figures around.

Despite his relatively high salaries, Ruth was a bargain for the Yankees. At his peak he was worth a third of a million to half a million dollars to the franchise. To baseball as an industry, his value was simply incalculable. We can only say that every club benefitted from the greater popularity of the game. His presence with the Yankees, according to their ablest scout, Paul Krichell, also had a good deal to do with the success of the Yankees in winning 22 pennants after Ruth left the team. In the days when the recruiting of beginners was an auction and not a kind of lottery, the Yankees found it easier to sign promising rookies because they wanted to be Yankees. The American League profited in the same way. By outdrawing the National League, every American League club was better able to outbid National League rivals for young talent. (This advantage lasted until the National League earned the gratitude of blacks by breaking down the skin-color barrier.)

Babe Ruth is better remembered than his contemporary presidents Harding, Coolidge, Hoover, better than his contemporary ethical hero Lindbergh, better than the foxy hero Cobb. He needs no rescue from oblivion. Proofs of his lasting fame are everywhere, as a few instances will show:

An organized baseball program for boys too old for Little League and too young for American Legion junior baseball, called the Little Bigger League, changed its name in 1953, to the Babe Ruth League and, with Claire Ruth's help, has been flourishing ever since.

As of this writing, the city of Baltimore is renovating Pius Shamberger's house, where George Ruth was born and lived for a few days, in order to make it a Babe Ruth shrine.

The National Commemorative Society, which commissions souvenir silver medals, polled its members in 1968, asking whose memory should be perpetuated in the 1969 medal. Babe Ruth won over Alexander Hamilton by a score of 760 to 724.

Der Sport Brockhaus; alles vom Sport von A-Z (Wiesbaden, 1971) gave Ruth seven lines (with three errors of fact) and a portrait.

In the part of Israel's "youth woodland" called the "freedom forest for Soviet Jewry," an ex-New Yorker named Jeff Shaya planted a tree in 1972, to memorialize Babe Ruth.

This list could be much longer.

Another kind of evidence is the interest of collectors. Dr. Helen Cripe of the American Antiquarian Society, studying the public sales of Americana, found in the catalogs of well-known dealers 17 pieces of Ruthiana listed in the years 1963–1973, at prices from $6.50 to $250. Advertisements in the *Antique Trader* (Summer 1973) give us a relative evaluation: three Mickey Mouse watches of 1931, from $95 to $135, and one Babe Ruth watch at $110.

Babe Ruth's fame is grounded on firm achievement. A baseball player can't hide mistakes or clumsiness; he stands alone and naked. There is no way to build up an ordinary player artificially for very long. A few hot dogs become well known, but their days of true popularity are few. Ruth was even more than a great player, he was a folk hero. He didn't have all the qualities Thomas Carlyle insisted a hero must have (nor has Mickey Mouse), but he still gets from ordinary people most of the homage Carlyle said was due a hero.

His fame will last. Once a living legend persists from the first generation into the third generation, that legend is secure and durable. Captain John Smith made it; John Rolfe is rarely spoken of. Abraham Lincoln is remembered; Douglas is recalled, if ever, only as Lincoln's foil. Babe Ruth's name draws crowds of small boys to the Ruth exhibit at Cooperstown. Do many small boys beg to visit Lindbergh's trophies in St. Louis or Grant's tomb in New York?

Babe Ruth could not know the real world as obscure people know it. After living his formative years in a kind of monastery for boys, he leaped into a heroic place as a winner on winning teams. He never saw anything anonymously; it was all shown to him from where he stood on his pedestal. The ordinary person's world, how it worked, what it looked like, what it did to people, he couldn't know. Which may explain his fellow feeling for people institutionalized in artificial worlds—orphanages, hospitals, prisons.

He became a normal person by working to be normal. It was a hard struggle for him to become an acceptable member of society, partly because of his physical endowment. His appetites were strong, and his muscular urges even stronger. Driven by his makeup to satisfy his gut and use his muscles more than he used his mental powers, he was initially out of balance. With effort he became what we call normal by the age of 30. If he had had less human sympathy and even greater physical strength, he might have been in a state of permanent emotional disturbance. But his generosity and affections were as large as his hungers and his need to use his muscles.

It is rather sad that he never learned how typical a man he was. A reading of his memoirs and a study of his behavior raise the suspicion that he thought of himself as a kind of freak. Yet, in every American cigar store, pool hall, barbershop, bar and grill, during his glory times, were specimens much like him—lacking only the ability to play baseball well.

Ruth had all of our faults, yet had the material success most Americans would like to have. Never did he try to be anything he was not; he never spoke on a subject he was unqualified to speak on, except in response to interviewers' questions, and rarely even then. The ballplayer was larger than the man. His mind was empty of practically everything but baseball, and packed tight with baseball. He never said a banal thing about baseball except in situations contrived by press agents, where he echoed the puritan bosh about the uplifting gifts of sport—platitudes he had heard others use, pro forma, with apparent success. Except when cornered in that way, he was intellectually honest.

Did his manner of life hurt his play? The matter of keeping in shape for baseball has in it a great deal of superstition. Inborn ability to make catlike movements is far more important than precise weight. Only in long games and doubleheaders does overweight take its price. He may have neglected to keep in condition, but that wasn't what killed him. Up to the age of 30 he tried hard to support the deathless belief of so many, that pleasure is happiness. Stories of the sins of popular heroes certainly grasp the attention of readers; so much has been written about Ruth's very ordinary and rather tiresome hedonism (but never with names, places, dates) that one is convinced there must be a real need to believe him a glutton who played best with a hangover. It reduces him to a smaller moral size so that some people can feel superior in some way to the otherwise titanic figure. And, as John McCabe well noted in his life of George M. Cohan, America sees itself as "Peck's Bad Boy," rough and hard to rule but instinctively doing good because it knows what is right. Ruth *had* to be a bad boy to be the paramount American. As Tristram Coffin said, "The hero must have a bit of the fool in him."

The record contradicts Ruth's reputation for self-destructive gluttony. As of 1972, only 61 players had played 20 full seasons in the major leagues. Ruth was one who played 20 full seasons, and parts of two others. Whatever he did, it didn't destroy him as a player or a person.

Babe Ruth was driven by ambition and love. The ambition was to be the most successful baseball player, and the standard of success was the salary. Having money, he saw no reason not to enjoy it. He was driven by love in the sense of an urge to do good, which he saw in two ways—as being kind to the helpless and as not hurting people on purpose. He was good at both. The home runs and the dollars are famous, but we overlook the absence of permanent enemies and the number of people who knew him well and loved him.

With most professional athletes, play is work. With Ruth, play was play. And it was his life. Was his life trivial? Because the Greeks taught us that what is universally popular is literally vulgar and ignorable, we think the business leader, the statesman, and the soldier are really living, while the athlete is wasting his and our time. (Euripides, for one, was very rough on athletes on this point; he had competing theaters to fill.) But there is a certain nobility in uniting mind and body in acts that need their perfect harmony. There is no need to apologize for athletes. The body has disorganized stimuli, gnawing hungers, and some unsystematic goals. The athlete makes it over into something controlled and directed toward its own excellence. If the mind merely lives in the body as a fish lives in the bowl, it would be folly to spend much time and effort to perfect the bowl. But man is mind and body in one, and the great athlete is a complete man who has found the limits of adventure within the bounds of the rules of his kind of play. That is not trivial.

Babe Ruth lived only 53 years, but not all shortened lives are unfinished lives. Some are well rounded off and end at a proper time. Since we have no reason to think he could have been a successful manager, and he had no other serious interest than baseball, we may say his was a finished, complete life. He was born at precisely the right time; it is hard to see how he could have been eminent if born earlier, or unique if born later. In the judgment of the people, no ballplayer has succeeded him. More than that, all others have diminished while he has grown. At the first election to the Hall of Fame in 1936, he ranked third. At mid-century, the Associated Press poll ranked him first over Cobb as the greatest ballplayer in the previous 50 years. In 1969, the centennial year of professional baseball, the Baseball Writers' Association of America voted him the best player in the history of the game. They were nearly all strangers to him personally. Somehow that fact seems to add credibility to Babe Ruth's history; one feels like saying it really *did* happen.

A puzzled dramatic critic, in 1948, asked Babe Ruth's close friend, Dan Daniel, why Ruth should have a funeral unlike any before in New York (or, one may add, since) and more obituary space than any New Yorker ever had, more memorializing than proposed for presidents, or scientists, or warriors. "Why all this? What did the man Ruth do? What did he have, to merit this?"

To answer, a generation later: He is our Hercules, our Samson, Beowulf, Siegfried. No other person outside public life so stirred our imaginations and captured our affections.

THE JUDGE WHO RULED BASEBALL

Bruce Watson

Back when baseball was widely considered a pastime and not a business, when fans wore fedoras instead of baseball caps and players had nicknames like Lefty and Pepper, the game's integrity rested in a single office. A player ordered to report to that office took a cab to 333 North Michigan Avenue in downtown Chicago. After riding the elevator to an upper floor, the player would tread softly on hallway carpet until reaching a door. On it was stenciled a single word—BASEBALL.

Behind baseball's door stood all the trappings of authority. Tall shelves were lined with law books. Greeting the player, a secretary told him to have a seat. The judge "would be right with him." As the player sat, a stream of populist profanity spewed from the adjacent office. "Pishtush! You tell that blankety-blank SOB that I said . . ." Moments later, the player was summoned into the next room. In the middle of it was a desk cluttered with papers. A box of chewing tobacco sat on the desk; a spittoon stood alongside. And striding forward, extending a bony hand, was the short, wiry man who served as baseball's judge, jury, and Julius Caesar.

From the seasons of a young Babe Ruth to the days of Joe DiMaggio and Ted Williams, Judge Kenesaw Mountain Landis was baseball's court of last resort. As commissioner, he imposed his iron will on every level of the game, from minor-league squabbles to major-league scandals. He overruled trades. He banished players for life. He suspended Babe Ruth as easily as he had once subpoenaed John D. Rockefeller. Ostensibly, Landis worked for the owners who hired him in 1920, yet his contract stated that he could not be fired, docked in pay, or criticized in public. He had the authority to investigate anything "suspected to be detrimental to the best interests of the national game," and he never hesitated to use that authority. These days, some call Landis "the only successful dictator in American history," while

Bruce Watson, "The Judge Who Ruled Baseball," *Smithsonian* 31, no. 7 (October 2000): 122–132. Reprinted with the kind permission of the author.

others regard him as "the savior of baseball." But throughout his nearly 25 years in charge of the game, owners, players, and fans called him "the judge."

With his perpetual scowl and bold shock of white hair, Landis looked like God in a three-piece suit. He lived in elite hotels, dining from room service, yet he chewed tobacco like a slugger and swore like a sailor. Where did baseball find such a character? "The legend has been spread that the owners hired the Judge off the federal bench," the feisty player and manager Leo Durocher remembered. "Don't you believe it. They got him right out of Dickens." Born in 1866, Landis was named for the mountain in Georgia where his father, a Union surgeon on the march with General Sherman, nearly lost a leg. (Abraham Landis, for reasons known only to himself, chose an alternative spelling of Kennesaw, dropping one "n.") When he was growing up in Logansport, Indiana, kids called the young Landis "every damned thing they could think of," he recalled. But his older siblings, noting his imperious air even as a boy, dubbed him "the Squire." Though he grew to just five feet, seven inches, he commanded respect. During the early 1880s, he played first base for the Goosetown, Indiana, semipro team and became its manager at 17. Offered a pro contract, he turned it down, preferring to play "merely for sport and the love of the game." He was also a fierce bicycle racer, winning many medals at county fairs, yet he did not seem likely to succeed at much else.

Unable to sit still in class, Landis dropped out of high school. He worked as a handyman, sold newspapers, and eventually became a court reporter. In the courtroom, the indifferent student proved himself adept at winning influential friends. In 1886, he began a rapid rise. First, an acquaintance who became Indiana's secretary of state made Landis his aide. A year later, Landis was admitted to the Indiana bar. Back then, he remembered, "All a man needed was to prove that he was 21 and had a good moral character." Eventually, however, he enrolled in a law school in Chicago, where, after graduating, he hung out a shingle. Then, in 1893, came another quantum career leap. Abraham Landis's former commanding officer, Walter Q. Gresham, became Grover Cleveland's secretary of state. Gresham quickly appointed the younger Landis his personal secretary. At the ripe old age of 26, Landis found himself hobnobbing with diplomats. Eventually, he even represented the U.S. Department of State at cabinet meetings. Cleveland later offered Landis the post of minister to Venezuela, but by that time he had met a charming socialite, Miss Winifred Reed. In 1895, he returned to Chicago, got married, practiced law, and became a fixture at Cubs games.

Baseball at the turn of the century was as different from today's game as Boston's creaky Fenway Park is from the Toronto SkyDome. Back then, players were raw farm boys, immigrants fresh from mill towns, and backroom brawlers with something to prove. The Chicago Cubs were by no means the best team in baseball—John McGraw's Giants, Connie Mack's Athletics, and Fred Clarke's Pirates were better—but by 1906 they would be.

Their games, all played under the natural light of the sun, made truants of schoolboys and a slacker of one feisty lawyer in particular. "Can't we get a postponement of the case until tomorrow?" Landis once asked an opposing lawyer. "Brownie is pitching against Matty and I just can't miss that." Mordecai Peter Centennial "Three Finger" Brown was the Cubs' star pitcher and Landis's favorite; Christopher "Christy" Mathewson was the star pitcher of the New York Giants. Landis loved baseball as much for its honesty as for its home runs, which in those "dead-ball" days were relatively infrequent. (The introduction, in 1909, of a cork-centered ball, and then, in 1920, of the so-called lively ball, which was made with a new kind of yarn that could be wound tighter, resulted in a sharp upturn in home run production.) "It is a great game this baseball, a great game," he mused. "It is remarkable for the hold it has on the people, and equally remarkable for its cleanness." Yet as crowds flocked to ballparks and gamblers to growing baseball pools, the "great game" was about to be dragged through the mud.

When two of his brothers were elected to Congress, Landis was encouraged to run for office. He declined but again backed the right horse. After one of his cronies helped Theodore Roosevelt win reelection in 1904, the man recommended Landis to the president for a newly created judgeship in Chicago. Roosevelt acceded to that request. As a federal judge, Landis treated the courtroom as his stage. His sense of justice, while occasionally blind, was never boring. If a lawyer's line of questioning seemed suspicious, Landis would screw up his nose as if smelling an odor. He sometimes bolted out of his seat and pointed his finger at a witness, saying, "Now, let's stop fooling around and tell exactly what did happen, without reciting your life history." And once, when an old felon protested that he'd never finish a five-year sentence, the judge scowled and said, "Well, you can try, can't you?"

Murder and mayhem, bribery and fraud, each case gave "the Squire" a reason to be righteous. But he might have remained as anonymous as most other federal judges had it not been for *United States v. Standard Oil of Indiana*. By 1907, Standard Oil of New Jersey controlled 85 percent of the country's refined oil and was the nation's most hated trust. In Landis's courtroom, its subsidiary, Standard Oil of Indiana, stood accused of colluding with the railroads and using its huge volume to obtain lower rates. When Standard's lawyers dodged questions, Landis furiously subpoenaed top officials, including the president, John D. Rockefeller himself. Rockefeller's lawyers tried to argue that the 67-year-old magnate was too frail to testify, but Landis thundered, "This court is no respecter of wealth or other claims of immunity!"

Saturday, July 6, 1907, was a hot, humid day in Chicago but a great day for a baseball game. Both the Cubs and Chicago's other professional team, the White Sox, occupied first place in their respective leagues. The Cubs were out of town, but the Sox were hosting Connie Mack's Philadelphia Athletics. Landis couldn't attend because he had a rendezvous with the richest man in America. Just before 10 a.m., hundreds gathered outside Landis's courtroom. "Here he comes!" someone shouted. Twenty Chicago policemen cleared a path as, wearing an icy blank stare, Rockefeller arrived for his day in court.

Under Landis's questioning, Rockefeller admitted his company ran "an oil refinery in New Jersey," but granted little more, evading and hesitating while Landis tapped his glasses. When the judge fined Standard Oil of Indiana $29.2 million, more than half the money then coined annually by the federal government, the public was ecstatic. The "frail" Rockefeller, receiving the news on the golf course, coolly drove a ball down the fairway and later remarked, "Judge Landis will be dead a long time before this fine is paid." He was right. An appeals court overturned Landis's verdict, something that happened frequently.

During World War I, Landis, by then known as a super-patriot, became fiercely intolerant. He lashed out at German Americans, saying, "Their hearts are reeking with disloyalty." In 1918, when members of the Industrial Workers of the World, or IWW (usually referred to as the Wobblies), were accused of draft evasion and other acts of sedition, Landis presided. Ignoring pleas for clemency from Helen Keller and other luminaries, Landis handed out sentences of up to 20 years and imposed fines totaling $2.3 million.

Five years later, President Calvin Coolidge commuted Landis's IWW sentences, but by then the judge had a job in which he could not be overruled. Even before eight Chicago White Sox threw the 1919 World Series, the team was known as the Black Sox. Along with paying baseball's stingiest salaries, Sox owner Charles Comiskey cut his team's laundry budget to the bone, hence the nickname. But as the heavily favored Sox were blowing the Series, rumors flew. The fix was in. An extensive cover-up kept the truth hidden until just before the 1920 Series. That fall, with the game's image tarnished, club owners voted to disband their governing National Commission.

The Black Sox Scandal wasn't the owners' only concern. For several years prior to that, political infighting between the leagues had all but nullified the Commission's ability to run things. Baseball was coming close to anarchy, and something had to be done. One strong man was needed to run the show, restoring both order and integrity to America's game. Among the candidates were former president William Howard Taft, Gen. John Pershing, and Landis. The judge had the inside track because in 1915, he had upheld baseball's reserve clause, binding players to teams for life. Now, thinking he was on their side, the owners turned to him.

On November 12, 1920, the most powerful men in baseball entered the courtroom where Landis was presiding over a bribery case. Seated, the team owners talked among themselves. "There'll be less noise in this courtroom or I will order it cleared," Landis boomed. After adjournment, tycoons—whose names adorned ballparks—Ebbets, Griffith, Comiskey, entered the judge's chambers with hats in hand. Flattered by the offer to become baseball's commissioner, Landis nonethe-less protested that he was "doing important work" on the bench. The owners in-sisted he could do both jobs. For the love of the game and the dual salary—$7,500 as judge and $42,500 as commissioner—Landis agreed.

Landis began rising at 5 a.m. to work as a federal judge and baseball's jury. He continued until the dual income led to censure by the American Bar Association and the threat of Congressional impeachment. In March 1922, he resigned from the bench to devote all his time to baseball.

Nearly a year after the Black Sox Scandal broke, all eight players were acquit-ted. Then it was Commissioner Landis's turn to overrule. "Regardless of the verdict of juries, baseball is entirely competent to protect itself against crooks, both inside and outside the game," he declared. Whether a player had taken $35,000, as had Chick Gandil, or had taken no money and thrown no games, as was the case with Buck Weaver, mattered little to Landis. He banished all eight men for life.

That was just the beginning of the judge's housecleaning. Landis loathed gamblers, those "vermin" who would "sell out their mothers or the Virgin Mary." They were bent on getting "their slimy fingers around baseball," he said. "But by God, so long as I have anything to do with this game, they'll never get another hold on it." Over the next four years, he blacklisted seven other players and suspended 38 more. A few had thrown games, but most, like Weaver, had merely been ap-proached by gamblers, then failed to tell their team. Landis banished a New York Giants pitcher for "treachery" after the man wrote a letter suggesting he was open to a fix. He ordered owners to sell any financial interests in racetracks, and years later, when crooner Bing Crosby tried to buy an interest in the Pittsburgh Pirates, Landis turned him down because he owned racehorses.

Players who flirted with the jazzier side of the Jazz Age could expect no mercy from the judge. One example was Benny Kauff. The New York Giants outfielder wore gaudy diamond rings, drove the kinds of cars usually owned by gangsters, and often carried thousands in cash. He played the 1920 season under indictment for grand theft auto. No one seemed to mind—until Landis became commissioner. Come spring, Kauff made the long trek from the Giants' training camp in San Antonio, Texas, to Landis's Michigan Avenue office. There Landis suspended Kauff until his auto-theft trial. When a jury acquitted the outfielder, Landis reviewed the case himself. "The acquittal smells to high heaven," he said. Kauff never played baseball again.

Banning a .274 hitter was one thing. But would the new commissioner have enough stature to take on the Sultan of Swat himself? It can be argued that no player has ever had a better season than Babe Ruth had in 1921. He hit more hom-ers, 59, than eight entire teams had that year. He also set records for extra-base hits, total bases, runs, and runs batted in, some of which still stand. By season's end, Ruth's name had appeared in American newspapers more often than anyone's except President Harding's. When Ruth booked a number of postseason exhibition games to cash in on his fame, Landis upheld a long-standing ban on such barnstorming by World Series players.

Summoned to the judge's office, Ruth refused to show, then called to tell Landis he was heading to Buffalo to play ball. Landis slammed down the phone, shouting, "Who the hell does that big ape think he is?" Ruth's reply? "Aw, tell the old guy to go jump in a lake." After Ruth went ahead, Landis fined him his entire World Series share and suspended him for the first six weeks of the 1922 season. When the two met in spring training, Ruth asked for a pardon; he got a two-hour lecture instead. "He sure can talk," Ruth said, but he never crossed the judge again.

Wayward players felt the judge's holy wrath, but others found him paternal. Despite his lordly status, Landis always addressed players formally as gentlemen—Mr. Gehrig, Mr. Hornsby, Mr. Cobb—and watched over them like a hen watches over her chicks. When players had personal problems, Landis helped them. He once sent an aide to take the great pitcher Grover Cleveland Alexander, a binge-drinking alcoholic, home to his family. When Landis heard that a player he had banished was nearly indigent, he sent the man a personal check. "He was always on the side of the ballplayer," Leo Durocher recalled. "He had no use for the owners at all. 'Don't worry about them,' he would tell me, 'They're not out to help you. You know where your friend is. Right here. I'm your man.'"

Players and fans loved Landis, but others did not. The powerful American League president Ban Johnson resented Landis's absolute authority and schemed against him. Finally, Landis, who always carried a letter of resignation in his pocket, threatened to quit unless Johnson did. The owners backed Landis.

The judge's arbitrary decisions baffled sportswriters. Why did he ban the Black Sox, then refuse to do the same to Ty Cobb and Tris Speaker when those two stars were accused of throwing a game back in 1919? Johnson suspended Cobb and Speaker, but Landis reinstated them. Public outcry may have swayed his decision, but Landis claimed there wasn't enough evidence. Besieged by other old scandals, he grumbled, "Won't these Goddamn things that happened before I came into baseball ever stop coming up?" and put a statute of limitations on such cases.

By the late 1920s, Landis, with a little help from his friend Babe Ruth, had restored the luster of the national pastime. In big new stadiums, attendance was soaring. Baseball's number-one fan was Landis himself. He seemed to be at every important game, watching from his box, his head resting on the railing, his snow-white hair signaling his presence like a beacon. He rarely spoke, just watched and scowled, like an eagle casting a cold eye down from his aerie. Here was Landis at the World Series in Yankee Stadium. There was Landis dedicating minor-league parks in Montreal, Columbus, Terre Haute. . . . He chose announcers for the Series, lecturing them about the perils of partisanship. He signed every World Series check. Once an official scorer asked if Landis had any advice. "No," the judge replied, "just go ahead and score the game in your usual damned incompetent fashion." Yet just as he preserved baseball's integrity, the judge also preserved its timeworn traditions.

During the Depression, owners sought ways to boost sagging attendance. Landis opposed every change. He vowed night baseball would never happen under his watch, but as it turned out he could not stop it. He fought the farm system through which clubs bought minor-league teams to develop their own talent. He upheld baseball's unwritten ban on black players and did nothing to push owners toward integration.

But by the 1940s, pressure was mounting. In 1943, the Pittsburgh Pirates tried to sign Josh Gibson, the legendary slugger who played for the Homestead Grays. Landis put a stop to it. "The colored ballplayers have their own league," he said. "Let them stay in their own league."

The most famous story of his opposition to integration was told by the maverick owner Bill Veeck. According to Veeck, Landis stopped him from buying the Phillies after Veeck told him he planned to sign black players. By the time he got from the judge's office to Philadelphia, Veeck claimed, control of the Phillies had been turned over to the National League, and the team was soon sold to another buyer. Yet some now doubt the story. "Veeck may have made it up out of whole cloth, and it has distorted Landis's image tremendously," says veteran sportswriter Robert W. Creamer. "Landis was no angel. He reflected the institutional racism of his times. But he wasn't quite the devil he's been portrayed." Baseball remained segregated until 1947, when the Brooklyn Dodgers' owner, Branch Rickey, signed Jackie Robinson. By then, Landis was no longer watching from his box.

In 1944, the judge missed the World Series for the first time since becoming commissioner. Two days before the Series began, he entered the hospital complaining of shortness of breath. At 78, he had survived prostate cancer and chronic respiratory problems, but friends expected he would soon be visiting ballparks again. When he didn't emerge to vote against Franklin Delano Roosevelt, whom he despised, they knew his condition must be serious. In mid-November, the owners renewed Landis's seven-year contract, but a week later the judge died in his sleep. His departure was the least theatrical act of his life. There was no funeral. He was cremated and buried beneath a modest headstone in Chicago. Two weeks later he was given a more fitting memorial when the Baseball Hall of Fame named him a member. His plaque in Cooperstown reads: "His Integrity and Leadership Established Baseball in the Respect, Esteem, and Affection of the American People."

Today the judge is remembered for the independence he brought to his office. No subsequent commissioner has measured up to his standards of power and authority. Not long after Landis died, the owners regained ascendancy and have guarded it jealously ever since. Landis's immediate successor, A. B. "Happy" Chandler, a onetime Kentucky governor and U.S. senator, never approached the judge in stature, and when he did begin to exert power on his own, the owners voted him out in a hurry. Every commissioner since has had to pay attention to what the owners want.

These days no one bothers to pretend that baseball is a mere pastime. The "Steves" and "Matts" who replaced the "Leftys" and "Peppers" make more money than any gambler could offer them. Yet in spite of everything—the rampant commercialism, the spitting on umpires, the trash talk, and the drug scandals—at least one of the old judge's verdicts on the game's meaning and importance has not been overturned. "Baseball is something more than a game to an American boy," he declared. "It is his training field for life work. Destroy his faith in its squareness and honesty and you have destroyed something more; you have planted suspicion of all things in his heart."

CHAPTER 6

The Depression and World War II, 1931–1945

Dark Days for America and Baseball

By the opening of the 1931 baseball season, the Great Depression was entering its second year. Hope that the Depression would be temporary slowly faded away. The Stock Market Crash of October 1929 had taken a terrible toll on the economy. By one measure, it had wiped out 20 years of economic growth and created the gravest economic and social crisis in U.S. history. The gross national product went from $104.4 billion in 1929, to $74 billion four years later, by far the sharpest drop in U.S. history. Unemployment was the worst aspect of the Depression, especially coming as it did after the booming prosperity of the 1920s. The unemployment figures slowly rose through 1930 and 1931, until by early 1932, the number had reached 20 percent. It would crest at 25 percent the next year.

Even the hugely successful automotive industry was hard hit. General Motors, one of the stars of the 1920s prosperity cycle, laid off 100,000 of its 260,000 workers. No group avoided the Depression. Farmers who had done well during World War I and then suffered from overproduction in the 1920s saw the price of their products drop to all-time lows. African Americans discovered that the "last hired, first fired" philosophy still prevailed. In Pittsburgh, home of the steel industry, African Americans constituted 8 percent of the population but accounted for 40 percent of the unemployed. By one estimate, among recent immigrants one-third of the Poles, Slovaks, and Croatians; one half of the Italians; and more than one half of the Greek immigrants returned to their native lands. The middle class couldn't escape either. Approximately 4,000 banks failed between late 1929 and early 1933, in many cases taking the life savings of millions.[1]

No institution, not the church, not the academy, not any political party, could satisfactorily explain what had happened. President Herbert Hoover, who had won a massive victory in 1928; the American banking system; European debtors; and Wall Street were among those blamed for the Depression. A particular victim of the Depression was the habitual confidence in the future of the American public.

As with other major events in U.S. history, baseball could not escape the consequences of the Depression. Baseball had prospered as never before in the 1920s, and the game became more popular than at any time in the past. That all changed quickly as the Depression deepened. The total attendance figure for the decade of the Depression decade was 81 million, a net drop of 12 million from the 1920s, the biggest single percentage decline decade from decade in baseball history. In 1930, attendance had reached an all-time high, topping the 10 million mark for the first time. Three teams, Brooklyn, Chicago, and New York, drew more than 1 million fans, while the Giants accounted for 868,000. For the rest of the 1930s, the million mark would be achieved just four times. The Yankees, baseball's biggest drawing card, would not draw 1 million fans again until after World War II.

For teams like the St. Louis Browns and the Philadelphia Phillies, the decade was an unmitigated disaster. The Browns, for example, drew the fewest fans in both leagues every year during the 1930s. In three seasons, the Browns drew less than 100,000 fans. The Phillies were only slightly better. Playing in perhaps the worst ballpark in baseball, Baker Bowl, the Phillies averaged a little more than 200,000 per year during the decade. Baker Bowl had been the first modern ballpark in the 1890s, but it had become decrepit. On two occasions, the stands collapsed and fans were killed. The right-field wall was covered in tin and had rusted so badly throughout the years that some line drives actually went through the wall for ground-rule doubles. The Phillies were the poor relation in Philadelphia baseball. The A's had produced a dynasty in the late 1920s, while the Phillies had exactly one winning season between 1917 and 1949; however, the A's dominance ended in the 1930s.

Connie Mack saw attendance for his great A's team go from 800,000 in 1929, to 233,000 six years later. The reason was obvious. Beginning in 1932, to pay his bills, Mack had to sell his best players—Jimmie Foxx, Mickey Cochrane, Al Simmons, and Lefty Grove, just to mention future Hall of Famers. The situation in St. Louis for the Browns was equally grim. The Browns had built their ball field, called Sportsman's Park in the teens, and made some money renting it out to the Cardinals. The Browns' problem was that throughout the late 1920s and the 1930s, the Cardinals had a good club and completely overshadowed them.

The reason for baseball's grim balance sheet was obvious. Baseball, except to the dedicated fan, was a luxury. People during the Depression did not have the kind of disposable income that characterized the Roaring Twenties. The teams kept ticket prices low, but even so a baseball game was more expensive than a movie, for instance. You could usually walk to a movie because they were found in every neighborhood, while if you wanted to go to a baseball game you had the added expense of trolley fare. Also, the 1930s saw the full emergence of radio as a form of entertainment, with three networks, NBC, which controlled two, and CBS, providing free material, ranging from drama and mystery to comedy and music, every night. The only cost was the one-time price of the radio, which could be bought on time. As we will see, baseball tried to keep the sport off the radio, believing it encouraged people to stay home instead of going to the games.

Organized baseball did not know how to respond to this crisis, one that proved worse than anything in its past, including the Black Sox Scandal. Major-league teams lost $1.2 million in 1932. The next season was worse because the government had enacted a 10 percent entertainment tax on baseball's gate receipts. The owners slashed salaries. Babe Ruth's $80,000 a year in 1930 would not be topped until after World War II. After hitting .346 and leading the American League in home runs and RBIs in 1937, Joe DiMaggio had to fight for a salary of $25,000. Although it is difficult to get accurate figures, it appears that the average salary in the 1930s was about $5,000. Despite these grim statistics, it is interesting that during the 1930s there was no effort to organize baseball players as had happened so often in the past. Even in the mid-1930s, when the union movement became radicalized and aggressive, there wasn't a shadow of interest in creating a players' organization. Baseball players were an elite in the nation, and they acted like and believed they were fortunate to have jobs that paid so well.

BASEBALL'S RESPONSE TO THE DEPRESSION

It is one of the contradictions of baseball history that the sport's response to the crisis of the Depression was one of remarkable creativity. It was almost a textbook example of historian Arnold Toynbee's thesis of challenge and response. The men who guided baseball in the 1930s, beginning with Judge Kenesaw Mountain Landis and including the owners, managers, and players on the field, were completely caught off guard by the downward economic spiral from late 1929 until the Depression bottomed out in 1933. The first reaction of the baseball leadership was summed up by Judge Landis in the midst of the decline in attendance. The American people, he said, love their sport, and they will return to it as soon as the economy picks up. He was correct, but his optimism must have seemed out of place in 1933, when baseball attendance took a nosedive.[2]

Baseball's first response to the economic downturn actually had been brewing for some time. Beginning in 1931, baseball finally systematized the granting of an award to the best player in each league. Called the Most Valuable Player (MVP) Award, it caught the attention of the public and was one way of keeping baseball alive during the offseason, as well as dramatizing the season's greatest accomplishments. A postseason award first had been tried in 1910, when the Chalmers Automobile Company announced it would give a car to the batting champion in each league. The outcome was ugly because players on the St. Louis Browns who hated Ty Cobb laid down so the more popular Napoleon Lajoie could win the title, allowing him to bunt successfully seven times to pass Cobb. Following an outcry, Chalmers gave a car to both men.

To avoid that in the future, a committee of leading baseball writers was formed and selected the outstanding player in each league. The first winners were Cobb and a solid hitting outfielder for the Cubs, Wildfire Schulte. That system prevailed for a couple of seasons and then faded away. The concept was revived in the 1920s, and the players named in each league were a representative group of great players: Babe Ruth, Rogers Hornsby, and Hack Wilson. The award didn't seem to generate that much interest, perhaps because both leagues followed different rules for selection. That changed in 1931, when the Baseball Writers' Association of America (BBWAA) took over. As the men who followed the game intimately and wrote about it for the public, they were equipped to render a fair verdict. The *Sporting News* also named a Most Valuable Player each season and vied with the BBWAA for popularity, but the latter's choices were generally accepted. In reality, the choicest were often the same player. Both groups, for example, picked Jimmie Foxx in 1932 and 1933, and Lou Gehrig in 1936, as American League MVP.

The real importance for the MVP Award lay in the fact that it kept the discussion and debate about baseball alive during the off season, the so-called Hot Stove League. Baseball was the first sport to adopt the MVP concept, and its success led others to duplicate it, making it commonplace in almost every sport today. The owners were not always thrilled with the idea since it provided a group of players, singled out for distinguished service, leverage to ask for a raise; however, the public relations value was too positive to reject, and the MVP concept did not disappear but throughout the years was expanded to other aspects of baseball play: Rookie of the Year, the Cy Young Award for outstanding pitching performance, Manager of the Year, and so forth.

At about the same time that the MVP idea caught on, Arch Ward, a writer for the *Chicago Tribune*, came up with a concept to honor the 1933 centenary of the founding of the city, the "Century of Progress." His idea was to have a team of the best players in each league play against one another. The concept of an All-Star Game had been talked about in the past, but nothing had come of it. With the backing of the *Tribune*, the most influential newspaper in the Midwest, labeled by its owner, Colonel Robert McCormick, with all humility, as the world's greatest newspaper, Ward's concept won over the baseball owners and even the always skeptical Judge Landis.

The first All-Star Game was staged on July 6, 1933, in Comiskey Park. Connie Mack managed the American League team, and John McGraw came out of retirement to manage the Nationals. Fans chose the players. The game was a huge success. Babe Ruth, at 38 and in decline, hit the first home run in All-Star Game history. The game also was a sellout, and the money earned was turned over to a fund to aid indigent baseball players. The next season, the concept was revived and since then has been a hallmark of the baseball season. Staged in the middle of the season, it became a popular way to honor the best players in the game. Like the MVP, the concept has been adopted by almost every sport. Baseball's All-Star Game, however, has been the one that most resembles the regular game. Those all-star games in other sports have been largely meaningless. The Pro Bowl in football is hardly paid attention to and resembles something like touch football. No one wants to get hurt playing a game that means nothing. Professional basketball and hockey's all-star games are usually wild shoot-outs.

While the owners were enjoying the success and popularity of the All-Star Game, they made the first move to tap into the success of radio. Baseball had broadcast games in the past but basically hadn't figured out a way to profit from them. The consensus of the owners was that radio broadcasting would hurt attendance by allowing fans to enjoy the game at home and, what is worse, for free. But the economic crisis of the 1930s forced even these conservative men to contemplate a revolutionary idea, charging for the broadcasting of their games.[3]

In 1933, Judge Landis, a skeptic about baseball on the radio, negotiated a lucrative deal with the Ford Motor Company to sponsor World Series broadcasts for $400,000, a huge sum in those days, easily the equal of $7 million today. Those broadcasts (and the potential economic return) were a great success, but most team owners remained convinced that doing their games on the radio would drive down attendance. It took a genuine innovator to first exploit radio's economic possibilities.

Leland "Larry" MacPhail was a baseball original. Nicknamed the "Roaring Redhead" because of his temper, he was a lawyer, had served in World War I, and had tried a series of unsuccessful business ventures. He bought the American Association Columbus team, made it one of the most successful minor-league teams, and sold it to the St. Louis Cardinals for a profit. In 1933, radio manufacturer Powel Crosley bought the bankrupt Cincinnati Reds and gave MacPhail a free hand to run the team. MacPhail modernized the ballpark; made a series of shrewd trades; and then, in one of his masterstrokes, hired a little-known southerner, Walter "Red" Barber, to broadcast the Reds games on the radio. Barber was a great success who combined the idea of teaching the game with his laconic style of announcing it. The Reds began to improve and, by 1938–1939, were one of the best teams in the National League.[4]

In 1938, MacPhail was brought in to revive the Brooklyn Dodgers, a team that had been in the doldrums and in poor financial shape for a decade. He followed the same path he had taken in Cincinnati. He spruced up the ballpark; hired a new manager, the young Leo Durocher, to take over the team; and began a series of trades and acquisitions that made the Dodgers a power in the National League.

Perhaps MacPhail's greatest contribution to the sport in general came when he discovered that the three New York area teams had entered into an agreement to not broadcast their games. He thought that was nonsense and set out to change New York baseball forever. As with Cincinnati, he brought Red Barber with him with the same orders, to teach and sell the game. Barber was a great success and became synonymous with the Dodgers for the next two decades. His pet phrases, "Oh, brother" and "We're sitting in the Cat Bird seat," and arguments with umpires, which were fights in the "rhubarb patch," set a standard that those who followed him in radio sought to copy.

Given the success of the Dodgers on the radio, the Giants and Yankees were forced to broadcast their games. The Yankees came up with their own version of Barber, another southerner, Mel Allen. Unlike Barber, Allen was noted as a "homer," rooting for the Yankees and supplying the players with nicknames that caught the public's fancy. Joe DiMaggio was the "Yankee Clipper," Phil Rizzuto was "Scooter," and Tommy Henrich was "Old Reliable." With all three New York teams doing their games on radio, the rest of baseball fell in line. Most teams were sponsored by products identified with males, young and old. Breakfast cereal with General Mills set the pace, advertising Wheaties for 14 of the 16 major-league teams. Sellers of gasoline, cigarettes, and beer found that baseball broadcasts were a good way to reach the public, especially males. Each team strove to find its own Red Barber and Mel Allen, and in a short time, every team had a personality that helped define them to the public.[5] On another level, baseball expanded old sources of revenue—advertising on the fences and selling scorecards. Some teams in the late 1930s and early 1940s were getting $40,000 a year for the rights to broadcast their games, a sum large enough to help offset the cost of players' salaries.

Along with radio broadcasts adopted during the Depression, nighttime baseball changed the game forever. It was MacPhail who introduced the idea, despite the protest of the baseball establishment and the opposition of Judge Landis. When MacPhail ran the Columbus team for the Cardinals, he had installed lights and found that they not only didn't present a problem for playing the game, but also consistently outdrew day games. Almost as soon as he took over the Reds, MacPhail began pushing his plan to install lights. Other National League teams refused to go along, but MacPhail, with Crosley's backing, insisted that the Reds had the right to play in the day or at night. After some back and forth, the other owners agreed to allow their teams to play in Cincinnati at night, but they insisted there would be only one game for each team.

The first nighttime game took place on May 24, 1935, between the Reds and a poor Phillies team. President Franklin D. Roosevelt agreed to throw a switch in Washington, DC, that turned the lights on. The game went off without incident, and a crowd of 20,000 turned out to see two second division teams compete. MacPhail believed that seven games in a season would soon turn into more. One of his strongest arguments was that a nighttime game in the middle of the week would be like another Sunday game, the day when attendance was at its peak. He had the figures to back up that view. The seven nighttime games attracted 130,000 customers, an average of about 19,000. The remaining Reds home games drew an average of 4,700 fans. Baseball owners could count, and night baseball quickly began to win them over.[6]

Night baseball caught on quickly, especially when the National League owners saw that nighttime games outdrew day ones by a factor of three. The Dodgers, with MacPhail in charge, installed lights in 1938, and saw attendance increase by 100,000 fans for the season. Connie Mack followed shortly thereafter, and by the outbreak of World War II, only a handful of teams didn't have lights. And they would have adopted them, except the war rendered the materials scarce.

The last of the creative actions by baseball during the Depression was the creation of a Hall of Fame honoring the greatest players in baseball history. The Hall was founded in 1936, and opened for the first time in 1939, the supposed anniversary of Abner Doubleday's invention of baseball. There had been discussion of a monument to baseball in the 1920s, but baseball wanted the government to vote the funds. Those in power in Washington then didn't believe in this kind of government action, so the plan for a Hall of Fame lay dormant. The idea was adopted by the Clark Foundation, which was seeking a way to honor the city of Cooperstown and attract tourists there. The idea was for a museum of baseball history, featuring artifacts and memorials to the sport's past. As a former public relations man, Ford Frick, president of the National League, saw great possibilities in the idea. He convinced a skeptical Judge Landis of its value for popularizing baseball's connections to America's past. Major League Baseball owners endorsed the idea, and the construction of a museum was begun in 1936.

There was only one problem: Everyone with more than a passing knowledge of baseball history knew Doubleday had nothing to do with baseball. The closest thing to a founder would have been Alexander Cartwright or Henry Chadwick, who served as the proponent of the uniqueness of American baseball. Once again, as in some aspects of baseball history, myth triumphed.

The Hall of Fame concept turned out to be a brilliant success. The museum was kept intimate and from the beginning highlighted baseball's past in an imaginative manner. In a sense, it became baseball's holiest shrine, almost a Fátima of the diamond. The idea of picking the "greats of the game" also was a masterstroke. It meant that each year, a ballot would take place choosing honorees for the Hall. The balloting would foment discussion and was precisely the kind of action that kept baseball in the news when the season ended.

The first class, consisting of Ty Cobb, Babe Ruth, Christy Mathewson, Walter Johnson, and Honus Wagner, was about as representative a sample of baseball greatness as one could imagine. Subsequent elections added others of equal stature: Grover Cleveland Alexander, George Sisler, Tris Speaker, and Napoleon Lajoie among them. When the Hall opened in 1939, those living greats were gathered in one place for the first time. It was a brilliant public relations stroke. The Hall became a site for baseball pilgrims despite the difficult location in Cooperstown, in the northern reaches of New York State. The yearly election continues to garner discussion and attention, and reminds the public of the role baseball played in America's development.[7]

The 1930s, with its grim economic record, also saw an ultimately successful attempt to revive Rube Foster's idea of an independent Negro League. Foster had tapped into the desire of the African American community to create their own version of professional baseball, showing that the sport belonged to them as much as white America. When his league slowly collapsed in the early 1930s, the best African American teams, for instance the Kansas City Monarchs, Hilldale from Philadelphia, and the Pittsburgh Crawfords continued playing exhibitions, usually against white teams, as a way of making money.

In 1933, a group of African American businessmen led by Pittsburgh restaurant owner and big-time numbers banker Gus Greenlee got together to revive the Negro League. The new Negro National League gathered the best African American teams to form one professional league. The organizers sought to avoid the problems that plagued Foster's old league. With the Depression entering its worst year, the timing was terrible given how hard hit the African American community was. The new league struggled and barely survived. It did have some successes.

The idea of an East–West All-Star Game, pitting the best African American players against one another, was established in 1933, and drew well. For the rest of the decade, that game was the one sign of hope. Set in Chicago, the game became the highlight of the season. The 1939 East–West All-Star Game drew a record crowd of 33,000, a figure that matched the attendance of the major-league All-Star Game. Sunday doubleheaders in Chicago, New York, Washington, and Philadelphia displayed the best players in the league for not only African American audiences, but also white fans and sportswriters.

The work of players like Satchel Paige, Josh Gibson, and Buck Leonard, among others, demonstrated a level of play equal to the best of Major League Baseball at the time. In some ways, the quality of baseball in the Negro Leagues reached a peak in the late 1930s and early 1940s. This raises an interesting question: Why wasn't there greater pressure to integrate the major leagues? The reasons are complex.

There was little interest in integration in the country, obsessed as it was during the Depression with economic problems. There was no outstanding pressure group with political influence pressing for integration. Even some of the best African American newspapers didn't think the timing was right. It also is important to note that the Negro Leagues were one of the biggest businesses run and controlled by African Americans. As much as the leaders of the league wanted recognition, they didn't want to lose their identity and become controlled by white baseball people.

In the final analysis, the white baseball establishment reflected the racism of American society at the time and didn't see any reason to take action. Nor did they see a way to profit financially by adding African Americans to their roster, which might have led them to overcome their racial prejudice. Despite whites going to Negro League games, the baseball leadership, like the nation at large, still believed in segregation in their sport. Racism confirmed the view that African American players would not significantly improve their chances on the field. It took the genius of Branch Rickey to recognize the potential significance of tapping into African American baseball talent.

It should be said the Negro League owners didn't show much interest in integration either. The league struggled but, by the late 1930s, was beginning to show signs of success and turn a profit. White baseball owners like Clark Griffith, Connie Mack, and even Ed Barrow of the Yankees were happy to rent their stadiums for a good price for Negro League games. By creating a stable business model and demonstrating the high quality of play, many of the African American team owners were hoping to show that eventually, the Negro Leagues would be recognized as part of Major League Baseball. There was no realistic chance of that happening, however, and when baseball opened its door to African American players, it came in a way that eventually destroyed the Negro Leagues.[8]

The game on the field in the 1930s was an extension of what had begun with the introduction of the lively ball in 1920. Offense dominated over pitching. There were plenty of pitchers who had won 20 games and two 30 game winners, Lefty Grove in 1931 and Dizzy Dean in 1934, but pitching ERAs were high. The American League consistently produced higher ERAs than the National League, often by a considerable margin. In 1936, the American League ERA was 5.04, a full run higher than the Senior Circuit. The consensus of the baseball community was that the American League maintained the offensive superiority that had begun in the 1920s with Babe Ruth. With the exception of 1930, when Hack Wilson led the National League with 56 home runs, and 1935, when the two leagues were separated by one home run, the American League consistently outhomered the Senior Circuit. Part of the reason for this was the existence of a steady supply of home run hitters produced by American League teams: Ruth until 1934, Jimmie Foxx, Lou Gehrig, Hank Greenberg, and Joe DiMaggio. The National League had no one to match them, especially after Wilson went into a rapid decline due to excessive drinking.

This offensive dominance was reflected in the outcomes of the All-Star Game, which the American League won five of the seven years after its introduction in 1933. The lack of balance was more noticeable in the World Series, which the American League dominated, winning in seven years versus three Series victories for the National League. The National League lost the World Series for five consecutive years from 1935 to 1939. The last four years of this string of victories was accounted for by the second great New York Yankees dynasty.

After Babe Ruth left the Yankees in 1935, the team was led by his hitting partner, Lou Gehrig, but he was not the charismatic figure Ruth had been. The emergence of Joe DiMaggio in 1936 brought a new hero to New York. The Yankees once again had a player of rare talent, a quiet leader, unlike Ruth, but still an iconic figure. DiMaggio had that unique quality of self-assured greatness often associated with charisma. With the power of the New York press behind him, he became the face of American baseball for a decade and half.

It is no accident that after DiMaggio's arrival, the Yankees won six American League pennants in eight years and six World Series. They won nine consecutive World Series games, taking the last game of the 1937 series against the Giants; four straight from the Cubs in 1938; and another sweep of the 1939 Series against the Cincinnati Reds, a record that lasted until the Yankees dynasty of the late 1990s and early 2000s set a new standard by winning 14 consecutive Series games. Even the year they lost the pennant, 1940, they finished just two games out of first place.

Along with DiMaggio, the American League in the 1930s produced a group of future Hall of Fame players, easily outstripping the output of the National League for that period. Hank Greenberg, Bob Feller, Ted Williams, Earl Averill, Early Wynn, Lou Boudreau, and Bobby Doerr all began their careers in the 1930s. No National League player, for instance, could match the quality of play of DiMaggio or Williams, or the pitching domination of Feller. As an interesting sidenote, DiMaggio, Williams, and Doerr were from California, which had begun to turn out a string of quality players, perhaps because the Pacific Coast League was the best minor-league circuit of the decade and baseball could be played year-round in sunny California.

The best players produced by the National League in the 1930s were pitchers. Dizzy Dean and especially Carl Hubbell were on par with Bob Feller as dominant hurlers. Dean won 30 games in 1934, and 20 or more for four consecutive years. He won 130 games before the age of 26, only to suffer an arm injury that ended his career at 28. Hubbell, a lean left-hander, had mastered the screwball, the pitch that had made Christy Mathewson so successful. Pitching for the New York Giants, he won 20 games six years in a row and 253 for his career. One of his claims to fame was striking out Babe Ruth, Lou Gehrig, Al Simmons, Jimmie Foxx, and Joe Cronin consecutively in the 1934 All-Star Game. Despite the solid pitching performance of the National League, the 1930s belonged to the American League. The National League drew many of its players from the South: Pepper Martin, the Dean brothers, Johnny Mize, Enos "Country" Slaughter, and Travis Jackson. The only explanation for this may have been the success of the St. Louis Cardinals in scouting the South and the fact that St. Louis games were broadcast throughout the South.

The closest thing to the Yankees in the National League was the St. Louis Cardinals. Under the guiding genius of Branch Rickey, the Cardinals built the first great farm system, which, by the late 1930s, controlled 15 minor league teams and had working agreements that gave them first call on players with 17 others. Rickey's farm system helped propel the Cardinals to four pennants and two World Series in the late 1920s and early 1930s. But the franchise really blossomed in the early 1940s, when the Cardinals won three-consecutive pennants, with a fourth one coming right after the war, along with three World Series championships. The Cardinals system produced some of the best players in the National League in the 1930s: the Dean brothers, Enos Slaughter, Joe Medwick, and Johnny Mize, among others. Rickey's success with the farm system concept deeply offended Judge Landis's sense of fair competition. But by the end of the 1930s, every team in baseball had accepted the idea, and the best, Brooklyn and the Yankees, produced systems as good as Rickey's.

There was better balance in the National League in the 1930s than in the American League, dominated as it was by the Yankees. Four National League teams won pennants during the decade. The Cubs won three but no World Series. The Giants also won three pennants and one World Series. The Cardinals won three pennants and two World Series, while Cincinnati won the pennant in 1939, but was swept in the World Series by the Yankees.

WORLD WAR II'S IMPACT ON BASEBALL

Professional baseball did not have a good experience during World War I. The government was unsympathetic to the sport and would have closed it down if the war had lasted into 1919. World War II proved a different experience. Baseball was untouched by the war from September 1939, when it broke out in Europe, until the fall of 1940, when a peacetime draft was instituted. In fact, baseball hardly noticed the war in Europe as the new decade began because the game was showing signs of pulling free from the economic problems of the Depression. The 1940 season saw baseball attendance approach the record set a decade earlier. There are a number of possible explanations for this.

The American economy was showing signs of recovery. Although unemployment was still at 10 percent, it was dropping as war orders poured into the United States. It also looked like a good figure when compared to the 25 percent unemployed just seven years earlier. The country appeared to have recovered its self-confidence and some of the optimism that had been an American tradition.[9]

The emergence of such new, popular players as DiMaggio, Williams, and Feller brought some excitement back to baseball—excitement that had been lacking since the retirement of Babe Ruth. DiMaggio had won back-to-back batting titles in 1939 and 1940, and was hitting over .400 in 1939, before an eye infection slowed him down. Williams erupted on the scene in 1939, and as a 20-year-old, he set a rookie record by driving in 145 runs. Feller was even more spectacular. In 1939, as a 20-year-old, he won 24 games and struck out 246 batters. The next year, he did even better, winning 27 games and fanning 261 batters. At this time, it was rare for pitchers to strike out that many batters. Since 1916, only one American League pitcher had topped the 200 mark, and that was Lefty Grove. Feller also was a great drawing card, the best since Ruth. When he pitched, the fans came out to see something special, and he usually gave it to them.

The 1941 season proved a legendary one; two remarkable records were set. Beginning in May, Joe DiMaggio launched the greatest hitting streak in baseball history, 56 consecutive games. After being stopped, he then hit in 17 more games. Some statisticians argue that given the nature of the game today, it is a record that will never be broken. The closest anyone has come to DiMaggio's record is Peter Rose's 44 consecutive games with a hit, still 20 percent behind the Yankee slugger's mark. That same season, Ted Williams, just 22 years old, reached the .400 batting mark for the last time in baseball history, another mark that will probably never be matched given the nature of modern-day baseball. Feller, DiMaggio, and Williams achieved an iconic stature on the eve of World War II. All three, in their prime, saw their careers hurt by the war.

The rise of the Brooklyn Dodgers to respectability helped boost attendance in the National League in the early 1940s. In popular culture, Brooklyn had become synonymous with a kind of lower-class, but lovable, roughneck populace, speaking in a strange patois of "deez" and "doze" labeled Brooklynese. Brooklyn jokes were commonplace on the radio and in the movies. The Dodgers, under MacPhail, and with Leo Durocher directing them on the field, changed that image of Brooklyn losers. They turned the Dodgers into a competitive team and made a run at the pennant in 1940. They finished second and introduced two of the most exciting new players in the league, shortstop Pee Wee Reese and outfielder Pete Reiser. The next season, the Dodgers won the pennant and, in 1942, finished second to the Cardinals, while winning 104 games. No one ever made jokes about the Dodgers again.

By the time of the attack on Pearl Harbor, Major League Baseball players were starting to be affected by the draft. The first major leaguer drafted was Phillies pitcher Hugh Mulcahy, whose claim to fame was his nickname, "Losing Pitcher." Hank Greenberg had enlisted even before Pearl Harbor, exchanging his $55,000 salary for a private's $21 a month. Bob Feller volunteered for the U.S. Navy right after Pearl Harbor.

Given the emotional anger felt in the United States by the attack on Pearl Harbor, the real question facing baseball was: Should the game continue for the duration of the war? In January 1942, Judge Landis, no admirer of President Roosevelt, sent a letter asking what he expected of baseball during the war. Landis and the baseball owners knew how close the game came to being shut down in World War I and would not have been surprised if, in the aftermath of Pearl Harbor, baseball was suspended for the duration of the war. Instead, the president gave baseball what is often referred to as a "green light" to continue playing. He believed it would be good for morale and added that more night games should be scheduled so that workers could get to see baseball played.

The 1942 season turned out to be the last normal one for baseball. The major leagues lost 61 players to various branches of the armed services, but many of the stars, like DiMaggio and Williams, were able to play out the season before joining the military. During the next two seasons, major-league rosters were decimated. By 1945, Major League Baseball had been, in the words of one author, reduced to playing "teenagers, graybeards, and 4 Fs."[10] That wasn't much of an exaggeration.

The quality of play declined rapidly after the 1942 season. Statistically, baseball began to resemble the game of the Deadball Era. Runs per game, for example, dropped to levels before the long-ball era of the 1920s changed baseball. In 1925, the major-league average was 10.25 runs scored per game. That figure dropped to a little more than seven runs per game by 1943. Home run figures were down considerably, partly a result of baseball using inferior material for its baseballs. In 1941, the last normal, that is, prewar, season, nine men in the American League hit 20 or more home runs, while five in the National League matched that figure. In 1943, five batters from both leagues hit 20 or more home runs. The American League leader that year, first baseman Nick

Etten of the Yankees, hit 22, the lowest figure since before Babe Ruth launched the long-ball era in 1919.

By 1945, 500 current or former major leaguers were in the military. Baseball was desperate to fill the void. Older players were recruited for the majors, one of whom had been out of baseball since 1936. Jimmie Foxx, who hadn't played after the 1942 season, returned to baseball in 1944, and the next season, at 37, he played 89 games for the last-place Phillies and even pitched in nine games. At age 16, Tommy Brown played in 46 games for the Dodgers, while the next season he played one-third of the team's games at shortstop. The most remarkable example of how desperate baseball was came in 1945, when the St. Louis Browns played a one-armed man, Pete Gray, in the outfield.

An unpredictable by-product of the war was the creation of the first professional league for women. Women had played softball in schools and college, and on company teams, for years, so there was a baseline of skill available to draw from. The All-American Girls Professional Baseball League was formed in 1943. Its major backer was Phil Wrigley, the immensely rich and somewhat eccentric owner of the Cubs. With the minor leagues collapsing during the war—their total number dropped to just nine functioning leagues by 1943–1944, Wrigley saw an opening for quality baseball in the area of the country he knew best and that had been the heart of good minor league baseball, the Midwest. Women were recruited from girls' softball leagues, and teams were placed in such cities as South Bend, Rockford, Battle Creek, and Kenosha. The players were given an introduction to charm school and paid a salary commensurate with quality minor-league players.

At first, women's baseball was a novelty, but it continued to grow during the war and reached a peak of success in 1948, when, with 10 teams, the league drew close to 1 million fans. Women's baseball was forgotten in the more traditional 1950s, but it was finally given recognition by the successful film *A League of Their Own* in 1992. The film went on to earn $107 million, two and a half times what it cost to produce.

When the 1945 season began, it looked as if at least the war in Europe would soon be over. The Pacific War was another story, with rumors flying that it would last for a couple more years. "The Golden Gate in 48" was one of the phrases that circulated at the time. The atomic bomb changed that. The war in Europe ended in May, just as the season started. The Pacific War lasted until mid-August. Thus, the 1945 season was the closest one to normality since 1941. At the same time, the quality of play, especially in the American League, reached an all-time low. The American League batting champ, George "Snuffy" Stirnweiss, hit .309, the lowest figure for a batting champ since Elmer Flick in 1905.

In all, the 1945 season was a surprise for Major League Baseball, if not for the quality of play, at least as far as numbers were concerned. Attendance topped the 10 million mark for the first time since before the Depression. Even a couple of the big stars made it back to baseball that season, Hank Greenberg and Bob Feller. Greenberg was released from the U.S. Army in time to play half of the Tigers' games and show he still could hit. He batted .311, hit 13 home runs, and drove in 60 runs. In the World Series that year, he hit two home runs and drove in seven. Feller was able to get into nine games, but he looked like the Feller of old. He won five of the games and had an ERA of 2.50, and struck out 59 batters in 72 innings. DiMaggio got out of the Army in time to play in 1945, but he believed he wasn't in condition to play up to his usual standards. He was right. At 31, he was no longer the great player he had been before the war. Major League Baseball looked to the future with glee.

Baseball had met the crisis of the Depression and the war, and shown its adaptability. In 1944, Judge Landis had died, and this time the owners made sure to select a commissioner they could control. The job went to a former Democratic governor and senator from Kentucky, A. B. "Happy" Chandler. He seemed a good choice. He admired baseball and had good connections in the corridors of power in Washington, DC. More importantly, the owners made sure he did not have the right to interfere for what Landis had called the "good of the game." Baseball survived, and just like the country, the owners and fans looked to the future with a sense of optimism.

Questions for Consideration

1. Discuss the impact the Great Depression had on Major League Baseball. What were some of its responses?
2. Of the various new concepts baseball introduced in the 1930s—radio, night baseball, the Hall of Fame, the MVP Award, the All-Star Game—which was the most significant in your view?
3. Compare the performance of the National League to that of the American League in the 1930s. Which was better, and why, in your view, was this the case?
4. Discuss the revival of Negro League baseball in the worst economic decade in American history. What were some of the reasons baseball didn't integrate in the 1930s?
5. Compare the Yankees dynasty of the 1920s with the one that emerged in the late 1930s. How were they similar and different?
6. How did baseball handle the problems created for it by World War II? Contrast baseball's experience in World War II with what happened in World War I.

7. What were some of the distinguishing characteristics of World War II baseball?
8. Why was a professional league for women introduced during the war? What does that say about the social changes brought about by the war?

Notes

1. David Kennedy, *Freedom from Fear: The American People in Depression and War, 1929–1945* (New York: Oxford University Press, 2001), especially chapters 1 and 2, provides a good overview of the impact of the Depression in the United States.

2. For how baseball dealt with the Depression, see Charles Alexander, *Breaking the Slump: Baseball in the Depression Era* (New York: Columbia University Press, 2004).

3. G. Edward White, *Creating the National Pastime: Baseball Transforms Itself, 1903–1953* (Princeton, NJ: Princeton University Press, 1996) has an excellent chapter, "Baseball on the Radio," dealing with radio's impact on baseball.

4. For MacPhail's influence on baseball, see Don Warfield, *The Roaring Redhead: Larry MacPhail, Baseball's Great Innovator* (South Bend, IN: Diamond Communications, 1987).

5. White, *Creating the National Pastime*.

6. White, *Creating the National Pastime*; Leonard Koppett, *Koppett's Concise History of Major League Baseball* (Philadelphia: Temple University Press, 1998).

7. For an overview and analysis of how the Baseball Hall of Fame functions, see Bill James, *The Politics of Glory: How Baseball's Hall of Fame Really Works* (New York: Macmillan, 1994).

8. One of the best new overviews of the history of the Negro Leagues can be found in Neil Lanctot, *Negro League Baseball: The Rise and Ruin of a Black Institution* (Philadelphia: University of Pennsylvania Press, 2004).

9. For baseball during World War II, see Bill Gilbert, *They Also Served: Baseball and the Home Front, 1941–1945* (New York: Crown, 1992).

10. Harrington Crissey, *Teenagers, Graybeards, and 4 Fs: An Informal History of Major League Baseball during the Second World War* (privately printed).

THE HISTORY OF WOMEN'S BASEBALL

Kerry Candaele

From 1943 to 1954, "America's pastime" was a game played in skirts. At its peak in 1948, the All-American Girls Professional Baseball League (AAGPBL) fielded 10 teams in Midwestern towns like Rockford, Illinois (Peaches); South Bend, Indiana (Blue Sox); Racine, Wisconsin (Belles); Grand Rapids, Michigan (Chicks); and Fort Wayne, Indiana (Daisies)—entertaining a million paying fans. Over time, the bases got longer and the mound higher. The play got better, and the league evolved from underhand softball to overhand baseball. During its 12-year existence, more than 600 woman athletes had the phrase "professional baseball player" attached to their names.

Before describing the league in greater detail, a dusting off of home plate is in order. My mother, Helen Callaghan Candaele, played center field for five seasons with the AAGPBL, first with the Minneapolis Millerettes and then with the Fort Wayne Daisies. Yet I didn't know about her AAGPBL history until I was in my late 20s.

For many years my four brothers and I knew there was something a bit odd about my mother. Once a year our Little League Baseball program in Lompoc, California, put on a "Powder Puff" game, where the mothers took the field to provide comic entertainment for dads, who watched from outside the fence. The 5-foot-1 woman who cooked our meals and washed our dirty uniforms year in and year out could throw, swing, and catch not only like a man, but like a man who knew how the game should be played—with the physical skills to accompany her baseball sense. Frankly, few men could match her. No one who watched from behind the backstop laughed. Helen Callaghan Candaele was no Powder Puff: sportswriters had dubbed her the "feminine Ted Williams" just 20 years earlier.

Kerry Candaele, "The History of Women's Baseball," *Gilder Lehrman Institute of American History*, April 27, 2012, https://www.gilderlehrman.org/history-by-era/world-war-ii/essays/history -women%E2%80%99s-baseball. Courtesy of the Gilder Lehrman Institute of American History.

Her five sons, self-absorbed and no doubt dreaming of the big leagues, never bothered to ask the basic question: "Mom, how the hell did you learn to throw and hit like that?" Shy and unwilling to talk about what was in part a painful past, my mother didn't volunteer her biography. Her rules were clear: There is no whining in life or in baseball, and the past is past. Vivian Kellogg, a Daisy first baseman, summed up the historical disappearing act that was their league: "You see, when I quit and came home, I never said anything to anybody because nobody believed that there was a girls' baseball team. So rather than be embarrassed by talking of something that it seems no one had ever heard of, I never said anything."

Not until my brother Kelly began making a documentary about the league in 1987, a film called *A League of Their Own* (later translated into a feature film starring Tom Hanks and Madonna), did the AAGPBL find its slot in sports history. Until then, the league had a history but no historians. Outside of those who played and watched, the AAGPBL was a nonentity for 40 years, with nothing of significance said or written about the women who demonstrated, vigorously and with considerable panache, that they could play ball.

Women had of course played baseball before the 1940s. A team at Vassar College first formed in 1866, and Bloomer Girls teams toured the country from the 1890s through the 1930s. One historian reports that three women played in the professional Negro Leagues: Toni Stone, Mamie Johnson, and Connie Morgan. (The AAGPBL was a lily-white affair.) Yet no women's league before the AAGPBL had expected to play professional hardball and decently remunerated its players.

The league was the experiment of Philip Wrigley, owner of the Chicago Cubs. In 1942, he looked at the future of professional baseball and found it bleak. Half the players in the majors were in military uniform, the farm system that groomed new players was decimated, and there was talk that the 1943 season would have to be cancelled. Who would watch professional baseball without Joe DiMaggio in Yankee pinstripes?

Wrigley approached Dodger owner Branch Rickey, and after making sure the women's league would stay in the Midwest to be watched over from Chicago, the four-month opening season was secured for the summer of 1943.

But who would fill the 15 spots for each team? And how would a women's league be presented to a populace who Wrigley and friends felt might accept Rosie in the factory but not Shirley at shortstop?

The solution combined paternalism, an appeal to civic duty during wartime, and a contradictory sexism that both mirrored the times and hinted at a more liberated future, summarized nicely in the management mantra: League members would "look like ladies and play like men." Women could play to win, but not under conditions of their own choosing. Looking like ladies meant playing in tunic-like uniforms with short skirts. Sliding into second base with spikes high and bare thighs, well, that's the very moment when contradictions in league ideology revealed themselves with a brutal clarity.

These contradictions revealed themselves further in the selection and training process. Wrigley sent scouts to the softball leagues across the United States and Canada, seeking women with appropriate skills, demeanor, and looks, then brought them to camps for lessons in baseball and comportment. If the new left fielder's baseball chops were in order yet she hadn't found time to learn the finer points of drinking tea with an outstretched pinky, off to the Helena Rubenstein Charm School she went. If successful, she brought in $80 a week (a lot of money for working women in 1943).

Complete with books balanced on the head while walking and fully enunciating "bounce the ball" as if in imitation of William F. Buckley Jr., charm school curriculum offered plenty of advice, head to toe. About teeth? Brush them. On using the mouth? Don't talk too loud. About "A Woman's Crowning Glory," her hair? "Keep your hair as neat as possible, on or off the field." Wrigley failed to see that he was dealing with professional ballplayers, not women who would be primping their curls in the middle of a double play. The charm school was chucked after the first few seasons.

And lest the ladies begin to act like their male counterparts, who—decades before steroids and generalized decadence—could still behave like bands of Visigoths, league players were kept under strict observation and guidelines, with team chaperones attempting to enforce traditional gender roles. No smoking, no drinking, and "avoid pests and autograph hounds" (i.e., men) "gracefully . . . without hurting their feelings."

The women played six days a week, with a doubleheader on Saturdays, exhibition games at army camps, and paid visits to veterans' hospitals. Competing teams shaped a "V" for "Victory" down the first- and third-base lines prior to each game. With these appeals to civic patriotism, combined with a shortage of gas and the democratization of television a decade away, the Daisies, Belles, Peaches, and Chicks drew hundreds of thousands of fans out to watch stellar baseball.

Soon enough, the league outgrew the hybrid of baseball and softball, and inched closer to regulation hardball. The pitcher's mound moved from 40 to 60 feet from home plate, distance between bases grew, and the ball got smaller each year. As play became more ambitious, so did owners' dreams for the league. Postseason play included tours to Cuba and South America, where film footage shows a polite but lively bunch of women enjoying El Malecon beaches in Havana.

However, the AAGPBL was unsustainable in postwar/Cold War America and folded up the tent in 1954. Management miscalculations and the increasingly transient nature of American society were to blame. Another angle on the league's demise is what Elaine Tyler May calls the "family fever" of the 1950s. Arising amidst the dangers, both real and manufactured, of the world outside our borders, a vigorous domestic ideology nudged and sometimes pushed women in the direction of domesticity and suburban isolation.

As a result, no one seemed to remember the league's amazing 12-year ride for over 30 years after its conclusion. As one former player put it, "In 1954, when the league ended, it fell off the face of the earth." In my own family, my mother just "didn't want to talk about it." In today's celebrity-besotted culture, the "glory days" are all people want to talk about, even if the glory is nothing more than having been thrown off the island.

The women of the AAGPBL did not consciously set out to break taboos or over-turn the worst stereotypes of gender difference. Nor were they part of a movement against the sexism and repression of women in almost every sector of American life during the '40s and '50s. For these ball-playing women, making good money and playing the game provided ample rewards.

But with hindsight and historical recovery, we can now see the contours of their achievement. As one historian of the league describes its pioneers, "They were not behind the scene, they were the scene." And in the long revolution for women's equality that stretches from the first Woman's Rights Convention at Seneca Falls in 1848 to the present, the AAGPBL finds its rightful place. Today, as I watch my three daughters choose whether to play volleyball, baseball, and/or soccer, or to pick up the cello bow in place of the bat, my mother and the women of the AAGPBL are present, responsible for the freer ground upon which today's girls walk, run, swing, and play.

BASEBALL AND WORLD WAR II: A STUDY OF THE LANDIS–ROOSEVELT CORRESPONDENCE

James A. Percoco

Baseball, along with apple pie and motherhood, is synonymous with the United States and its popular culture. Our national pastime is tied to the American way of leisure life. The 50th anniversary of United States involvement in the Second World War presents an opportunity for students to examine the correspondence between baseball commissioner Kenesaw Mountain Landis and President Franklin Delano Roosevelt regarding the wartime status of baseball. Facsimiles of the correspondence appear at the end of this lesson. The original documents are preserved by the National Archives at the Franklin D. Roosevelt Library in Hyde Park, New York. The documents are part of the President's Personal File (P.P.F.), number 227.

Introduction

Shortly after the Japanese attack on Pearl Harbor, baseball commissioner Kenesaw Mountain Landis questioned if professional baseball should be played while the nation was embroiled in war. On 14 January 1942, Landis wrote to President Roosevelt seeking his advice. Roosevelt responded the next day with what has become known as "the green light letter," offering Landis his personal opinion that baseball should continue even though the nation was at war. Roosevelt suggested that the benefits of the game would provide a much-needed morale boost to those on the home front and to American service personnel overseas.

James A. Percoco, "Baseball and World War II: A Study of the Landis–Roosevelt Correspondence," *OAH Magazine of History* 7, no. 1 (1992): 55–60. http://www.jstor.org/stable/25162857. Used with permission.

Background

One of the most interesting periods in United States sport history is the period between 1942 and 1945, when professional baseball played an important role on the home front and around the world. With the entry of the United States into the Second World War, baseball teams endured tremendous short-term changes. Many baseball stars such as Hank Greenberg, Joe DiMaggio, Bob Feller, and Ted Williams were drafted or volunteered for military service. In most cases, those stars became players for army or navy baseball teams that played to entertain service personnel. Others, like Bob Feller, found themselves in the midst of combat against the Japanese or the Germans.

A hodgepodge assortment of players, both young and old, filled the vacuum left by those who served in the armed forces. Fifteen-year-old phenom Joe Nuxhall pitched for the Cincinnati Reds; Pete Gray, a one-armed outfielder, suited up for the St. Louis Browns; and former slugger Jimmie Foxx came out of retirement to play for the Philadelphia Phillies. These players kept the game alive in the big-league cities, as did their counterparts on the minor-league circuit, and provided lighthearted entertainment for millions of fans.

Black Americans did not fail to notice that the white major-league teams preferred to employ schoolboys, overaged journeymen players, or the physically handicapped over able-bodied and incredibly talented black men. Nevertheless, the Negro Leagues continued to play and draw respectable crowds during the war years. In addition, Philip Wrigley, owner of the Chicago Cubs, organized the professional All-American Girls Baseball League (1943–1954)—the only time women have played professional baseball in U.S. history. Principally from the Midwest, teams such as the Rockford Peaches, Kalamazoo Lassies, and Grand Rapids Chicks provided an interesting chapter in the annals of wartime baseball. Both black and women's organizations contributed to the diverse history of the national pastime by serving the nation in a valid and valuable capacity—promoting patriotism and emphasizing American values of teamwork and victory.

During the war, the tradition of playing the national anthem prior to the start of games began. Team owners and both major leagues felt that it was appropriate to honor America while reminding fans of our soldiers and sailors overseas. Home-front baseball also saw an increase in the number of night games so that working-class Americans could frequently attend, a point to which Roosevelt alluded in his response to Landis.

Perhaps World War II's greatest effect on baseball was in the area of deseg-regation. With the Axis powers defeated by black and white soldiers who fought a war against totalitarian governments, the hypocrisy of professional baseball's seg-regated status was pushed into the spotlight. It seemed evident that a nation supposedly committed to the ideals of equality could not long condone the fact that a color barrier divided its preeminent sports institution. In late 1945, when United States Army war veteran Jackie Robinson signed with the Brooklyn Dodgers' top farm club, the Montreal Royals, the first crack in organized baseball's wall of racial apartheid appeared. As one chapter in the history of America's pastime closed, another chapter had begun.

JUDGE LANDIS'S LETTER TO PRESIDENT ROOSEVELT—JANUARY 14, 1942

Dear Mr. President:

The time is approaching when, in ordinary conditions, our teams would be heading for spring training camps. However, inasmuch as these are not ordinary times, I venture to ask what you have in mind as to whether professional baseball should continue to operate. Of course my inquiry does not relate at all to individual members of this organization whose status in this emergency is fixed by law operating upon all citizens.

Normally we have, in addition to the 16 major-league teams, approximately 320 minor teams—members of leagues playing in the United States and Canada.

Health and strength to you—and whatever it takes to do the job.

With great respect
Very truly yours
Kenesaw M. Landis

PRESIDENT ROOSEVELT'S ANSWER

January 15, 1942

My dear Judge

Thank you for yours of January 14th. As you will, of course, realise the final decision about the baseball season must rest with you and the baseball club owners—so what I am going to say is solely a personal and not an official point of view.

I honestly feel that it would be best for the country to keep baseball going. There would be fewer people unemployed, and everybody will work longer hours and harder than ever before.

And that means that they ought to have a chance for recreation and for taking their minds off their work even more than before.

Baseball provides a recreation which does not last over two or two hours and a half, and which can be got for very little cost. And, incidentally, I hope that night games can be extended because it gives an opportunity to the day shift to see a game occasionally.

As to the players themselves, I know you agree with me that individual players who are of active military or naval age should go, without question, into the services. Even if the actual quality of the teams is lowered by the greater use of older players, this will not dampen the popularity of the sport. Of course, if any individual has some particular attitude in a trade or profession, he ought to serve the government. That, however, is a matter which I know you can handle with complete justice.

Here is another way of looking at it—if 300 teams use 5,000 or 6,000 players, these players are a definite recreational asset to at least 20,000,000 of their fellow citizens—and that in my judgment is thoroughly worthwhile.

> With every best wish,
> Very truly yours,
> Franklin Delano Roosevelt

CHAPTER 7

Boom, Bust, and Expansion, 1946–1960

Baseball Returns to Normal

With the end of World War II, the United States entered two and a half decades of unprecedented prosperity and growth. The war had put an end to the Depression, and contrary to many fears, the reconversion from war to peace proved relatively painless. In the immediate aftermath of the war there were a series of strikes and, once wartime controls were lifted, a sharp rise in prices. But the economy soon picked up and inflation fears faded. The standard of living rose sharply, increasing by 28 percent in the 1950s alone. With the GI Bill pointing the way, veterans flocked to colleges, bought homes, and opened new businesses. Automobile ownership, which had been essentially level since 1929, tripled. Television emerged from nowhere after the war until in less than a decade 87 percent of Americans owned a set. The postwar era also witnessed the great Baby Boom, which reflected the country's optimism about the future.[1]

Major League Baseball shared in this optimism. The game had a good war in contrast to World War I and looked eagerly to the first peacetime season. The decade and a half after World War II would be labeled another "Golden Age" for baseball, on par with the 1920s. In reality, as prosperous as baseball was in the aftermath of the war, between 1946 and 1960 it faced a series of traumatic events that eventually changed the sport forever: the ending of baseball's policy of racial segregation, two threats to set up a third major league, a strange decline in attendance, the disappearance of four of the original franchises, and expansion to the West Coast. These years were no Golden Age, but rather troubled ones that forced Major League Baseball to finally transform itself into a truly national sport open to everyone.

Major League Baseball eagerly awaited the 1946 season. *Who's Who in Baseball* heralded the return of baseball's elite by devoting a full page to the game's greatest stars back from the war, including the iconic figures of Joe DiMaggio, Ted Williams, and Stan Musial, among others. While many players were happy to restart their careers, the war had taken a toll on some major leaguers. Cecil Travis, the hard-hitting shortstop/third baseman of the Washington Senators, suffered frozen feet during the Battle of the Bulge. Travis, a lifetime .300 hitter who finished second to Ted Williams in batting in 1941, with a .359 average, never regained his prewar level of play. After two mediocre seasons, he retired at age 34. His teammate, outfielder Buddy Lewis, another career .300 hitter, after flying the "Hump" in Burma during the war, found that he had lost his taste for baseball. The same was true for the great slugger Hank Greenberg. Despite leading the American League in home runs and runs batted in in 1946, Greenberg found that baseball just "wasn't that important." He said, "I had seen a lot of things happen in the world, and I didn't think that baseball was the only thing in my life."[2] He played one more season and then retired at age 36.

Not all players shared Greenberg's outlook. George Kell, Greenberg's teammate on the Detroit Tigers, spoke for many of the returning players. "We've all been through this terrible war, and now here's baseball, the one great constant in our lives. Everyone was happy that the great game had survived."[3]

The 1946 season was a booming success. Attendance shattered the 1930 record of 10 million-plus by 8 million. Nine of the 16 major-league teams drew more than 1 million fans. The Yankees, despite falling out of contention, topped all past attendance records by drawing 2.3 million fans. Even the lowly Phillies surprised everyone by topping the 1 million mark.

It appears that the thirst for baseball as part of normality played a major part in attracting such a large turnout. The season itself saw some of the returning players revert to prewar quality of play. Ted Williams hit .342; Stan Musial led the National League in batting; and Bob Feller won 26 games and struck out 348 batters, establishing a record for right-handed pitchers. Other players had difficulty adjusting, of whom the most prominent was Joe DiMaggio; who ended the season hitting under .300 for the first time in his career.

The American League pennant race was over almost before the season started. The Red Sox won their first pennant since 1918, winning 104 games and finishing 12 ahead of the second-place Tigers. The National League saw a return to the prewar rivalry of the Dodgers and Cardinals. They battled to a tie after 154 games and forced the first playoff in baseball history. The Cardinals won, finishing the season two games ahead of the Dodgers and 14 over the 1945 champion Cubs.

Off the playing field the 1946 season witnessed some of the most dramatic developments in baseball history. These developments began during spring training. With everyone eager for baseball to begin, rumors spread of another attempt at unionization. Robert Murphy, a Harvard-trained lawyer from Boston, launched a campaign to organize a new players' organization, interestingly enough not called a union, but rather the American Baseball Guild. He claimed that he had been shocked by how baseball treated its players, noting that Jimmie Foxx, having won back-to-back MVP Awards in 1932 and 1933, saw Connie Mack reduce his salary from $18,000 to $12,000. Murphy thought the time ripe for another attempt at organizing baseball. He avoided the term union because he knew baseball players didn't like to think of themselves as employees. Murphy's timing couldn't have been better. A wave of strikes swept the country after the war as workers tried to enhance their position and solidify the gains they made during the war. A record wave of strikes took place in 1946. It seemed to some that, just as after World War I, radicalism was in the air.

Murphy met with players, asking them to sign up for membership in his guild. When he felt he had a sufficient number, he outlined the program he wanted to secure from the baseball establishment. He kept his goals moderate: a minimum salary of $7,500 a year (at the time it was closer to $4,000), half of the purchase price of any player sold, and an arbitrator for disputes between player and management. He steered clear of tampering with the reserve clause.

By June, Murphy believed he was in a position to threaten a strike unless some of his demands were met. He targeted the Pittsburgh Pirates as the team most sympathetic to his strike strategy. On June 7, he met with the Pirates players, arguing if they refused to play the game, the owners would be forced to negotiate. Pirates ownership threatened to sign up sandlot players to field a team. The manager, Frankie Frisch, and coaches, including 72-year-old Hall of Famer Honus Wagner, said they would take the field if necessary. The vote to strike, 20 to 16, fell short of a needed two-thirds majority, and Murphy's threat failed. He tried to rally his supporters, but by the end of the season he had lost support, partly because he was an irascible individual who was often his own worst enemy. One by-product of his war with baseball was a decision by management to pay money to the players for spring training expenses. This money is still called "Murphy Money," although it is doubtful if any of today's players know who Murphy was.[4]

At the same time Murphy was touring spring training camps signing up players for his new union, a much more serious threat to baseball emerged—the possibility of a rival major league in Mexico. The five Pasquel brothers were multimillionaires who owned teams in the Mexican League. The league had thrived during the war, but the Pasquels wanted recognition as a major league. After the war, they decided to upgrade their league by a strategy similar to how the American League had begun. They would raid Major League Baseball by offering lucrative salaries to the players who they knew were underpaid. Starting in spring training, Jorge Pasquel began contacting players with lucrative offers to join the Mexican League. The sums they offered were beyond anything major-league players were earning. Average players like Mickey Owen, a catcher for the Dodgers, and Danny Gardella, a mediocre outfielder with the Giants, signed for sums that dwarfed what they earned in the majors. Owen got a $12,500 bonus for signing, while Gardella's bonus was $8,000.

The Pasquels targeted the biggest names in baseball. Pitcher Hal Newhouser of Detroit said he was offered a bonus of $300,000, plus a three-year contract for $200,000.[5] Stan Musial, then 26, was making $13,500 for the Cardinals. He was offered $75,000 to sign. Newhouser and Musial turned the Pasquels down. They even targeted Jackie Robinson, who had signed a contract to play with the Dodgers farm team in Montreal. They signed a handful of players from the Negro Leagues.

Eventually, the Pasquel brothers signed 17 major leaguers, mostly second-line players. Their biggest catch, shortstop Vern Stephens of the St. Louis Browns, probably was responsible for cooling enthusiasm for the Mexican League. Stephens signed for big money, went to Mexico, and returned quickly with stories of how bad playing conditions were, as well as pretty much everything else about Mexican baseball.

To thwart the Pasquel brothers' raiding, the new commissioner of baseball announced that any players "jumping" to the Mexican League would be banned from baseball for five years. Along with the stories coming back from the Mexican League, that put an effective end to the Pasquel brothers' practices.

What really destroyed the Mexican League was a matter of timing. The Pasquels' challenge came just when the major leagues were experiencing a tremendous period of success and prosperity following the war. The majority of players in baseball wanted to get back to normality, and that meant playing in the majors. The Mexican League seemed too exotic, too risky, no matter how much money was involved.

It took years for the so-called Mexican "jumpers" to get back to the majors. A lawsuit against Major League Baseball by Danny Gardella was eventually resolved in 1949, when Commissioner Happy Chandler allowed his return. Only a couple of the players who went to Mexico managed to resume their careers. Gardella was paid off handsomely with a check for $60,000 for dropping his lawsuit. The best of the Mexican jumpers by far was pitcher Sal Maglie, a Giant farmhand, who admitted he really learned to pitch during his time in Mexico and would go on to become one of the dominant pitchers in the majors in the early 1950s.[6]

The threat to baseball posed by Murphy and the Pasquels caused management to take preventive action. With Chandler and a handful of more enlightened owners, Major League Baseball convened a meeting in July and August to try to meet some of the players' demands. A minimum salary of $5,000 was established; travel expenses of $500, if traded during the season, were guaranteed; and a player, if injured "in his employed capacity," was to receive his full salary and funds to be paid during spring training, that is, the Murphy Money. Given the conservative nature of most players, the most important consideration was the creation of retirement pay for players, coaches, and trainers. At age 50, if they had five years in the majors, they would receive sums of $50 to $100 a month. The money eventually was to come from the receipts from the All-Star Game. Dubbed "Baseball's Magna Carta," it effectively satisfied players' demands for a decade or more.[7]

By far the biggest story of the 1946 season was baseball finally taking a step to end racial segregation in the sport. The idea of bringing African American players to the majors had been around and talked about for years, but no progress had been made. World War II changed the atmosphere surrounding the issue. Having fought a war in the name of democracy against a brutal form of Nazi racism, it was difficult to argue for the continued exclusion of African Americans from white professional baseball. Two men are responsible for ending baseball's racial bar: Branch Rickey and Jack Roosevelt Robinson.

Rickey was a blend of preacher, huckster, and shrewd businessman. Nicknamed the "Mahatma," after Gandhi, for his well-known moralizing about life in general and baseball in particular, Rickey had taken over the Dodgers in 1942, when Larry MacPhail went into the U.S. Army. At some point during the war, he decided it was time to integrate the majors. His instincts were not altruistic. He once observed that there was one untapped source of baseball talent in the United States: African American players. He wanted to be the first to draw on that pool of talent. He started signing every young ballplayer he could during the war, on the grounds that when peace came, he would have endowed the Dodgers with a group from which he could build a championship team. The fact that for any excess talent he sold he would get a percentage of their sale price was something he kept in mind.

Rickey ordered his aides to begin scouting the Negro Leagues. He wasn't interested in the big names like Josh Gibson or Satchel Paige. They would be too expensive. He wanted someone young who would serve as a role model for the integration of baseball. The story he gave out was that he was thinking of organizing a team for his own version of the Negro League. Rickey had no respect for the Negro Leagues, arguing they were a "racket." He had his eye on a solid player from the Kansas City Monarchs, shortstop Jackie Robinson. His scouts told him Robinson was a good all-around player better suited to second base than shortstop and, most importantly, had the temperament to withstand the abuse he would face as the one who broke baseball's color barrier.

In October 1945, Rickey signed Robinson to play for Brooklyn's number-one farm team, the Montreal Royals. By beginning his career in Canada, Robinson would avoid racial abuse for at least half the season. It didn't bother Rickey that he got Robinson cheap: a $3,500 bonus plus $600 a month to play for the Royals. The baseball establishment was angry at Rickey, accusing him of going after the money of the African American fans and posing as a pious bleeding heart. Many players were of two minds about the signing of Robinson. Some, like Bob Feller, argued that he was too muscular and would not be able to hit major-league pitching. The *Sporting News*, the so-called Bible of Baseball, was not supportive, accusing Rickey of caving to liberal political opinion in New York.[8]

Even after Robinson quieted doubters by winning the International League batting title with a .349 average, leading the league in runs scored, and winning the MVP Award, the *Sporting News* implied he was playing over his head. That matter was resolved the next season when Robinson joined the Dodgers and helped them win the National League pennant, leading the league in runs scored. He also was named Rookie of the Year. He did all that while suffering abuse from fans and other players in the league, attempts at spiking him, and even death threats. New York sportswriter Jimmy Cannon described Robinson as the "loneliest man in baseball."[9]

When Ford Frick, president of the National League, got word that the St. Louis Cardinals planned to walk off the field rather than play against Robinson, he threatened the potential strikers with a lifetime ban even "if it wrecks the National League." Frick was backed by Commissioner Chandler, a southerner who put matters more starkly: "If a black boy can make it on Okinawa and Guadalcanal, hell he can make it in baseball."[10] The strike threat fell through.

Along with his skills as a player, Robinson also proved to be the greatest gate attraction in baseball since the days of Babe Ruth. The African American community, heretofore an insignificant group attending major-league games, now turned out in droves to see Robinson play. The Dodgers drew huge crowds in just about every city he visited. Philadelphia, whose Phillies team had taunted him brutally in Brooklyn, saw the largest crowd in city history, with more than 40,000 fans packing into a ballpark that held 34,000 to see Robinson play in a doubleheader in early May. The same was true in Cincinnati, Chicago, and St. Louis when the Dodgers visited those cities on a road trip. Whatever else the baseball establishment was, the owners knew how to count and saw a gold mine.

In July, the iconoclastic Bill Veeck signed Larry Doby from Newark of the Negro Leagues and integrated the American League. Veeck claimed he had wanted to do so as far back as 1942, but was thwarted by Judge Kenesaw Landis and the baseball owners. There is little support for this story, and it is probably rooted in Veeck's dislike for Rickey, whom he labeled a pious fraud.[11] Veeck grabbed the biggest name in Negro League baseball in 1948, when he signed Satchel Paige to help Cleveland win the American League pennant. Other American League teams did not rush to follow Veeck's lead.

Baseball was slow to integrate despite Robinson's obvious success on the field and at the gate. The nation's residual racism may have faded by the end of the war, but it was still there. The St. Louis Browns brought up a couple of players from the Negro Leagues after Veeck signed Doby, but they flopped. American League clubs lagged behind the National League in integrating their teams. The Giants, bitter rivals of the Dodgers since the 1920s, were the next National League team to integrate, adding Monte Irvin, probably the best player in the Negro Leagues, in 1949. In the meantime, the Dodgers had strengthened their hold on African American talent by signing the best catcher in the Negro Leagues, Roy Campanella, and one of the best pitchers, Don Newcombe. Any excess talent Rickey got from the Negro Leagues (and the Dodgers couldn't use, like Sam Jethroe) he sold and pocketed a share of the selling price. He got $150,000 for Jethroe, so integration paid, at least for Rickey.

One by-product of the integration of baseball was the eventual destruction of the Negro Leagues. As Major League Baseball signed more and more African American players to major- and minor-league contracts, the Negro Leagues saw their fan base shrink. Fans would rather go and see Jackie Robinson, Monte Irvin, and, later, Willie Mays and Hank Aaron than players in the Negro Leagues. To make matters worse, Robinson himself voiced a low opinion of the Negro Leagues. He told a reporter in 1948 that, "Negro baseball needs a housecleaning from bottom to top." In a follow-up article for *Ebony*, Robinson said the Negro Leagues were poorly administered and treated their players shabbily.[12] The Negro American League, which had branched off from the Negro National League, folded as early as 1948. The Negro National League continued for a few more years but had lost its identity by the mid-1950s. It is an interesting commentary that the very thing that African Americans had clamored for for so long, ending the racial barrier in baseball, would lead to the destruction of one of the most unique constructions of African American society, the Negro Leagues.

The interest and new group of fans Robinson and later great African American players brought to Major League Baseball is one of the reasons why baseball thrived in the immediate aftermath of the war. There were other explanations. A series of great pennant races between 1946 and 1951 also contributed to this rise in attendance. In 1948, there was a three-way race in the American League, with Cleveland defeating the Red Sox in a one-game playoff. The Dodgers edged the Cardinals by one game in 1949, while the Yankees did the same to the Red Sox that season. The National League season went down to the final game in 1950 before the Phillies prevailed over the Dodgers. The next year saw the exciting comeback from a 13-game deficit by the Giants to beat the Dodgers in a playoff, highlighted by Bobby Thomson's famous home run in the ninth inning of the final game of the playoff. These exciting pennant races featuring the three New York teams, with their huge press contingent, are largely responsible for the Golden Age image taking hold.

In 1949, attendance reached a record of 20.9 million. Thereafter, there was a sharp drop, with 3 million fewer in 1950, a huge decline from one season to the next and one with no clear reason. But the worst was yet to come. In 1952, attendance was just a little more than 14 million, a decline of 30 percent. For the rest of the decade, baseball struggled to reach the record achieved in the peak season of 1949. Only in the last year of the decade did baseball top the 19 million mark in attendance, and that was largely accounted for because two teams, the Dodgers and Giants, had invaded the California market. Just about everyone else was still struggling. Even the vaunted Yankees, having won eight of nine pennants during the decade, drew more than 400,000 fewer fans in 1958 than they had in 1950. This was the problem that beset baseball in the 1950s. What was happening to explain this phenomenon?

BASEBALL CHALLENGED

While enjoying the burst of prosperity and booming attendance figures of the late 1940s, baseball was on the brink of a revolution. Lost in the huge crowds that flocked to the Major League Baseball games was a confluence of forces that in a decade would change the sport forever: television, the population move to the suburbs, and the first shift of franchises in 50 years. Each of these created problems that the men who ran baseball were totally unprepared for.

Television had been around since the late 1930s and had even experimented with baseball by televising a Dodgers game in 1939. The war held back the development of television. It burst onto the scene beginning in 1947, when sets began to be produced in large numbers. The 1947 World Series was the first to be televised. Although the audience was limited to the East, it was estimated that 3.7 million fans saw the games, many in bars and restaurants, where the first televisions appeared. In 1948, the price of a television, at about $300 for a 12-inch set, began to slowly drop, ownership grew, and such popular shows as Ed Sullivan's *Toast of the Town* and Milton Berle's *Texaco Star Theater* comedy program garnered large audiences. The growth of television ownership was phenomenal, with 200,000 sets in use in 1948 and more than 80 percent of the homes in the United States having a set a decade later. No technology had ever caught on as quickly.

Baseball didn't know how to react to this new technology. Some teams began televising their games but still regarded radio as the most important way to reach their fans and bring in extra revenue. In the late 1940s and early 1950s, the three networks, CBS, NBC, and Dumont, needed baseball to fill their broadcasting time. They paid teams for the right to broadcast home games. The Giants got $50,000 for their games, while the Yankees were paid $75,000 by the Dumont Network to broadcast their games in 1947. Major advertisers like Ford, Buick, Chesterfield cigarettes, and various breweries bought the right for commercials. Baseball pocketed the money, but not everyone was sanguine about the future of baseball on television.

Branch Rickey, always an innovator, didn't understand television. He believed radio created fans, as was the case in Brooklyn, while television satiated them. As attendance sagged in the early 1950s, with teams televising more and more of their games, the baseball owners blamed television. The problem for ownership was simple: They were hooked on the revenue television was bringing in.

It is difficult to prove an absolute link between the growth of television broadcasting of baseball and the decline in attendance; however, given that the very years during which television viewership grew also witnessed the dramatic drop in baseball's attendance is suggestive. By the mid-1950s, both the size and quality of the television picture had improved to the point where watching a game from your home was a pleasure. This was especially true once the major networks took over how to best exploit baseball. The *Game of the Week* concept, introduced in the 1950s, showed baseball throughout the country, and it did so with imagination. Announcers like Dizzy Dean, Red Barber, Mel Allen, Jack Brickhouse, and Russ Hodges helped create new fans.

What is beyond dispute is that the spread of television broadcasting hurt the minor leagues. Now, instead of going to watch the local Class B team play, the fan could stay at home and watch major-league games almost three or four nights during the week. As far as baseball was concerned, it turned out to be a double-edged sword, improving the appreciation of the game for many fans, while almost killing off the minor leagues.

If baseball was confused about the proper role of television in the sport, another trend that developed in the late 1940s and early 1950s spelled potential doom for the game. One of the themes of the postwar era in the United States was the drift of population from the cities to the suburbs, fueled by the growth in automobile ownership and the huge building boom of the late 1940s to the 1960s—the era of what one historian called the "crabgrass frontier." The spread of mass housing in the suburbs, the Levittowns that sprang up around the major urban areas, helped draw fans away from where baseball was played. The ballparks, built in the first two decades of the twentieth century, were located near the central core of the cities. Built before the spread of automobile ownership in the years after World War II, they supplied little parking space.

To further complicate the problem of location, most of the ballparks were located in decaying areas of the city and ones that became minority-occupied neighborhoods. Suburban fans avoided public transportation and stayed away from the ballparks. When the Boston Braves moved to Milwaukee in 1953, their new stadium had parking space for 20,000 cars. The success of the Braves, who averaged almost 2 million fans a year from 1953 to 1959, indicated that if you wanted to expand attendance you better have two things: a good team and plenty of parking spaces. For teams like the Phillies, White Sox, or Washington Senators, this was an insoluble problem unless they moved to the suburbs or at least the fringe of the city. The costs of such moves were prohibitive, and teams would need public money if they wanted to do what individual owners had done early in the century: build their own ballparks. The solution to this problem for baseball only began in the late 1960s, when teams pulled up roots and, backed by government funds, moved away from the center of the city.

There are other possible explanations for the decline in attendance at baseball games. For the first time, baseball had rivals for fan interest. College football boomed in the late 1940s and early 1950s. This was led by a series of great Notre Dame, Michigan, and Alabama teams. What had once been a sport for college alumni now developed a working- and middle-class audience. Pro football in the 1940s and 1950s wasn't much of a threat to baseball's popularity. That challenge would emerge in the early 1960s. But activities like golf, tennis, and skiing, once limited to the upper classes and wealthy, now were being adopted by the postwar generation. It wasn't that they detracted from baseball attendance as much as they created alternative interests.

One minor matter undoubtedly contributed to baseball's problems in the 1950s: the dominance of New York teams. Consider that from 1947 to 1958, Brooklyn won six pennants, the Giants two, and the Yankees a remarkable 10. During those years, the only non-New York teams to win pennants were Cleveland (1948 and 1954), the Boston Braves (1948), the Phillies (1950), and Milwaukee (1957 and 1958). There was a reason for this New York dominance. The three teams from the Big Apple were clearly the best in baseball at the time. The Yankees team that Casey Stengel managed from 1949 to 1960 was noted for good starting pitching, anchored by Vic Rashi, Allie Reynolds, Ed Lopat, and, later, Whitey Ford. The Yankees made the offensive transition from Joe DiMaggio to Mickey Mantle and Yogi Berra. The Dodgers had great offense built around Gil Hodges, Roy Campanella, Carl Furillo, and Duke Snider. These men dominated in the National League. The Giants were the least balanced of the three, but they had Willie Mays, perhaps the best all-around player from the 1950s to mid-1960s.

This may seem to have been good for New York and was certainly heralded as such by the powerful New York media. But a close look at attendance shows that this one-city dominance hurt everyone, including the New York teams. The Dodgers drew a record 1.8 million fans in 1947, attributable to some degree to Jackie Robinson. Ten years later, despite their success on the field, attendance had declined by 800,000. The story is the same for the Giants, whose fan turnout declined by 400,000. The Yankees, who had set a team record in 1946, with 2.3 million fans, while winning their tenth postwar pennant in 1958, drew 1.3 million fewer fans. When writers talk about the 1950s as a Golden Age, what they really mean is a Golden Age for New York baseball, and even that glow lessens when you examine the record in detail.

By the mid-1950s, baseball was facing a major crisis: declining attendance, a lack of competition on the field, too many ballparks in poor locations, and no clear idea how to exploit television. Part of the solution came from a direction baseball hadn't seriously contemplated for 50 years: franchise movement.

BASEBALL CHANGES LOCATION

Since 1903, Major League Baseball had been located in the same 11 cities. Five of the cities housed two teams: Boston, Philadelphia, Chicago, New York, and St. Louis. This didn't make much sense, even in 1903, as neither Boston nor St. Louis had the population to sustain two teams. But like many other aspects of professional baseball, the structure created in 1903 went unchallenged. There was some talk before the war of taking advantage of the growth of Los Angeles and San Francisco, but the problem was one of travel time and cost. It took 20 hours by train to go from Boston to St. Louis. Train travel to California was out of the question. The Pacific Coast League was a success in its own right and wanted recognition as a major league. Major League Baseball liked its monopoly and would have nothing to do with granting the Pacific Coast League equality. There matters stood for years, and then the logjam broke almost without warning.

In 1952, the Boston Braves drew just a little more than 200,000 fans. They had never been as popular in Boston as the Red Sox and had no stars like Ted Williams, Bobby Doerr, or Dom DiMaggio to attract fans. In 1948, they surprised everyone by winning the pennant. They drew more than 1 million fans that season, but from that point onward the team went into decline. Their owner, construction millionaire Lou Perini, believed he would never be able to complete with the Red Sox. Perini was popular with other owners in the National League and, in the spring of 1953, requested permission to move to Milwaukee. Milwaukee had been a major-league city in the nineteenth century and had a strong tradition of minor league baseball. More importantly, they had just built a new ballpark with plenty of parking space.

With little warning, the National League voted to approve the move, and the Boston Braves became the Milwaukee Braves almost overnight. Two factors came into play. First, the Braves constituted a team in transition. They had a good minor-league system and, even with their poor showing in 1952, were on the brink of becoming a powerhouse. They had one of the best pitchers in baseball, Warren Spahn, and had made a trade for another good pitcher, Lew Burdette. Between them they would win more than 550 games. The Braves' minor-league system produced another outstanding pitcher, Bob Buhl, and a couple of future Hall of Famers in Eddie Mathews and Hank Aaron.

Milwaukee fans embraced the Braves with the kind of affection rarely seen in baseball. The players were showered with gifts: free cars, cheap apartments, and free food. The Braves responded by shocking everyone, winning 92 games and finishing in second place in 1953. For baseball owners, the most important part of their move was the fact that they drew 1.8 million fans and made a profit for Perini.

The Braves' success broke the logjam. During the next two seasons, the structure of baseball was changed forever. In 1954, the woeful Browns, wilting given the popularity and Budweiser-backed money of the Cardinals, moved to Baltimore. The next season, the Athletics, unable to keep up with the spending of the Phillies, backed as it was by DuPont money, pulled up stakes and moved. Connie Mack no longer ran the team. It was guided by his two sons, who literally ran the team into the ground. The A's moved to Kansas City for the 1955 season.

As radical as these three moves seemed at the time, baseball was only returning to cities that had housed major-league teams in the past and been abandoned for a variety of reasons. The real significance of these actions was that it broke the logjam of opposition to franchise moves.

In Brooklyn, Walter O'Malley, who had taken control of the Dodgers from Branch Rickey in 1950, recognized that the Dodgers, despite their impressive record, were in trouble. Ebbets Field, which held just 34,000 fans, had virtually no parking spaces, was in the middle of a slowly changing neighborhood, and was in need of a thorough overhaul. O'Malley was concerned that while the Dodgers were winning pennants, attendance continually declined. In 1953, he saw what Milwaukee had achieved, outdrawing the pennant-winning Dodgers by 700,000 fans. He believed the long-term consequence would be that Milwaukee would have more money to spend on player development and, in a short time, outperform his Dodgers. Drastic action was needed. O'Malley had a plan.

He wanted to stay in the city and offered to build a ballpark with his own money if he was granted a parcel of land in downtown Brooklyn where a confluence of trolley and train lines met. He ran into the opposition of someone better politically connected than he was. Robert Moses controlled building projects in New York even though he was not an elected official. Moses vetoed downtown

Brooklyn and offered O'Malley a modern ballpark in Queens, the future Shea Stadium. O'Malley wanted no part of Queens.

At the same time that the Dodgers were becoming concerned about the future, Charles Stoneham was worried about the future of his Giants. The Polo Grounds was falling into disrepair and needed major structural improvements. The neighborhood around the ballpark also was deteriorating. Stoneham had an option denied to O'Malley: He had a farm team in Minneapolis and could see the possibility of duplicating the success of the Braves if he moved the Giants there. The city was in the process of building a state-of-the-art baseball facility in preparation for the arrival of a major-league team.

All this came to a head in the mid-1950s. With O'Malley stopped by Moses, he upped the pressure to prove he was serious by selling Ebbets Field to a New York real estate broker for $300,000. He also scheduled a handful of games in Jersey City to show he had other options. Moses wouldn't budge. At this point, officials from Los Angeles came calling to see about moving the Dodgers to California. The idea was no longer unrealistic. With commercial jet travel, it would be possible to fly to the West Coast in a matter of hours. Stoneham was being approached by officials from San Francisco, one of whom was the politically connected mayor, George Christopher, with offers to move and promises to build a new ballpark if he did. During the 1957 season, the Giants were playing mediocre baseball, and attendance was averaging a little more than 8,400 per game. Stoneham was ready to pull up stakes. O'Malley saw a problem. It would be impossible to have just one team in California. He knew of Stoneham's discontent and suggested their two teams move to California, keeping alive one of the great baseball rivalries.

The Giants moved first, in August. Stoneham said he was sorry to leave New York and hurt the feelings of his young fans, but he didn't see many of their fathers at the games. O'Malley waited until the season was over and decamped for Los Angeles in October. He had carefully laid the groundwork for his move. For $2 million, he bought the rights to the Cubs farm team in Los Angeles. This gave him exclusive rights to the fastest-growing area in the nation. He clearly got a better deal than Stoneham, despite San Francisco's offer to build a ballpark for the Giants.

O'Malley's plan was to play in the Los Angeles Coliseum, which had been built for the 1932 Olympic Games and had to be modified to suit baseball, while he built his own ballpark with his money on land given him by the city. It turned out to be one of the greatest steals in baseball history. O'Malley built Dodger Stadium, which opened in 1962. It remains one of the best modern ballparks. And he owned everything: parking, concessions, as well as television rights.

Stoneham's Giants didn't do as well. They played for two years in the small downtown ballpark that had been the home of the Seals team in the Pacific

Coast League. In 1960, they moved into Candlestick Park. The location proved a problem. The temperature dropped in the evening, and a steady wind blew out to right field during night games. People remembered Mark Twain's quote: "The coldest winter I ever remember, was the summer I spent in San Francisco." Possessing the greatest right-handed hitter in baseball, Willie Mays, the Giants wound up with a ballpark better suited to left-handed power hitters. Stoneham had been outfoxed by O'Malley. If he had stayed in New York, he would have gotten a new ballpark in the biggest city in the nation.

If the Dodgers got the better of the deal, both teams still did well. The Giants had a good team in 1958, and were in the pennant race in the National League until the final days of the season. They doubled their attendance from the 1957 season. The Dodgers had a terrible year in 1958. The team had grown old and needed to be revamped. They finished tied with the Phillies for seventh place. Even so, by playing in the Coliseum, which could hold 80,000 fans, they broke the team's all-time attendance record set in Jackie Robinson's first season, 1947.

It is easy to treat Stoneham and especially O'Malley as great villains, betraying their fans. But they were only doing what other owners had done in the past—putting the bottom line first. If there was a villain, one could argue it was Robert Moses. He was unwilling to meet O'Malley fairly and sought to get his way, as he had in many political deals in New York political history. He didn't believe O'Malley would really move and thought he was bluffing. O'Malley got the last laugh.[13]

The 1950s ended with baseball on an upswing. Attendance was slowly rising. The 1959 campaign was the best year for baseball attendance since the boom of the late 1940s. Finally, every team had integrated, with Detroit, the Phillies, and the Red Sox being the last three. An important by-product of integration was the arrival of the first generation of great Latin players.

There had always been a handful of Latin players in the majors, people like the great pitcher Adolfo Luque from Cuba, who amassed 194 wins hurling for Cincinnati, the Giants, and the Dodgers. Clark Griffith of the Senators was notorious for scouting Cuba for cheap players. But there was a caveat. These players had to be white Latins. With the color barrier broken, baseball could now bring in Latin players who were black. The first Latin star, and a truly great player still not recognized today, was Orestes "Minnie" Minoso, who was signed by Cleveland in the late 1940s but traded to the White Sox in 1951, because the Indians already had too many "blacks" on their team. Minoso played 17 years in the big leagues and compiled a lifetime .298 batting average. He was an exciting forerunner of the Latin talent that emerged in the 1950s: Chico Carrasquel; Bobby Avila, who won a batting title in 1954; Roberto Clemente; and Luis Aparicio, who revived base stealing, leading the league in stolen bases for nine-consecutive seasons, among others. Interestingly, it was the American League, not the National, that tapped the best Latin talent at first. In the next two decades, Latin players would emerge as one of the most powerful forces in baseball.

Questions for Consideration

1. What made the year 1946 so special for baseball?
2. How do you explain the explosion in baseball attendance in the years immediately after World War II?
3. Discuss the challenge of the Mexican League and the attempt at unionization. How did management deal with these threats?
4. Discuss the integration of baseball, in particular, the role of Branch Rickey in bringing about this change. What were his motives?
5. Compare the record of the two leagues in dealing with integration. What were some of the consequences of the differences in how the two leagues handled this issue?
6. Baseball faced a number of challenges in the 1950s: declining attendance, failed franchises, and the threat from television, among others. How did baseball deal with these problems?
7. Was Walter O'Malley justified in moving to Los Angeles? Discuss some of the ramifications of this move for baseball.
8. What explains the emergence of Latin players in Major League Baseball in the 1950s?

Notes

1. Landon Y. Jones, *Great Expectations: America and the Baby Boom Generation* (New York: BookSurge, 2008).

2. Ira Berkow, *Hank Greenberg: The Story of My Life* (New York: Ivan R. Dee, 2009), 165.

3. Daniel Peary, ed., *We Played the Game: Sixty-Five Players Remember Baseball's Greatest Era, 1947–1964* (New York: Hyperion, 1994), 9.

4. Robert F. Burk, *Much More Than a Game: Players, Owners, and American Baseball since 1921* (Chapel Hill: University of North Carolina Press, 2001).

5. Burk, *Much More Than a Game*.

6. Robert Weintraub, *The Victory Season: The End of World War II and the Birth of Baseball's Golden Age* (New York: Little, Brown, 2013) is the best overview of baseball's first season after World War II.

7. John Carmichael, *Who's Who in Baseball*, 15th ed. (Chicago: B. E. Callahan, 1947), 52–53.

8. Jules Tygiel, *Baseball's Great Experiment: Jackie Robinson and His Legacy* (New York: Oxford University Press, 1983).

9. Tygiel, *Baseball's Great Experiment*, 188.

10. Murray Polner, *Branch Rickey: A Biography* (New York: Atheneum, 1982), 74.

11. Veeck's claim to have attempted to integrate baseball before Branch Rickey is dealt with in David Jordan, Larry R. Gerlach, and John Rossi, "A Baseball Myth Exploded," *National Pastime: A Review of Baseball History* 18 (1998): 3–13.

12. Neil Lanctot, *Negro League Baseball: The Rise and Ruin of a Black Institution* (Philadelphia: University of Pennsylvania Press, 2004), 333. Lanctot's volume is the best overall history of the Negro Leagues.

13. Neil Sullivan, *The Dodgers Move West* (New York: Oxford University Press, 1989) is the best overview of baseball's transcontinental move.

BLACKS IN MAJOR LEAGUE BASEBALL: THE EXPERIENCE OF THE FIRST GENERATION, 1947–61

John Rossi

World War II was many things to the American people: the good war, the war that ended the Depression, the victory of democracy over totalitarianism. As such, it marks one of the great dividing lines in American history comparable to 1865, 1898, 1917, or 1933. Among the themes that were emphasized during the war was the evil of racism, whether the Nazi form, which singled out the Jews and other so-called undesirables, or the Japanese version, less vicious but equally pernicious.

The United States and its Allies believed that they were victorious, partially because their enemies' racist policies were self-defeating. The hatred of racism that emerged from the war, especially the Nazi version, brought into focus the single greatest flaw of American democracy, the nation's historic racial prejudice toward African Americans. One area where this flaw was obvious was in America's game, baseball.

Major League Baseball had a good war. After Pearl Harbor, many baseball people expected that the game would be shut down for the duration. But Franklin D. Roosevelt's famous green light letter to Commissioner Landis was a godsend to the sport. Baseball not only survived, but gloried in the contribution it made to the war effort. Free tickets to service personnel, revenue from the All-Star Game of 1944 to war relief, patriotic parades, war bond sales, etc., enabled baseball to boast that not only had the game survived intact, but baseball again had demonstrated its central role in America's life. More importantly, baseball actually prospered during the war. Attendance in 1945, 10,841,000, was the highest in baseball history. During the four years of the war, 1942–45, Major League Baseball attracted slightly over 35 million fans [1]

John Rossi, "Blacks in Major League Baseball: The Experience of the First Generation, 1947–61," *International Journal of the History of Sport* XIII, no. 3 (December 1, 1996): 397–403. Reprinted by permission of the publisher, Taylor & Francis, Ltd. http://www.informaworld.com.

But the years of the war raised questions about baseball's color bar. How could a nation (and a sport) that fought one form of racism continue to maintain and support an equally obnoxious version, the segregation of the races? Major League Baseball's response to the crisis over the color bar was typical of the game. A conservative, hierarchical institution was forced to confront its past failures. The "Lords of Baseball" would have preferred that the issue go away. But it would not. Sportswriters, civil rights activists, politicians, and even fans brought pressure on the baseball establishment to integrate the game.[2]

The way baseball handled the problem of desegregation in the generation after World War II is the subject of this essay. It is my contention that baseball managed to achieve a degree of integration that was superior to most other branches of American society. The record of blacks in baseball between World War II and the early 1960s compares favorably to the level of integration in education, politics, the church, or business in those years. Black baseball players had achieved a wide degree of acceptance by this time, as measured by awards won, All-Star selection, statistical excellence, or even general popularity. In the early 1960s, Willie Mays was probably the single most popular baseball player in the majors, inheriting a position once held by the likes of Babe Ruth, Joe DiMaggio, and Stan Musial.

When in October 1945, Branch Rickey of the Brooklyn Dodgers announced that he had signed a black, Jackie Robinson, to a professional contract, he ended nearly six decades of baseball segregation. Rickey acted in the face of unanimous opposition of other baseball executives. Rickey's motivation was a blend of idealism and opportunism. He genuinely wanted to end baseball's color bar, but he also saw a chance for the Dodger organization to tap the last great reservoir of baseball talent in America. While there was no guarantee that Robinson would make it to the majors, it was clearly understood that the color bar in baseball was doomed. In fact, Robinson's success at Montreal in the International League, where he led the league in hitting and won the Most Valuable Player Award, assured that he would be brought up to the majors.[3]

Robinson's first season in Brooklyn, 1947, was a huge success. He hit .297, led the league in stolen bases, scored 125 runs, and was voted Rookie of the Year. More significantly, he had broken the ice, and almost immediately other blacks were signed by major-league clubs. In July 1947, Larry Doby, a young, talented hitter, joined Bill Veeck's Cleveland Indians, thus integrating the American League, while other players from the Negro League, Willard Brown and Hank Thompson, were signed by the St. Louis Browns·in what one of the leading St. Louis papers, the *Gazette-Democrat*, called "an eyebrow-lifting experiment."[4] None of these players made much of an impact in 1947. They only got into between 21 and 29 games among them, although Brown had the distinction of being the first black to hit a homer in the American League—an inside-the-park drive against future Hall of Famer Hal Newhouser of the Tigers.

Despite great credentials as one of the Negro League's premier long-ball hit-ters, Brown could not adjust to the pressures of being an innovator. He was also at least 36 when he got his chance in the majors. The St. Louis Browns were a ter-rible team in 1947, and their owner, Robert Muckerman, saw the huge crowds that Robinson had attracted to the park. The Browns, according to Buck O'Neil, were looking for a franchise saver, hoping that Brown and Thompson would do for the floundering Browns what Robinson had done for the Dodgers.[5] But the Browns were a last-place team, not a pennant contender, and neither Brown nor Thompson had the charisma, intelligence, or drive of Robinson. Brown, in particular, was laid back and lacked intensity. Both players were cut by the Browns after a matter of weeks.

Thompson was young and resurfaced with the Giants as an everyday regular in the early 1950s. Brown, an immensely strong right-handed hitter, continued to play in the minors and, as late as 1954, when he was 43, hit .314, with 35 homers, for the Cardinals top Triple-A farm club, Dallas-Houston.[6] Doby became a star in the American League for over a decade beginning in 1948. In his first full year in the majors Doby hit .301 and helped lead the Indians to the pennant and World Series. He hit the first homer by a black in the Fall Classic.

The success of Robinson and Doby opened the way for other talented blacks to reach the majors. Baseball executives followed Rickey's lead and instead of try-ing to develop young black players, they raided the Negro Leagues, whose owners were only too happy to sell off their most talented players. The process of adding players was slow for seven years. Those blacks who made the majors in almost every case were stars of the Negro Leagues who already had proven themselves. Good examples would be Monte Irvin and Luke Easter, who had carved out distin-guished records in the Negro Leagues. All told, 35 Negro Leaguers played in the majors between 1947 and 1953. Their overall quality was high. Thirteen of them were All-Stars at one time or another, while six reached the Hall of Fame: Robinson, Ernie Banks, Roy Campanella, Willie Mays, Monte Irvin, and Satchel Paige. Paige's selection was for his long career as the premier pitcher in the Negro Leagues, although as a "rookie" at age 42 he helped the Indians win a pennant in 1948, winning six games while losing one with a low ERA of 2.48. Four years later, while pitching for a terrible St. Louis Browns team, he went 12–10 with a 3.07 ERA, pitched 2 shutouts, and saved 10 games. Not bad for a 46-year-old.

In 1950, there were nine African Americans among the 400 players on the major-league roster, 20 in 1953, 36 four years later, and 64 in 1961. Up to the early 1960s, there was an unspoken agreement among baseball executives to limit the number of blacks playing in the majors.[7] A form of racial tokenism prevailed. Larry Doby remembers first becoming aware of a black quota of no more than three regulars during spring training in 1951. The Indians had four blacks capable of making the majors: Doby, Luke Easter, Minnie Minoso, and Harry "Suitcase" Simp-son. Before the season began Indians general manager Hank Greenberg traded

Minoso and got washed-up pitcher Lou Brissie in return. Greenberg's justification was that he preferred the long-ball-hitting Simpson to Minoso.[8] But this begs the question—why not keep both?

Those blacks who did reach the majors had to be clearly superior to their white counterparts. Very few of the black players were benchwarmers or of below average ability. At first, as Don Newcombe observed, you didn't "see too many black substitutes, either you were a regular or you didn't get on the team."[9] Aaron Rosenblatt has analyzed the records of black players between 1953 and 1965, when their numbers were sufficiently large enough to draw inferences. His research showed that the batting average of black hitters in those years was anywhere from .012 to .031 higher than white batters.[10] There were not enough pitchers to make any meaningful comparisons, a reflection of yet another prejudice, i.e., that blacks could not handle those positions that required analytical thought—pitcher, catcher, or shortstop. It was believed that they were better at the instinctive side of baseball, hitting and baserunning.

This is remarkably shortsighted considering that Roy Campanella had already demonstrated by the early 1950s that he could call a game with the best backstops and was by far the best defensive catcher in the National League and perhaps all baseball. Don Newcombe won 20 games three times, including 27 victories in 1956, the most in the National League since Bucky Walters won that many for the pennant-winning Cincinnati Reds in 1939. For his 27 victories, Newcombe was the first winner of the newly created Cy Young Award for an outstanding pitching performance.

The pace of baseball integration was painfully slow until around 1954, reflecting the slowly emerging conviction that segregation was wrong both morally and practically. It is interesting that the year in which the pace of baseball integration quickened saw the unanimous Supreme Court *Brown v. Board of Education of Topeka Kansas* ruling outlawing separate but equal education. By 1954, it was clear to baseball executives that blacks could make a major contribution to winning. For example, from Robinson's breaking the color bar in 1947, blacks took part in every World Series but 1950's, when two lily-white teams, the Yankees and Phillies, played. In some Series, blacks made a crucial contribution, such as rookie Joe Black's starting the first game in the 1952 Series, Doby's team-leading .318 average in the 1948 Series, or Monte Irvin's .458 average in the Giants' loss to the Yankees in 1951.

The so-called Bible of Baseball, the *Sporting News*, initially no supporter of integration, noted this phenomenon as early as 1952. Roger Birtwell, a Boston sportswriter, argued that baseball teams were making a mistake if they failed to recruit talented black players. During the 1951 season, he pointed out that three of the top four clubs in the National League, the winning Giants, second-place Dodgers, and fourth-place Boston Braves, fielded blacks at key positions. Robinson at second,

Campanella behind the plate, with Don Newcombe on the mound, were Dodger regulars. The Giants carried four blacks: outfielders Willie Mays, Monte Irvin, and infielder-outfielder Hank Thompson, while Ray Noble was a backup catcher. The Braves had Sam Jethroe leading off and playing center field, while Luis Marquez was a reserve infielder. Jethroe was an immensely fast and talented outfielder whose career was cut short by chronic eye problems and a poor throwing arm. Despite this he led the National League in stolen bases for two years in a row, 1950–51, and was a close second in 1952. His total of 98 stolen bases over three seasons was the most in the National League since 1928–30.

In the American League, the second-place Indians and fourth-place White Sox had black players at key positions. Huge Luke Easter played first for Cleveland, hit a solid .270, and led the Indians in homers with 27 and runs batted in with 103. Doby had another good year in center with 20 homers to go with a .295 average. The White Sox were the surprise of the American League in 1951, moving into the first division for the first time since 1943. They were led by Minnie Minoso, who was also baseball's first great black Latin player. He finished second in batting with a .326 average and led the league in triples with 14 and stolen bases with 31. For this he was named Rookie of the Year by the *Sporting News*.

As Birtwell noted, only five teams in the majors used African Americans at key positions in 1951, and all five finished in the first division. Three of the top six men in the voting for the MVP Award in the National League were blacks, while Minoso finished fourth in the voting in the Junior Circuit. Of the 11 teams in the majors without black players, eight finished in the second division. "It looks," said Birtwell, "as though second-division teams have something to ponder."[11]

He was correct. Major League Baseball may have been slow to respond to integration, but as in the case of night baseball and radio broadcasting, the game's owners were not invincibly ignorant. In 1954, the majors started to integrate more rapidly. By one count 32 blacks played in the majors that season.[12] Black players were now being developed in the minor leagues, as well as purchased from the Negro Leagues, which were in the process of breaking up. There were eight players from the old Negro Leagues who made their debut in 1954. All told, 72 Negro Leaguers made it to the majors after Robinson began baseball's integration. Of those entering the majors from the Negro Leagues after 1954, only Hank Aaron and Elston Howard of the Yankees could be considered superstars.[13]

Five teams in 1954 integrated their rosters, six if one adds the Athletics, who had brought up pitcher Bob Trice for a "cup of coffee" in September 1953. The A's failure to integrate was costly. According to Judy Johnson, a black scout for the A's, at one time or another Connie Mack was offered the services of Larry Doby or Minoso for $5,000. He also could have purchased the contract of Hank Aaron from the Negro Leagues for $3,500. If Mack had signed these three, said Johnson, "the A's would still be in Philadelphia."[14]

The Pirates, Cardinals, and Reds in the National League added black players in 1954; the Senators and Yankees did so in the Junior Circuit. Only one of these teams produced a player comparable to the talent of the first generation of black stars. The Yankees added Elston Howard to their roster as a backup catcher to Yogi Berra and part-time outfielder. Howard eventually took over for Berra behind the plate and became in 1963 the first black to win the Most Valuable Player Award in the American League.

The other black rookies, Tom Alston for the Cardinals, Curt Roberts for the Pirates, Nino Escalera for the Reds, and Carlos Paula for the Senators, were journeymen at best, although the Cards had high hopes for Alston, which he never fulfilled. He had hit well in the minors and was a fine first baseman, but he never panned out in the majors, hitting just .244 over four years with the Redbirds from 1954 to 1957.[15]

Only three teams after 1954 were without blacks on their rosters: the Phillies, Red Sox, and Tigers. All three teams played in cities with reputations for hostility toward blacks, although it should be noted that the Boston Braves had integrated that city in 1950, with Jethroe, while the Philadelphia Athletics had added their first black player in 1953. The Athletics also had a black regular in Philadelphia during the 1954 season. Vic Power came over in a trade with the Yankees but made little impression that season, as the Athletics were a last-place team on their way out of Philadelphia. Power became a star after they moved to Kansas City in 1955.

The final integration of baseball smacked of tokenism. The Phillies added a black player, shortstop John Kennedy, in 1957, who got into just five games with two at-bats. But he was sop to outside pressure to integrate. In 1956, the local chapter of the NAACP accused the Phillies' front office of harboring "anti-Negro feelings."[16] The charge was not groundless, as the Phillies' players and executives had been among the most adamant in harassing Jackie Robinson during his rookie season. In reality, the first black regular for the Phillies was Chico Fernandez, a Cuban who came over to them in a trade, appropriately enough with the Dodgers. The first black star they developed in their minor-league system was Richie Allen, who did not reach the majors until 1963, a full generation after Jackie Robinson broke the color bar. Allen's sojourn in the city of Brotherly Love was a painful and tempestuous one.[17]

Detroit and Boston were not any better at integration, although the size of the minority population was not always an accurate indicator to how a city would react to integration. The Motor City had a significant black population—18 percent according to the 1950 census, while Boston's figure was just 5 percent. The Tigers added reserve infielder Ossie Virgil to their roster in 1957, while the Red Sox had the unenviable distinction of being the last team in baseball to integrate when they signed Pumpsie Green, a benchwarmer, in 1959. At least the Tigers thought that Virgil might be the answer to their perennial problem of finding a regular third baseman. Green was pure tokenism. The Red Sox had no intention of playing him. It took another six to seven years or so before either team produced a first-class black regular.

The first great black star for the Tigers was Willie Horton, who broke in with the team in 1963 but became a regular in 1965, when he hit 29 homers and drove in over 100 runs. The Red Sox had to wait until 1966 to produce their first talented black player, first baseman George "Boomer" Scott. Scott broke in with a splash that year, hitting 27 homers, while driving in 90 runs. Both Horton and Scott went on to have long and distinguished careers. And both proved popular with the fans.

Despite these flaws and hesitation, Major League Baseball was committed by the mid-1950s to exploiting existing black talent whether American or Latin born. An analysis of blacks entering the majors between 1954 and 1960, the end of the first generation of integration, is revealing. Largely because of Jackie Robinson and the commitment of the Dodger and Giant organizations to search out black players, the National League attracted a few higher-quality players.

Two hundred and fifty-six players made their major-league debut in these years, 136 in the National League, 120 in the American. Thirty-one blacks entered the National League, 11 in the American. This disparity is even greater if one examines the quality of those 42 players. Six National Leaguer, Juan Marichal, Hank Aaron, Bob Gibson, Roberto Clemente, Willie McCovey, and Frank Robinson, are in the Hall of Fame, while none of the American League blacks have been named. Among other blacks in the National League during these years are such outstanding talents as Curt Flood, Maury Wills, Bill White, Vada Pinson, Orlando Cepeda, and Felipe Alou. At least two of these players, Cepeda and Pinson, are serious candidates for the Hall of Fame. That cannot be said for American League blacks.

Of the 11 blacks who made their major-league debut in the Junior Circuit between 1954 and 1960, the best would probably be catchers Earl Battey and Elston Howard, while first baseman Vic Power was an above-average player. Only Howard approaches the quality of the best National League blacks. Only three black pitchers broke in with the American League during these years: Pedro Ramos, Jim "Mudcat" Grant, and Earl Wilson. Wilson and Grant each had one 20-game-victory season, while Ramos pitched competitively for a series of terrible Senator teams. Grant won 145 games in his career, Wilson 121, Ramos 117, but their records do not compare with those of Gibson and Marichal. Gibson won 251 games, including five 20-win seasons; Marichal had 243 victories, while winning 20 games six times. Gibson also won two Cy Young Awards.

The qualitative advantage of the National League is further revealed if one looks at how blacks statistically dominated the game during the 1950s. Between 1950 and 1960, blacks won nine Most Valuable Player Awards: Robinson once; Campanella three times; Ernie Banks twice; Mays, Aaron, and Newcombe once each. No black earned that award in the American League. Blacks won nine Rookie of the Year awards in the National League: Robinson, Newcombe, Jethroe, Mays, Joe Black, Jim Gilliam, Frank Robinson, Cepeda, and Willie McCovey. There were no black Rookie of the Year awards in the Junior Circuit. There were four black batting champs in the National League, none in the American. Four times blacks led the National League in homers, while Doby duplicated this feat twice in the American League.

The imbalance in favor of black talent in the National League is clear, and it helps explain the growing dominance of the National League from the mid-1950s on. One of baseball's reigning statistical experts, Bill James, believes that the success of the Senior Circuit was a team-by-team phenomenon. But what was at the heart of that difference was a simple fact: The National League since Jackie Robinson was more accepting of blacks than the American League. Since the emergence of Babe Ruth and the home run revolution in baseball he brought about in the 1920s, the American League had been clearly superior to the Senior Circuit. This began to change in the mid-1950s as the black talent helped swing the balance in favor of the National League.[18] Between the end of the war and 1954, the National League won two World Series, 1946 and 1954, as the all-white New York Yankees dominated baseball. Beginning in 1955, this began to change. The National League went on to win the Series in 1955, 1957, 1959, and 1960, to finish out the decade with four out of five victories. Their domination would continue all through the 1960s and into the early 1970s, when the American League would begin to catch up with the National League by developing their own great black players: Reggie Jackson, Rod Carew, Tony Oliva, etc.

If you use the All-Star Game (a much more debatable concept) as a measure of skill, the same outcome can be seen. When Jackie Robinson broke the color bar the American League was leading in the All-Star Game rivalry 10–3. By the end of the 1950s, the National League had won nine of the 15 games played, with two games played in 1959 and 1960. It was commonly believed that blacks provided the talent edge to the National League. In the words of player and manager Bobby Bragan, by failing to fully integrate, the American League "was left holding the sack for a long time."[19]

By any measure, the record of the black athlete in baseball was an impressive one. The 64 black players on major-league rosters as the 1961 season began constituted 14.5 percent of the total, this at a time when the black population in the country according the 1961 census was 10.5 percent.[20] That year Gene Baker was named to manage one of Pittsburgh's minor-league teams, the Batavia Pirates. The record of integration in baseball had come a long way from Jackie Robinson's terrible isolation in 1947, when sportswriter Dick Young labelled him the loneliest man in baseball.

Baseball, with all its many flaws and foibles, could be proud of its record during the first generation of integration. The success of blacks in what was still regarded as America's game played a significant role in reconciling the nation's tensions in the 1950s, when the Korean War and McCarthyism had inculcated a terrible sense of fear and division.[21] The on-the-field performance of Robinson, Campanella, Willie

Mays, Hank Aaron, et al., gave fans of all races new heroes to cheer on. Not a bad epitaph for any sport.

Notes

1. Bill Gilbert, *They Also Served: Baseball and the Home Front, 1942–45* (New York: Crown, 1992) provides an overview of World War II baseball.

2. See Bill Weaver, "The Black Press and the Assault on Professional Baseball's Color Line, October 1945–April 1947," *Philon* XL (December 1979): 303–17.

3. The best studies of Rickey and Robinson are Murray Polner, *Branch Rickey: A Biography* (New York: Atheneum, 1982) and Jules Tygiel, *Baseball's Great Experiment: Jackie Robinson and His Legacy* (New York: Oxford University Press, 1983). Robinson also wrote an autobiography with Alfred Duckett, *I Never Had It Made: An Autobiography of Jackie Robinson* (New York: Ecco, 2003), which has some revealing material.

4. Tygiel, *Baseball's Great Experiment*, 219.

5. John B. Holway, *Black Diamonds: Life in the Negro Leagues from the Men Who Lived It* (New York: CyberBooks, 1991).

6. Holway, *Black Diamonds*.

7. James E. Miller, *The Baseball Business: Pursuing Pennants and Profits in Baltimore* (Chapel Hill: University of North Carolina Press, 1990).

8. J. Thomas Moore, *Pride against Prejudice: The Biography of Larry Doby* (New York: Praeger, 1988).

9. Art Rust, *Get That Nigger Off the Field: An Oral History of Black Ballplayers from the Negro Leagues to the Present* (New York: Golden-Lee Book, 1992), 132.

10. Aaron Rosenblatt, "Negroes in Baseball: The Failure of Success," *Transaction* IV (September 1967): 51–53.

11. Roger Birtwell, "A Comprehensive Review of the Negro in Organized Baseball," *Sporting News*, February 6, 1952, 3–4.

12. *Sporting News Guide, 1955* (St. Louis, MO: Sporting News, 1955).

13. Dick Clark and Larry Lester, *The Negro League Book* (Cleveland, OH: Society for American Baseball Research, 1954).

14. Bruce Kuklick, *To Everything a Season: Shibe Park and Urban Philadelphia, 1909–1976* (Princeton, NJ: Princeton University Press, 1991), 147.

15. For a discussion of the chronology of integration in baseball, see Merl Kleinknecht, "Integration of Baseball after World War II," *Baseball Research Journal* 12 (Fall 1983): 100–105.

16. Kuklick, *To Everything a Season*, 148.

17. Tim Whitaker, *Crash: The Life and Times of Dick Allen* (New York: Ticknor & Fields, 1989).

18. Bill James, *The New Bill James Historical Baseball Abstract* (New York: Free Press, 2001).

19. Tygiel, *Baseball's Great Experiment*, 336.

20. *Sporting News Guide, 1962* (St. Louis, MO: Sporting News, 1962).

21. This point is made clearly in Ron Briley, "Amity Is the Key to Success: Baseball and the Cold War," *Baseball History* 1, no. 3 (Fall 1988): 4–19.

CHAPTER 8

Baseball's New Frontier, 1961–1977

The Continental League

The United States entered the 1960s with a sense of optimism and confidence in the future. After a brief but sharp recession in 1958–1959, the economy was booming. The population had hit the 180 million mark, and the gross national product (GNP) totaled $500 billion. For some perspective, the GNP had more than doubled in 20 years. Per capita income was a record $2,166. Car ownership was at a record high, with 20 percent of the families in the country owning more than one car. Television ownership had reached the 85 percent mark, with a handful of families now having two or more televisions, something once unthinkable. Color television was now practical and would arrive in a serious way in the mid-1960s.

This sense of optimism was also reflected politically. In November 1960, a 43-year-old John F. Kennedy won the presidency and would replace the then-oldest president in U.S. history, 70-year-old Dwight Eisenhower. Kennedy brought with him to the White House a handsome young family and a stylish, beautiful wife. Although he had won a narrow victory over his Republican opponent, Richard Nixon, Kennedy was soon embraced by the press and the public at large. Politically, he was something American politics hadn't seen since Theodore Roosevelt: an intellectual with an interest in literature and culture. What the press dubbed the "New Frontier" caught the public's imagination, and Kennedy, despite his narrow election victory, soon saw his approval ratings approach record highs.

The nation's optimism was further fueled by the expanding of education to virtually every sector of society. The first Baby Boom generation would start to enter college in 1963–1964. There were 12 million students in high school in

1960. College enrollment had expanded dramatically because of the GI Bill in the years after World War II. There was a smaller growth when the Korean War ended. Almost as important was how these groups broke the cake of custom as far as college was concerned. Students who wouldn't have considered college an option in the past began enrolling in the 1950s. African Americans also were entering college by 1960, in record numbers, despite the disadvantages they labored under because of existing segregation laws. Through legal action they had won admission to law schools in parts of the South. But despite the historic *Brown v. Board of Education of Topeka* decision in 1954, educational opportunities for African Americans were slow to open up. Most of the Southern states were in full resistance to integration throughout the 1950s, and this fueled the civil rights revolution of the 1960s.[1]

Baseball remained optimistic about the future. Attendance was slowly approaching the records set in the late 1940s. It would finally top those figures in 1962, but with a caveat: There were four more teams operating that season as a result of expansion. It would take another decade to match the per game attendance figure of the record year. In 1969, when baseball drew 27 million fans, a figure that made the baseball owners happy.

Total attendance for the decade was 224 million, an increase of 59 million from the 1950s, a better than 20 percent increase. The improvement was across the board. Twelve of the 16 major-league teams drew 1 million or more fans at least once during the decade. The Los Angeles Dodgers averaged 2 million for the decade. In 1962, they moved into Dodger Stadium, the state-of-the-art ballpark Walter O'Malley built on land supplied by the political authorities in California. It was and is one of the iconic ballparks in baseball history and, other than Fenway Park in Boston and Wrigley Field in Chicago, the oldest ballpark still in use today. The move to California set off a building boom in baseball construction. Ten new or overhauled ballparks opened during the decade, a testament to baseball's financial success.

This baseball success came amid a threat from a new league that emerged in the last years of the 1950s. Beginning in 1958, after the shift of the Giants and Dodgers to California, the political authorities in New York set out to lure a team to fill the gap. The mayor, Robert Wagner, and the governor, Averell Harriman, both Democrats, and neither much of a sport fan, realized there was a political dimension to losing the Giants and Dodgers. They created a committee of distinguished New Yorkers led by lawyer and sportsman William Shea to find a discontented team that would be willing to move to the Big Apple with its potential market. Even in their last season in New York, the Giants and Dodgers had attracted 1.6 million fans.

Shea approached three teams that were doing poorly in attendance and baseball success—Cincinnati, Cleveland, and the Phillies—about moving. They all turned him down. It was clear that the answer might not be luring an existing team to New York, but rather forming a new league. This was the genesis of the Continental League. Along with some big-money people and Branch Rickey, who was always eager for a new challenge, Shea set out to create a competitor to the existing major leagues.

Using his financial connections and Rickey's baseball ones, he soon lined up an impressive group of backers for the Continental League. Toronto, Denver, Houston, and Minneapolis, along with New York, would form the core of the new league. Eventually, three more cities would be added. Rickey, who recently had left the Pirates, would serve as front man and president and advise on baseball matters. He knew the minor-league systems of the major-league teams and what players might be worth pursuing once the Continental League got the go-ahead.

Major League Baseball hadn't faced a serious threat since the Federal League—they hadn't regarded the Mexican League challenge as real. With Texas oil money and Whitney money in New York backing the new league, this threat couldn't be dismissed. In any case, Major League Baseball had been thinking of expanding on its own terms since the move to California. The majors had their eyes on Texas, Florida, and even the Northwest, especially Seattle, as potential areas for development.

Major League Baseball also was concerned because even though they had dodged a bullet in 1953, when the Supreme Court didn't overturn Holmes's 1922 decision on baseball's exemption from antitrust legislation, congressional committees were looking into the issue. Major league-owners, mostly Republicans, had considerable support in Congress, but politics was a tricky business. No matter, owners had no intention of caving to a new league and watching the value of their franchises be watered down. It might be better to take the lead in expansion.

Talks were held throughout 1959–1960 between the major-league owners and the leaders of the Continental League, but the discussions went nowhere. To undercut the Continental League, Commissioner Ford Frick suggested that an organized expansion plan be carried out. American League owners wanted to move quickly. In December 1960, despite the objections of the National League representatives, who preferred the two leagues acting together, the American League announced that they would move in 1961. They transferred the Washington franchise to Minneapolis, while establishing a new team in Washington to please the politicians. Then they secured the financial support of cowboy actor and businessman Gene Autry to invade the California market by putting a team in Los Angeles. The cost would be prohibitive. Autry would have to pay an indemnity to Walter O'Malley, who controlled rights to Los Angeles, and then have to play in Dodger Stadium, paying rent while he had a stadium built in Anaheim.

The National League was more cautious. They preferred to carefully lay the groundwork and establish new teams during the 1962 season. Franchises were created in New York, with the team to revive the nineteenth-century name, the Metropolitans, and in Houston, where, in honor of Texas' western reputation, the team was called the Colt 45s.

To satisfy the Continental League backers and avoid a potential lawsuit, a deal was struck. The richest and most powerful of the league's supporters were given control of the new franchises: Joan Payson of the Whitney family in New York, as well as oilman Craig Cullinan in Texas. Along with Autry, this was the kind of new blood baseball needed: fresh money but with traditional tastes. It also turned out to be a better deal than a baseball war that might eventually invite a congressional investigation.

To stock the new teams, the baseball owners came up with a plan that a) protected the best players in their organizations, and b) forced the new teams to pay an exorbitant price to stock their teams. In the American League, the cost of players was $2,150,000 for each team. The Angels drafted well and took some youngsters who turned into decent players: infielder Jim Fregosi, pitcher Dean Chance, and catcher Bob Rodgers. The new Washington team picked older players with recognizable names and paid the price, finishing last in 1961, while losing 100 games.[2]

When the National League's turn came in October 1961, the owners learned from the American League's mistake. The price for players was higher and the quality even lower. Houston paid $1,850,000 but chose wisely, mixing some young players with proven veterans. They finished in eighth place, ahead of one of the existing teams, the Cubs, and the new Metropolitans. The Mets went for veterans with names that would be recognizable in New York: Gil Hodges, Roger Craig, Richie Ashburn, and Charlie Neal. In a shrewd public relations move, they captured the biggest name to lead the team, former Yankees manager Casey Stengel. He gave the new team identity and personality. Sportswriters loved him because he gave them good quotes and insights about baseball instead of the usual flat comments of other managers. Despite Stengel, the Mets paid the ultimate price for their choices, losing a record 120 games for the season. With the help of sportwriters, instead of being rejected for their awful record, the Mets became the darlings of the city, the lovable Mets, who always found a new way to lose.[3]

The Mets were popular, perhaps because the world loves a good-natured loser, and they drew well in the old Polo Grounds, where they played for two years. During the 1964 season, in their new home, while again losing 100 games, they outdrew the pennant-winning Yankees by more than 400,000 fans.

NEW CHALLENGES FOR BASEBALL

The opening years of the 1960s saw a series of balanced races in the National League with five different teams winning the pennant: Pittsburgh, Cincinnati, San Francisco, Los Angeles, and St. Louis. The 1962 and 1963 races were exciting ones. In 1962, the Giants and Dodgers tied for the pennant and forced the fourth playoff in National League history. In an exciting three-game series, the Giants prevailed, winning the last game in dramatic fashion. With the Dodgers ahead, 4–2, going into the top of the ninth, Dodgers pitcher Ed Roebuck ran out of gas. Exhausted after pitching three innings, he was shelled for four runs.[4]

The National League's 1964 pennant race was even more exciting. The surprising Phillies came out of nowhere and held first place from July until the end of September. The team captured the hearts of the wary Philadelphia fans, beset with a decade of woeful teams. Behind the pitching of Jim Bunning, who hurled a perfect game in June, and the hitting of rookie Richie Allen, the Phillies built a seemingly safe six-and-a-half-game lead. Beginning on September 21, they lost 10 consecutive games, giving Cincinnati and the Cardinals a chance to win. At one point, a three-team tie was possible. The Cardinals won on the last day of the season and went on to defeat the Yankees in the World Series.

The American League was dominated in the opening years of the 1960s by a Yankees team that still looked invincible. The Yankees won handily in 1961 through 1963, and narrowly in 1964. The Yankees were getting old, and their once-vaunted farm system was dry. The heart of the team, Whitey Ford, was 36, Yogi Berra was 39, Roger Maris was a part-time player after 1962, and injuries had sapped Mickey Mantle's talent. The Yankees won the 1961 and 1962 World Series but were swept by the Dodgers in 1963, and beaten by the Cardinals in 1964. The team collapsed the next season and was out of contention for a decade until George Steinbrenner took over and remade the squad.

After the Yankees collapse, there were no dynasties in baseball. In the National League, a good Dodgers team, built around the pitching of Don Drysdale and Sandy Koufax, as well as the speed of Maury Wills, fell out of contention. Koufax's arthritic elbow forced him to give up after the 1966 season, and Drysdale was finished in 1968. The Cardinals won three pennants in the 1960s and two World Series, in 1964 and 1967, but they collapsed after the 1968 season and remained a nonfactor until the early 1980s.

In the American League, no one team emerged to match the excellence of the Yankees dynasty. The Baltimore Orioles were a solid team through the early 1960s, winning a pennant in 1966 and sweeping the Dodgers in the World Series. By the late 1960s, Baltimore, behind the managing of Earl Weaver, had constructed one of the most balanced teams in baseball. Combining the pitching of future Hall of Famer Jim Palmer with the solid hitting of Frank Robinson and Brooks Robinson, also Hall of Famers, and Boog Powell, they won three consecutive pennants and one World Series. Despite their talent, they lost the World Series to two teams that on paper were inferior to them: the 1969 "Miracle Mets" and a 1971 Pirates team led by the greatest Latin player of his time, Roberto Clemente. Talent often isn't enough.

The most dramatic development in baseball in the 1960s took place on the mound. After two monster hitting seasons in both leagues in 1961 and 1962, largely because of expansion, the baseball owners decided, beginning in 1963, to raise the pitcher's mound and expand the strike zone. The consequences changed baseball in ways no one had foreseen.

Ever since expansion, offense had been up sharply in both leagues. The offensive performance was most noticeable in the high level of home runs hit in 1962: 1,552 in the American League; 1,449 in the National. In 1968, players in the National League hit 891 home runs, almost 600 less than six years earlier. The average fan has always preferred offense to low-scoring games dominated by pitching. But in 1963, Major League Baseball decided to raise the height of the mound. While it is difficult to give an exact figure, it appears that the pitcher's mound was raised from 10 inches to 15. Some observers say the reason for the pitching dominance of the Dodgers in the mid-1960s was not the great talent of Sandy Koufax and Don Drysdale, but the fact that the mound in Los Angeles was 18 inches high. That 50 percent increase in height gave the pitcher an enormous advantage. The pitch would now arrive at the batter on a sharper angle, and the added height would give greater spin to fastballs and a sharper break for curveballs and sliders. The result, in a matter of years, was to return baseball to something approximating the Deadball Era. In the six years from 1963 to 1968, pitching totally dominated offense. League batting averages dropped to levels not seen since before Babe Ruth launched the long-ball era. In 1968, the American League batting average was .230, a record low. Only one hitter reached the .300 level, Carl Yastrzemski of the Red Sox. Things were only marginally better in the National League, where batting averages stayed in the .240 range.

The Dodgers' Sandy Koufax put together four years of dominant pitching not seen since the days of Lefty Grove. From 1963 to 1966, he won 97 games and lost just 27. He struck out 300 batters three times, including a record 382 in 1965. There even was a 30-game winner in 1968, Denny McLain of the Tigers. That season, Bob Gibson compiled a 22–9 record, including 13 shutouts. His ERA was 1.12, a figure not seen since the days of Grover Cleveland Alexander a half-century earlier. Both leagues had an ERA average under 3.00.[5]

One effect of this pitching dominance was to slow the growth of attendance. Fans always preferred offense to defense. After peaking at 25 million in 1966, attendance declined by more than 2 million in the next two years. Fans were staying away from America's game. The timing couldn't have been worse. For the first time in its existence, baseball was being challenged for dominance by rival sports. During the middle years of the decade, professional football began the process of becoming America's most popular sport. Football was better suited to television than baseball because the action was more exciting and even violent. Football made extensive use of instant replays and slow-motion footage to enhance the game and was ahead of baseball in using television creatively.

In the 1960s, led by a new, young, dynamic commissioner, Pete Rozelle, professional football took a series of imaginative steps that began to win new fans. Rozelle merged the American Football League and his National Football League, and then signed a lucrative television contract, which meant that pro football would dominate the sports scene every Sunday in the fall. Then, in a masterstroke, Rozelle organized a playoff between the two championship teams and brilliantly marketed it as the "Super Bowl." By the late 1970s, football had outpaced baseball as the country's most popular sport. For some idea of how successful Rozelle was, consider that in 1960, when he was named commissioner, there were 12 teams in the NFL worth approximately $1 million each. Twenty-eight years later, when he retired, there were 28 teams worth $100 million each. To further professional football's success, in 1977 Rozelle negotiated a television deal for $656 million with the three major networks.[6] Baseball had nothing comparable to that financial arrangement.

Professional basketball, which had been a minor sport in the 1950s, suddenly found a new audience in the 1960s and early 1970s. Exciting new players like Wilt Chamberlain, Elgin Baylor, Bill Russell, and Bob Cousy turned the National Basketball Association game into a polished and electrifying sport. Scoring increased dramatically, especially when the rule requiring a team to shoot for the basket within 24 seconds was introduced. A series of great Boston Celtics teams caught the public's fancy and basketball took off. NBA attendance increased from 2 million in 1960 to 10 million by the late 1970s.[7]

Baseball suffered in comparison with these new rivals for public attention. What hurt baseball was the sense that the game had grown stodgy. The large number of low-scoring games robbed baseball, a game that is slower moving than football or basketball, of its excitement. An even more serious problem was the fact that baseball was losing the best African American athletes to football and basketball. This was offset somewhat by the continued popularity of baseball in the Caribbean and other parts of Latin America. As the number of African American players declined, they were often replaced by Latin players. By the end of the 1970s, every team in the majors had Latin players. A check of *Who's Who in Baseball* of players on major-league rosters during the 1977 season reveals 57 hitters and 18 pitchers of Latin descent.[8] The breakdown shows the prejudice that Latin players were not good at pitching, which was regarded as requiring more thought.

Baseball finally awoke to its problem in 1969, taking action. First, they had the pitcher's mound lowered from 15 inches to 10, while at the same time narrowing the strike zone slightly. The American League, which had fallen behind the National in most offensive categories since the breakup of the Yankees dynasty, revived an idea that had been around baseball since the turn of the century: the designated hitter. In place of the weak-hitting pitcher, a team could "designate" a more offensive player to hit in the pitcher's place. In 1973 the rule was discussed, and the American League voted to adopt it. The National League held aloof, and as a result, the two leagues followed different playing rules for the first time since the major leagues were organized in 1903.

The result was immediately noticeable. In 1972, the American League had hit .239, while the league ERA was 3.07. With the designated hitter rule and new strike zone in operation, the figures for 1973 were .259 and 3.82, respectively. For the first time in years, the American League had outhit the National. The result was to return the American League to the dominance in hitting it had maintained since the days of Babe Ruth. For some comparison, the American League consistently outslugged the National League in almost all offensive categories. The rule didn't have the same impact on the World Series. There, the designated hitter could only bat in American League home games. During the next decade and a half, the two leagues were close in World Series play. The American League won eight Series titles to the National League's seven.

The designated hitter rule had another result: It extended the careers of players who from injuries or other factors could no longer play as regulars. Among them were such popular players as Orlando Cepeda, whose bad knees made it impossible for him to play regularly; Tommy Davis, former batting champ, who was also slowed down by injuries; and 38-year-old future Hall of Famer Frank Robinson, who in that role hit 29 homers and drove in 97 runs. For some comparison, Robinson had hit six home runs and driven in 59 runs as a part-timer in 1972. Cepeda's performance was even more remarkable. Slowing down and ready to retire in 1972, Cepeda hit just three home runs and driven in nine runs the season before the designated hitter rule was adopted. Despite these figures, the National League refused to adopt the rule.

One factor that offset offensive performance in both leagues was the greater emphasis on relief pitching. In the past, relief pitching was left to over-the-hill hurlers or starters who were pressed into service. In 1930, Lefty Grove, for example, led the American League in wins and saves. There were a handful of pitchers whose job was just relief: Firpo Marberry of Washington and Mace Brown of Pittsburgh in the 1930s. In the late 1940s, the Yankees used a fireballing lefthander, Joe Page, exclusively in relief. He saved 27 games in 1949, a remarkable total during a time when most leaders in saves had figures in the teens. The next year, the Phillies relied heavily on Jim Konstanty to win the pennant. Konstanty won 16 games and saved 22.

From that point onward, teams began to make greater use of relief special-ists. By the 1960s, every team had an expert in saving games, and the number of relief appearances and of saves rose steadily. In 1965, Ted Abernathy, a jour-neyman pitcher, saved 30 games for the first time. That figure then began to be topped with regularity. In 1973, a rule made it simpler to earn a save, and the figure began to rise: 37 in 1978, 45 five years later. More importantly, now every team had a relief specialist, no longer a starter who couldn't pitch nine innings any more, but someone with either a trick pitch like Konstanty's palmball or a fastball pitcher like Dick "the Monster" Radatz of the Red Sox in the mid-1960s.

What this meant is that a batter, instead of facing a starter who was begin-ning to tire in the seventh, eighth, or ninth innings, would now face a fresh hurler. Stan Musial, one of the greatest hitters of the 1940s and 1950s, was once asked what had changed the most about baseball in his time. Musial said it was two things: the development of the slider, once referred to as a nickel curve, and its use by more and more pitchers, and secondly, having to bat against a fresh pitcher, not a tired one, late in the game.[9]

With the addition of two new teams in each league and thus the further watering down of pitching, the offense immediately improved dramatically. Bat-ting averages rose sharply, as did home runs. The two leagues totaled more than 3,000 home runs, 1,100 more than the year before in 1968. Attendance showed an increase of almost 4 million fans. That season also saw baseball get a public relations boost when the lovable losers, now labeled the "Miracle Mets," won their first pennant and went on to defeat a heavily favored Baltimore Orioles squad in the World Series.

As the new decade dawned, baseball believed it had recovered its balance. There had been administrative problems when Commissioner Frick stepped down in 1965. The two leagues couldn't agree on a replacement and finally compromised by naming a military man, William Eckert, a U.S. Air Force gen-eral whose expertise was procurement of equipment, to the post. He knew noth-ing about baseball, which may have been the reason he was picked. The owners didn't want anyone interfering in their affairs. When his selection was made public, one baseball writer exclaimed, "Good God! They've named the Un-known Soldier."[10] Eckert was a front man and, as it turned out, not a very good one. He was bland, a charmless organization man. The two league presidents, Chub Feeney in the National League and Joe Cronin in the American League, had the confidence of the owners, having been baseball executives themselves. But the most powerful voice in baseball remained Walter O'Malley, who was deferred to because of his great success in Los Angeles.

Despite having seemingly solved its problems with better offense and a new commissioner, the mood in baseball circles turned sour. The late 1960s witnessed one of those moments when an entire nation's nerves seem to be frazzled. The war in Vietnam hadn't affected baseball until President Lyndon B. Johnson expanded the U.S. commitment in the conflict in 1965. Players started to be drafted. Antiwar protests, which began in a major way in 1966, occasionally spilled over to baseball, which was the most conservative and traditionalist of the major sports. By early 1968, there were 450,000 U.S. troops in Vietnam, and the death toll had exceeded 30,000. At the same time, the civil rights movement, which had begun in the late 1950s, reached a peak in the mid-1960s. With its large number of African American players, baseball couldn't avoid being influenced. When Rev. Martin Luther King Jr. was assassinated in 1968, Major League Baseball acceded to the demands of African American players to cancel scheduled games.

One interesting aspect for baseball in the 1960s and 1970s was the appearance of the first serious studies of the sport. Harold Seymour had broken ground in the 1960s and early 1970s with his history of the early years of baseball. That seemed to open the door for more scholarly research on baseball's past. David Voigt, in his three-volume history of baseball, called simply *American Baseball*, continued along the path Seymour laid out. His one-volume *America through Baseball* is filled with insights into baseball's relationship with American culture. Lawrence Ritter's *The Glory of Their Times* set the standard for baseball interview books. Steven A. Riess's suggestive essay "Race and Ethnicity in American Baseball, 1900–1919" broke new ground in thinking about the connections of baseball to the nation's ethnic history. Robert Creamer and Marshall Smelser, in their biographies of Babe Ruth, demonstrated what good scholars could do with a great subject. Roger Kahn's lament for the Dodgers of the past, *The Boys of Summer*, is beautifully written and started an industry of examining past teams. *Ball Four*, by Jim Bouton, began the trend of exposing the underside of baseball by a player. Only baseball, with its deep roots in America's past, was spawning an industry examining its past. Other sports would follow suit in later years but rarely reach the levels achieved in baseball writing.

One response to the atmosphere in the nation in the late 1960s and early 1970s was the growing sense of alienation of the players from management. As a group, they were better educated now than in the past and less willing to be treated with the owner's customary disdain. There were rumblings among the players that the Players' Association should represent them more aggressively. In 1966, the players decided to get rid of their representative, retired judge Robert Cannon, who they believed wasn't a strong enough advocate for their interests. At the time, the average salary for a major-league player was approximately $19,000. A rookie received $6,000, an increase of just $1,000 since 1946's so-called "Magna Carta of Baseball" settlement. Joe DiMaggio and Ted Williams made $100,000 in the early 1950s. Now only a handful of players received that salary, despite the vast increase in attendance, as well as the flow of money from television coming into the owner's coffers.

MARVIN MILLER RESCUES THE PLAYERS

In 1966, the Players' Association, at the suggestion of Robin Roberts, hired Marvin Miller, an economist who worked for the United Steelworkers Union in Pittsburgh. Miller was paid a salary of $50,000 a year, more than most baseball players made. He quickly discovered how conservative the players were when he studied their contracts with Major League Baseball. Every aspect favored management. They were little more than high-paid serfs. Most players were interested in two things: increasing their pay and a better pension system.

Shortly after taking over, Miller began the slow conversion of the Players' Association into a more aggressive union-like entity. He first went about meeting the players, attending spring training camps in 1967, introducing himself to the players, and listening to their complaints. Then, step-by-step, he started winning their confidence. He discovered that players received little money for appearing on baseball cards, instead being given a glove or some other minor compensation. He negotiated a deal with the card companies so that the players would receive $250 for appearing. He did the same thing with Coca-Cola for the rights to put the players' pictures inside bottle caps.

The next year, Miller negotiated a two-year labor contract with the owners. For many players, the key provisions were the minimum salary being set at $12,000, a large increase in funding for the pension program, and no salary reduction of more than 20 percent instead of 25 percent. By the deal, Miller had solidified his position with the players. For him, however, the key provision was the creation of a grievance committee to deal with disputes between the players and the owners, with the commissioner as arbitrator. Miller recognized that the commissioner was a creature of the owners, but he had gotten the concept of arbitration accepted in principle.[11]

In contract negotiations in 1970 and 1972 Miller strengthened his position by winning further concessions from the owners on pension matters with increases coming from the money baseball received from the televising of the All-Star Game and the World Series. Another provision popular with the players was the reduction from five to four years to qualify for the pension. But the key provision of the contract negotiation was an important change in the concept of arbitration. Initially the arbitrator of all disputes between the players and the owners was to be the Commissioner of Baseball. By 1970 the owners had gotten rid of Eckert and hired a lifetime baseball fan and lawyer for baseball, Bowie

Kuhn. Kuhn was an activist Commissioner and understood the importance of public relations. He believed that it was important to get contract matters settled and keep the focus on playing the game. In order to do so he and the owners agreed to a modification of the arbitration clause which was a colossal blunder on their part. Now the arbitrator would be an outsider agreed to by both sides. This was a major victory for Miller. He believed that the arbitrator would be neutral. He further believed that the players would win most cases. The stage was set for the most revolutionary change in baseball history, the ending of the reserve clause.

Under terms of the new baseball agreement signed in 1970 baseball players could challenge the salary offered them by appealing to arbitration. Even before that issue came to a head, baseball was challenged in court again. This time a player, Curt Flood, rejected his trade to the Phillies, claiming his rights were abrogated by the reserve clause and that he should have some say in where he played. The issue wasn't money. The Phillies were offering him more than he had been paid by his former team, the Cardinals. He decided to challenge the reserve clause on anti-trust grounds. Miller didn't believe a judicial challenge would work anymore than it had in the past, but Flood persisted. When the case reached the Supreme Court, they upheld the 1922 decision which exempted baseball from anti-trust rules, saying it was for the legislature to act and change baseball's anti-trust exemption. In the long run, the Flood case encouraged Miller and the players to see that they would have to be aggressive in their dealings with the owners. The courts were not going to step in and help.[12]

Baseball owners breathed a sigh of relief. For the third time, the exemption from antitrust rules had been vindicated. With regard to the question of salary disputes, they didn't think this would be a problem and felt that most disputes would be decided in their favor. What they discovered was that the arbitrator wouldn't split the difference between what the player wanted and what was offered. Instead, under classic arbitration rules, he would choose one or the other figure depending on the evidence in the case. In effect, what salary arbitration meant was that players always benefited. Even if the arbitrator decided on the side of the club offer, it would always be more than the player had made previously. Baseball owners didn't seem too concerned. They did win most of the cases, but the pressure on salaries slowly rose in the 1970s, despite their victories. The $100,000 figure was constantly broken, while the average salary climbed to $36,000. In 1973, Richie Allen of the White Sox and Hank Aaron of the Braves were making more than $200,000, and the trend was consistently upward.

In 1974, baseball's economic foundations were shocked. Charles Finley, the flashy owner of the Oakland A's, one of baseball's most successful teams, having won five consecutive pennants and three World Series, got into a dispute with one of his best pitchers, Jim "Catfish" Hunter. Before that season, Hunter had signed a two-year contract for $100,000 a year, with half of the money deferred for tax purposes. For some reason, Finley hadn't paid the deferred money by season's end, and Hunter sued that his contract was void and he was a free agent. Finley offered the money late, but Hunter turned him down. The issue went to arbitration, where the arbitrator, Peter Seitz, declared Hunter a free agent. That set off a rush of teams to try to sign him. Eventually, Hunter agreed to an unprecedented deal with George Steinbrenner's New York Yankees for $3.2 million for five years. The salary scale in baseball had been shattered. There had never been anything like this since Ruth signed for $80,000 in the midst of the Depression.

Once the arbitrator had ruled that a contract had not been fulfilled, Miller believed if he could get someone to play the entire season and not sign, he would have a test case for the reserve clause. The standard baseball contract simply said a player was signed for one year and that his services were reserved to the team. If a player didn't sign his contract, would he then be a free agent?

In 1975, Miller got his candidates. Two players, Dave McNally, a pitcher with Montreal who was getting ready to retire, and Andy Messersmith of the Dodgers, agreed to test the reserve clause by not signing their contracts during the season. In effect, they would be playing out their options. Messersmith was one of the best pitchers in the National League. He had won 20 games in 1974, followed by 19 the next year. The Dodgers offered him $115,000 during the 1975 season, and when he turned it down, they increased the offer to $540,000 for three years, which would make him one of the highest-paid players in the game. Again rejecting their offer, he decided to be the test case Miller was looking for and sued for his freedom.

Major League Baseball argued that the issue wasn't covered by the agreement signed in 1970, but that contention was rejected by the courts. The case then went to arbitration. The arbitrator, the same Peter Seitz who ruled in favor of Hunter in 1974, counselled both sides to resolve the issue. For some reason, Major League Baseball refused, believing they would prevail. In December 1975, Seitz ruled that the one year covered in the player's contract meant just that, one year. If no contract was signed, the player was free to offer his services to any team. Major League Baseball had lost the reserve clause, what it regarded as the rule that was the cornerstone of the game's success for more than a century, the security that came with controlling player movement.[13]

Miller was thrilled, but he also recognized that unlimited free agency would have the effect of leaving too many free agents and thus drive down their bargaining power. He negotiated a compromise where players could only exercise free agency after six years in the majors. This would provide the team with an opportunity to decide whether to keep a player based on his importance to the team.

The first batch of free agents, 24 in all, signed contracts for the 1977 season. The biggest name was Reggie Jackson, who signed a $3 million deal for five years with the Yankees. Bobby Grich, a solid second baseman with Baltimore, went to the Angels for $1.5 million for five years. For some idea of what was happening, consider that he had made $68,000 the year before. Even more shocking, Bill Campbell, a relief pitcher with Minnesota whose salary was $22,000 the year before free agency, signed with the Red Sox for $1 million for four years.[14]

Free agency stunned baseball and changed the game forever. Its immediate impact was negligible. Only Jackson's signing was of any importance. He helped the Yankees win the pennant in 1977. The other signings were inconsequential. But during the next few seasons, free agency would be a factor in a team's success.

The real problem that free agency and salary arbitration brought about was a sense among the baseball owners that Miller and the Players' Association were their enemies and had to somehow be brought under control. The new commissioner, Bowie Kuhn, believed that some kind of compromise acceptable to both sides could be worked out. But the owners were furious at Miller. They believed he was the source of their woes, and instead of working with him, they entered into a cold war with the players. As salaries rose because of free agency, they didn't recognize their role in the process as they bid for the services of freed players. Instead, they focused their anger at Miller. This was the root of the strikes of 1981 and eventually the 1994 catastrophe undertaken long after Miller was out of the picture.

Questions for Consideration

1. What was the significance of the Continental League for Major League Baseball? What are some of the reasons for its failure?
2. Discuss some of the factors behind baseball's expansion in 1961–1962. Which league benefited the most and why?
3. Analyze some of the reasons for the decline in popularity of baseball as compared to other sports during the 1970s.
4. Discuss the importance of the emergence of Latin American players in the 1960s and 1970s. Compare their experience in baseball with that of the African American players when they integrated the sport.
5. What were some of the factors behind the growth in baseball attendance in the 1960s and 1970s?

6. In what ways was baseball reflected in serious literature during the years after World War II? What does that tell us about baseball's connection to American culture?
7. Discuss some of the reasons behind the decline in baseball offense during the 1960s.
8. Why was Marvin Miller such an important figure in baseball during the 1970s?
9. Discuss some of the factors that led to the end of the reserve clause. Why was this so significant for the sport?
10. What was the significance of the Curt Flood case?

Notes

1. David Shannon, *Twentieth-Century America: World War II and Since* (Chicago: Houghton Mifflin School, 1969), chapter 27, provides an overview of some of the economic and social changes taking place in the 1960s and early 1970s.

2. For the Continental League, see Russell D. Buhite, *The Continental League: A Personal History* (Lincoln: University of Nebraska Press, 2014) and Michael Shapiro, *Bottom of the Ninth: Branch Rickey, Casey Stengel, and the Daring Scheme to Save Baseball from Itself* (New York: Henry Holt, 2009).

3. Leonard Shecter, *Once Upon the Polo Grounds: The Mets That Were* (New York: Dial, 1970) is a humorous portrait of the early years of the Mets.

4. Gary Parker, *Win or Go Home: Sudden Death Baseball* (Jefferson, NC: McFarland, 2002).

5. Bill James, *The New Bill James Historical Baseball Abstract* (New York: Free Press, 2001).

6. For a discussion on the reasons behind the rising popularity of professional football, see Benjamin Rader, *American Sports: From the Age of Folk Games to the Age of Televised Sports* (Englewood Cliffs, NJ: Prentice-Hall, 1983).

7. Rader, *American Sports.*

8. John Carmichael, *Who's Who in Baseball, 1947* (Chicago: B. E Callahan, 1947).

9. Rob Neyer, "The Pioneers of Modern Relief Pitching," *National History Museum*, December 20, 2013.

10. Leonard Koppett, *Koppett's Concise History of Major League Baseball* (Philadelphia: Temple University Press, 1998), 303.

11. For more information on the story of baseball's resort to arbitration, see Koppett, *Koppett's Concise History of Major League Baseball*, chapter 22.

12. Robert F. Burk, *Much More Than a Game: Players, Owners, and American Baseball since 1921* (Chapel Hill: University of North Carolina Press, 2001).

13. Koppett, *Koppett's Concise History of Major League Baseball.*

14. Leigh Montville, "The First to Be Free," *Sports Illustrated*, April 16, 1990.

A TALE OF MANY CITIES: THE WESTWARD EXPANSION OF MAJOR LEAGUE BASEBALL IN THE 1950S

Lee Elihu Lowenfish

Philip K. Wrigley, the chewing-gum millionaire who inherited and operated the Chicago Cubs baseball team until his death in 1977, was fond of saying, "Baseball is too much of a business to be a sport, and too much of a sport to be a business." As baseball emerged in the post–Civil War United States as the first "national pastime," the institution took on an almost sacred status. Politicians, churchmen, and ordinary citizens found something compelling and perhaps peculiarly American about a game which had a unique symmetry, a combination of guile and physical skill, and an inherent timelessness—the game was not over "until the last man was out. . . ."

Since 1903, a National Agreement had been enforced by which two "major" leagues of eight teams each, the National, established in 1876, and the upstart American League, agreed to respect each other's territories and player contracts. For 50 years, this agreement remained operative, with each league divided into a western and eastern division and the winners of the leagues meeting annually in one of America's greatest sporting events, the World Series. St. Louis was the westernmost city. . . .

By the end of World War II, however, the imbalance of the Major League Baseball map was glaringly evident. In 1903, the American population had totaled 73 million, by 1950 it would reach 160 million. Since 1921, the Los Angeles metropolitan area had grown 300 percent, compared to a national growth rate of 42 percent. In the 1940s alone, the growth rate of the entire Pacific Coast region was 24 percent, compared to a national growth rate of only 2 percent. Yet the number of Major League Baseball jobs, 400, remained exactly the same as in 1903.

Lee E. Lowenfish, "A Tale of Many Cities: The Westward Expansion of Major League Baseball in the 1950s," *Journal of the West* XVII, no. 3 (1978): 71–82. Copyright © 1978 by *Journal of the West*, Inc. Reprinted with permission of ABC-CLIO, LLC.

It is not surprising that the first pressure for western expansion of Major League Baseball came from the West Coast. College football had boomed in the Pacific area, as in the rest of the country, when it challenged baseball as a spectator sport in the 1920s. By the 1940s, professional football had come to the West Coast with successful franchises in Los Angeles and San Francisco. Although the cost of flying baseball teams several times a year to the West Coast was obviously far greater than an occasional jaunt for a Sunday football game, the teams in the Triple-A Pacific Coast League (PCL) . . . had regularly flown long trips from San Diego to Seattle and Portland.

By 1946, an impressive boom in spectator sports was in full force. . . . Attendance in the PCL reached new heights, the teams in Oakland, San Francisco, Los Angeles, and Hollywood combining for attendance well over 2 million. Clarence "Pants" Rowland, president of the PCL, decided it was time that his organization attained a special status. He went to the major-league meetings during the All-Star Game in July 1946, asking for a new designation as "the Pacific Major League," and for an exemption from the major-league clubs to purchase the best PCL players for a maximum price of $10,000. Rowland understood that immediate parity with the National and American leagues would not come merely from a changed name. But he argued that the PCL deserved special consideration because it clearly was more than a Triple-A league. . . . Rowland also wanted to protect his clubs "from the vultures who would like to descend on their little gold lode."

Unfortunately for Rowland, there were cities in the PCL, especially Los Angeles, which wanted immediate major-league status by admission to the big leagues. Los Angeles interests had almost bought the weak St. Louis Browns . . . franchise in 1941. . . . The bombing of Pearl Harbor abruptly ended those talks, but by 1946, Los Angeles spokesmen were again beginning to pressure the major-league owners. Crusading journalist Vincent X. Flaherty of the *Los Angeles Herald Examiner* and Los Angeles County board supervisor Leonard J. Roach both tried to speak before the owners' summer meetings of 1946 and 1947. Their anti-Rowland argument could be summed up in Flaherty's blunt statement, "Los Angeles shouldn't be shackled to little cities like Sacramento, San Diego, and Portland."

The haughty major-league owners, once described as compromising a club more exclusive than even the United States Senate, ignored both Rowland and the Los Angeles booster at their meetings. . . . The immediate response to Rowland's proposal was to table it, and then in December 1947, the other Triple-A leagues blocked any special status for the PCL at the minor-league meetings, leaving Rowland with absolutely nothing gained. . . .

But the drumbeats for Los Angeles as a major-league city continued their work. L.A. supervisor Roach, knowing how sensitive the owners were to charges of monopoly, blasted them as a conspiracy to keep L.A. from becoming a "member of the major-league family." In 1949, a federal court agreed to hear the first real test of the antitrust exemption since the 1922 Holmes decision. . . . Judge Jerome Frank described the controversial reserve clause in the standard player's contract as "peonage." . . . The reserve clause simply bound a player indefinitely to the team that owned him. . . .

With such weighty issues as the legality of the reserve clause . . . needing resolution, the House Subcommittee on Monopoly Power opened hearings in July 1951. Committee chairman Emanuel Celler (D, Brooklyn, N.Y.) provided a ringing opening to the investigation. "Organized baseball affords this subcommittee with almost a textbook example of what might happen to an industry which is governed by rules and regulations among its members rather than by the free play of competitive forces." Cellar . . . made it evident that he did not understand the complexities of baseball and had no desire to force government regulation upon it. . . .

The Celler Committee ended its first hearing in October 1951 and, in May 1952, issued a report without recommending legislation to specify or to limit baseball's antitrust exemption. The committee deferred to the courts, which were hearing several cases . . . most of them regarding the reserve clause. But the facts of demography and the lucrative fees of radio and TV broadcast remained for major league baseball owners to covet and to seek.

As the 1952 major-league season ended, the struggles of the smaller cities with two franchises were more obvious than ever. The Boston Braves . . . had slipped out of contention with the Red Sox and drew a woeful 281,000 spectators in 1952. The St. Louis Browns . . . faced extinction with the purchase of the Cardinals by the Busch Brewery Company. The Philadelphia Athletics . . . were falling behind the National League Phillies, who had been recently purchased by the wealthy Robert Carpenter.

At the December 1952 major-league meetings in Phoenix . . . the owners ruled that a team could move with the unanimous consent of its own league. . . . Brooklyn Dodger president Walter O'Malley, head of one of the most prosperous and successful franchises in baseball, called the news "most exciting" and wondered why the New York press was not covering it more.

New Yorkers would look back ruefully on this comment in five years, but in late 1952, attention switched to Boston and St. Louis. Louis Perini, a contractor, owned the Braves and vowed that he would "never" move the team. By October 1952, Perini . . . looked to greener pastures, especially Milwaukee, where he owned the Triple-A Brewers . . . and where a municipal stadium with parking for 14,000 cars was ready for occupancy by 1953.

Bill Veeck in St. Louis had his eyes on Milwaukee. . . . He had operated a highly successful Milwaukee Brewers team in the early 1940s. . . . Veeck had tried to revive the Browns, but not even hiring a midget at bat, an act which intensified the other owners' disdain for him, could bring lasting attendance to St. Louis. . . . When Veeck turned to Baltimore as a solid minor-league city which would likely support the Browns, the American League, led by the Yankees, rejected the move. . . .

Commissioner (Ford) Frick had been quoted in early 1953, as saying that a move of the franchise that close to the season was impracticable. But in early March, the National League unanimously approved the move of Boston to Milwaukee. The log jam of 50 years at last had been broken.

The immediate success of the Braves astounded even the most cockeyed optimist. By May 20, the Braves had matched the entire 1952 Boston attendance, en route to an impressive season attendance of 1,800,000. . . .

The triumph of Lou Perini was not lost on other owners. He had turned a large deficit in Boston into a profit in Milwaukee in two years. Moreover, his policy of not televising any games assured him of a large home attendance plus radio rights from all over the upper Midwest. By the mid-1950s, major-league owners were getting nearly 20 percent of their total income from broadcasting rights. In 1956, network money began to pour in as NBC started a Game-of-the-Week on Saturday afternoon national television. By 1957, even CBS had instituted a Sunday Game-of-the-Week. In keeping with the major-league owners' jealous regard for their own interests above all else, the second Game-of-the-Week was barred from major-league cities so better teams might not compete with the inferior local major-league product. . . .

(Walter) O'Malley was not born into baseball but had studied engineering and then law. He received his law degree in 1930, and far from suffering the effects of the depression, O'Malley established a sound practice dealing in bankruptcies. He joined the Brooklyn Dodger organization as a director in 1932, became counsel in 1942, and by 1946 was co-owner of the teamj along with the brilliant, shrewd Branch Rickey. It was only a matter of time before these two equally clever minds would clash. After the 1950 season, O'Malley bought out Rickey's share of the Dodgers for over $1 million, a staggering sum which reflected both Rickey's business acumen and the rising prices of baseball franchises.

O'Malley, who liked to be called *the* O'Malley . . . became the first executive to buy a plane for the exclusive use of his team and his farm clubs. If anybody in Brooklyn had doubts that the plane might soon fly West and stay there, as early as 1952 O'Malley had described the change in territorial rules as the "most exciting news" in years. The same year, he had hired architects . . . to plan a new stadium in Brooklyn to replace the antiquated Ebbets Field, which seated only 33,000, many behind poles, and had room only to park 700 cars. He even enlisted futurist planner Buckminster Fuller to sketch a domed stadium. O'Malley told sportswriter . . . Tom Meany in 1952, "There has been too much of a wait-till-next-year attitude in Brooklyn."

In June 1953, O'Malley met with the imperious New York City commissioner of parks, Robert Moses, whose actual power far exceeded the relatively minor, unelected post he had held for decades. O'Malley proposed a location for a new ballpark at an intersection of three subway stations and in an area where Moses was planning both a modern meat market and public housing projects. O'Malley added that he was willing to invest $4 million of his own money in a new stadium, which would make it the first privately financed ballpark since Yankee Stadium. Moses asked where the money was. O'Malley replied . . . that if Moses would provide the land, he would show the money. . . .

(O'Malley) saw the Milwaukee success and grew envious. His argument ran, "If they take in twice as many dollars, they will eventually be able to buy talent." . . . He bided his time as the Dodgers continued to dominate on the field, winning pennants in 1952 and 1953, and, at last, a world's championship in 1955. But hardly had the celebration died when O'Malley announced that seven Dodger home games in 1956 would be played in Jersey City's Roosevelt Stadium. *Newsweek* columnist John Lardner quipped that the Dodgers were already "1/600th of the way to Los Angeles." . . .

Belatedly, in April 1956, the state of New York approved a Sports Authority empowered to condemn land and to sell bonds to provide $30 million for a new stadium. But although the Sports Authority had bipartisan and multireligious backing, it did not have the blessing of Commissioner Moses. . . . It was probably too late anyway because in October 1956 O'Malley sold both Ebbets Field and the Dodgers' Montreal farm club stadium, raising the $4 million he promised to spend on a new stadium.

But if there was any doubt as to where that ballpark would be, February 21, 1957, proved the effective day of disaster for the Brooklyn Dodgers. On that day, the Chicago Cubs and O'Malley jointly announced that the Dodgers had purchased Wrigley Field and the Los Angeles Angels of the PCL in exchange for the Dodgers' Fort Worth franchise in the Class A Texas League and their working agreement with Portland in the PCL. The *Sporting News*, the authoritative baseball weekly, reported that Wrigley had received $3.25 million for his Los Angeles rights. . . .

In late May 1957, at a rare pre-midseason meeting of the National League, the owners brought Pacific Coast expansion even closer by voting unanimously to give the Dodgers permission to move to Los Angeles if they were joined by another club on the West Coast. O'Malley found a willing cohort in his crosstown rival, Horace Stoneham, whose family had owned the New York Giants since the 1920s. The Giants had come to hard times since their 1951 miracle pennant and their 1954 world championship. Fully one-third of their season attendance now came from the appearances of the hated Dodgers. The Polo Grounds ballpark, while far larger than Ebbets Field, was also short on parking space. Stoneham had his eye on Minneapolis, which had just built a new stadium with plenty of parking where the Giants' Triple-A farm team played. But San Francisco was also building a new stadium, and Stoneham was always easily enticed by the charms and business proposals of O'Malley. . . .

It was up to Walter O'Malley to show the world the most convincing display of the untrammeled power of the big-league owner. Appearing before a committee whose chairman's constituency was soon to lose a beloved institution, O'Malley posed as a hardworking businessman who only wanted to improve his facilities but had met rejection by New York City officials. By contrast, Los Angeles was willing to provide land in downtown Los Angeles, a site of 300 acres known as Chavez Ravine. He argued, with perhaps technical accuracy, that he never talked with Los Angeles officials until he saw the New York Sports Authority crumbling into insignificance. He continued, perhaps believing his self-portrait as a homeless waif, that after he sold Ebbets Field, he had "euchred" himself into a position where he had no place to play. Cooperative, friendly Angelenos came along, . . . "the first group of people that came up and showed that they had a little old-fashioned American initiative and whatnot. . . . They showed that they had political unanimity out there . . . and they said, 'We are for you, and when you tell us you don't want us to build you a ballpark, that is most refreshing and amazing.'"

When Cellar tried to get O'Malley to discuss his sizeable profits in Brooklyn, O'Malley countered, "I'm very proud of my profits. . . . It is a good old American custom, and I'm glad I'm doing well," to which Cellar could only reply, "I glory in your profits."

The Giants made their move to San Francisco official in August 1957, while O'Malley waited until the end of the season. . . . Many local L.A. groups considered the Chavez Ravine deal a bad one for the city. . . . Many poor Angelenos felt most of the land should be used for public housing. Their displeasure was fanned by the powerful interests who felt left out by O'Malley's toehold on a territory which was growing by 750 people a day in an area of already more than 5,000,000 people.

This clash of the temporary interest of rich and poor forced a referendum on the Chavez Ravine deal in June 1958. O'Malley wanted to keep a low profile in the campaign, but when the polls indicated he might lose, he went before the TV cameras in May to announce that he would provide free home television of eight of the Dodger road games in San Francisco. He also denied as a "red herring" the charge that he planned to boost his fortune from underground oil rights at Chavez Ravine.

His first months in California were thus uneasy. Only the attendance met expectations. Choosing to play in the cavernous Memorial Coliseum, a track and football oval, the Dodgers broke all attendance records. But they had to play on a bizarre field with a huge right-field area and a tiny left-field corner, which was buttressed by a 140-foot-long and 40-foot-high fence which some wags compared to the Brooklyn Bridge. The team's performance suffered surprisingly, as they plunged to seventh in 1958. . . .

But O'Malley had not made his daring move to fail. His TV appearance helped to swing the referendum his way by a narrow 25,000 votes. . . . Although a local court temporarily enjoined construction because of the priority of public housing on the land, a superior court overturned the decision. After all the delays, Walter O'Malley's dream Dodger Stadium, 55,000-seat jewel with room for 24,000 cars, opened in 1962. . . .

The O'Malley caper and its success left a lasting imprint on big-league baseball. It proved that the franchise rights and the ability to attract radio–television packages were more important than any community loyalties or concern for orderly minor–major league realignment. In one act, the move of the Giants and Dodgers disrupted the Pacific Coast League, which soon found its franchises stretching from Phoenix to Vancouver. . . . Although O'Malley and Stoneham had to share a $900,000 indemnity to the PCL for encroachment upon their territory, O'Malley was waiting to even that score. When the American League decided to expand to 10 teams for the 1961 season, it chose Los Angeles as a new city, in addition to Minneapolis–St. Paul. . . . Although Commissioner Frick considered Los Angeles an "open city," O'Malley insisted he was owed an indemnity. Before the American League Los Angeles Angels came into existence, the new ownership had to pay O'Malley a lump sum $100,000 . . . while agreeing to be his tenant in the New Dodger Stadium at a hefty rental of $200,000, plus a percentage of the concessions. . . .

Looking back at Walter O'Malley's momentous move in 1957, the words of veteran sports observer Lester Rodney resound: "This is not a very sentimental way of life, this get yours arrangement." So do the words of Arthur Mann's ignored plaint to the Cellar Committee, "I am a writer trying to tell the public that this is a national pastime, that it has certain quasi-public features to it, that the obligation to the public must be uppermost in any baseball operator's mind."

WALTER O'MALLEY WAS RIGHT

Paul Hirsch

Few men in sports history have been vilified to the extent Walter O'Malley was when he moved the Brooklyn Dodgers to Los Angeles in 1957. Over recent decades, New York City Parks commissioner Robert Moses has begun to share some, if not all, of the blame for the Dodgers' move. Countless trees have died supporting the contention that either O'Malley ripped the franchise from the bosom of a borough that has never recovered its identity or self-esteem, or that Moses did not understand the value of keeping the Dodgers in Brooklyn and was unnecessarily obstinate when it came to reaching a mutually satisfactory agreement with O'Malley to keep the team in the city. The purpose of this article is to provide a more dispassionate account without the assigning of blame and arrive at some conclusions regarding what choices O'Malley had to make when he brought Major League Baseball to Southern California.

From 1946 through 1957, the Brooklyn Dodgers won more games than any other franchise in the National League and were arguably the loop's most exciting team. Only the Yankees won more. The Dodgers were loaded with diverse and interesting personalities who immersed themselves in the community, and the core players were virtually constant over that entire period. A decade or more of success with basically the same crew meant one thing: On-field personnel were getting too old to maintain a championship level of play. By 1957, Pee Wee Reese was 38, Roy Campanella 35, Carl Furillo 35, Sal Maglie 39, Gil Hodges 33, and even the relative youngsters, Duke Snider, Carl Erskine, and Don Newcombe, were past 30.

Paul Hirsch, "Walter O'Malley Was Right," *National Pastime: A Review of Baseball History* 40 (Summer 2011): 61–63. Reprinted with permission from the Society for American Baseball Research with special thanks to Celia Tan.

216

In early 1957 Sandy Koufax and Don Drysdale were nothing more than promising youngsters; Johnny Podres was in the Navy; Maury Wills, John Roseboro, and Tommy Davis were minor leaguers; Wally Moon was a Cardinal; Ron Fairly and Frank Howard were in college; and Willie Davis hadn't finished high school. With all due respect to Brooklyn's regular second baseman, Jim Gilliam, he was hardly a cornerstone franchise player. No one could have known that this group would dominate the National League from 1962 through 1966.

It's one thing to lose games and quite another to struggle with the balance sheet when baseball is the family business. In Brooklyn, the history was either contention or bankruptcy. When the team went 20 years between pennants before 1941, it landed in receivership, and major decisions were being made or influenced by the Brooklyn Trust Company. Attendance dipped under 500,000 five times during this period.

Walter O'Malley was also justified in considering a move from Ebbets Field. By 1957, the right-field screen hung in tatters, the bathroom odors were stifling, and parking was available for only 700 cars. In 2003, Buzzie Bavasi wrote, "Ebbets Field was a great place to watch a game if you were sitting in the first 12 rows between the bases. Otherwise, we had narrow seats, narrow aisles, and a lot of obstructed views."

Mid-1950s attendance compared with the Dodgers' primary rivals of that time was also disturbing. From a high of 1.8 million in 1947, as the team won five more pennants and finished second three other times, Dodger attendance dwindled. When the Boston Braves moved to Milwaukee before the 1953 season, a worrisome situation grew dire.

Lower attendance compared with the primary competition meant fewer concessions sold, less money available for player procurement and development, and was perhaps a sign of waning interest. On the last Wednesday of the 1956 season, with the defending world champions one-half game out of first place, the day after Maglie had thrown a no-hitter, the Dodgers drew 7,847 to Ebbets Field. Player procurement would be more important than ever as the team rebuilt, and O'Malley would have been justified in worrying that he wouldn't have the cash to compete.

But wait, O'Malley critics claim the Dodgers were profitable during this period. They are right, but the claim is not as straightforward as it might seem. In 1955, for example, the Dodgers earned $787,155 from WOR TV. They accomplished that by televising all home games and 20 road games. Yet, in August 1955, Yankees owner Dan Topping was working hard to convince O'Malley and Giants owner Horace Stoneham to curtail or eliminate the practice of televising home games. O'Malley was receptive, in part because he believed the televising of home games cut into concession revenue, casting doubt on the net profit of the WOR deal. That income was crucial to the franchise's profitability. The importance O'Malley placed on concession revenue could be seen in his willingness to make every Saturday home date a Ladies' Day in 1956 and 1957, when female fans were admitted at no charge.

Brooklyn's net income from 1952–1956 ranged from a low of $209,979 in 1954 to a high of $487,462 in 1956, when Brooklyn hosted four World Series games. With an aging, deteriorating team and ballpark, slipping attendance, and the TV revenue in question, there was plenty of cause for concern in the Dodgers business office.

Another element of the profitability question had to do with Walter O'Malley's vision for his franchise. He needed profits to help build a new ballpark, regardless of where it was located. A new ballpark was his best chance of continuing to compete well in a three- or even a two-team market given that fans were staying away from Ebbets Field despite the winning ways of the team on the field. If fewer games were made available to television, and ticket and concession revenue declines were not reversed, it was debatable how much longer the franchise would be viable playing at Ebbets Field.

O'Malley was a devout capitalist, and that no doubt drove him. Yet finances were not his only problem. To build a new stadium in Brooklyn, he needed a cooperative city government. That's where he ran up against Robert Moses. As the head of many public agencies, including the cash cow Triborough Bridge Authority, Moses was the most powerful public works administrator in New York City. By all accounts, his influence was far-reaching and abundant . . . and he and O'Malley did not see eye-to-eye on the Dodgers' needs. In divorce court, this dichotomy might be classified as "irreconcilable differences." Moses's influence was such that nothing as significant as a major-league stadium could be built without his cooperation and approval. O'Malley owned the Dodgers, and his primary recourse was to move the franchise. Moses and Mayor Robert Wagner did not believe that the political fallout from losing National League baseball would be enough to cost them power. They were proved right about that.

Wagner's opponent in the November 1957 mayoral election, held about six weeks after the Dodgers and Giants played their last games in New York and well after their exodus had been confirmed, received fewer votes than Wagner's 1953 opponent. Brooklyn voters, meanwhile, gave Wagner a plurality of more than 330,000 votes. A reasonable person might wonder how much the typical Brooklyn resident cared about retaining the Dodgers. Moses did not face elections and retained enough influence to remain in power well into the next decade. The two had simply read the tea leaves and determined that there was no pressing need to keep the Dodgers and Giants in New York on anything other than the city's terms.

In *Twilight Teams*, his excellent accounting of postwar Major League Baseball franchise shifts through 1971, author Jeffrey Saint John Stuart makes the point that generally the new city made more attractive offers than the city from which a team was leaving. While Moses, Wagner, and other officials dithered in New York, Mayor Norris Paulson, Supervisor Kenneth Hahn, and Councilwoman Rosalind Wyman put together an offer in Los Angeles that was too attractive for O'Malley to dismiss. Space limitations preclude a detailed accounting of that offer, but suffice to say that the Dodgers wound up in 1962 with a privately owned, 56,000-seat stadium at the confluence of several major freeways surrounded by 16,000 parking spaces. Dodger Stadium remains functional and attractive to this day. Moses's vision, which turned into Shea Stadium in 1964, "looked old the day it opened," according to New York sportswriter Leonard Koppett. Shea was closed after the 2008 season and torn down that winter.

Those who have complained the longest and the loudest about O'Malley (primarily Dick Young, Dave Anderson, and Roger Kahn) were New York sportswriters left with less to cover. Rumblings about a move out of Brooklyn had begun in 1953, and Dodgers fans had responded by attending fewer games despite the team's success. New York officials were circumspect in their dealings with the Dodgers, while Los Angeles politicians were highly cooperative, if not downright accommodating. On top of all that, moving to Los Angeles meant that O'Malley would have the third largest city in the United States all to himself in terms of Major League Baseball.

If one views a baseball franchise as a public trust, then a case can be made that the Dodgers should have stayed in Brooklyn and taken what they could get in New York. If one views owning a baseball franchise as a competitive, profit-driven enterprise, then moving to Los Angeles was probably the best baseball-related gift O'Malley could give his family. In this case, at that time, for this author, the offer to move to Los Angeles made too much sense for O'Malley to ignore. The situation in Brooklyn was deteriorating and looked to get only worse, at least in the short term. It would have been an act of irresponsibility towards his stockholders and his family to remain in Brooklyn.

Despite all the finger-pointing over the past 54 years, it is very possible that there is no villain in the case of the Dodgers relocating to Southern California. It may be nothing more than reasonable people with understandable motivation responding rationally to a unique set of circumstances.

Sources

The 1980 Baseball Dope Book. Sporting News. 1980.

Brooklyn Dodger Yearbooks, 1956–1957.

D'Antonio, Michael. *Forever Blue.* Riverhead Books. 2009.

Fetter, Henry D. "Revising the Revisionists, Walter O'Malley, Robert Moses, and the End of the Brooklyn Dodgers." *New York History,* Winter 2008.

Goldblatt, Andrew. *The Giants and the Dodgers.* McFarland & Co. 2003.

Golenbock, Peter. *Bums: An Oral History of the Brooklyn Dodgers.* Putnam. 1984.

Kahn, Roger. *The Boys of Summer.* Harper and Row. 1971.

Kahn, Roger, and Al Helfer. *The Mutual Baseball Almanac.* Doubleday & Co. 1954.

Los Angeles Dodger Yearbooks, 1958–1962.

McGee, Bob. *The Greatest Ballpark Ever.* Rutgers University Press. 2005.

Moses, Robert. "The Battle of Brooklyn." *Sports Illustrated.* 22 July 1957.

Murphy, Robert E. *After Many a Summer.* Union Square. 2009.

Schiffer, Don, editor. *The Major League Baseball Handbook, 1961.* Thomas Nelson & Sons. 1961.

Stuart, Jeffrey Saint John. *Twilight Teams.* Sark Publishing. 2000.

Sullivan, Neal. *The Dodgers Move West.* Oxford University Press. 1987.

Baseball-reference.com.

Retrosheet.org.

WalterOMalley.com.

Personal conversation with Leonard Koppett. 2002.

E-mail exchanges with Buzzie Bavasi. 2001–2008.

CHAPTER 9

The End of Baseball Innocence, 1978–1994

Baseball Turns Sour

The late 1970s and early 1980s were some of the most traumatic years in U.S. history. The aftermath of the Vietnam War, which ended in 1975, left a sour mood among Americans. Combined with the Watergate scandal, these two events created a cynical attitude on the part of the public with regard to politics. At the same time, the U.S. economy, which had thrived since the end of World War II, suddenly was struck by runaway inflation beginning in 1972. The causes were obvious but difficult to do anything about. There were two oil crises, in 1973 and 1979, which shocked the American public with its love affair with the automobile. Lyndon Johnson's "Great Society," which tried to combine "Guns and Butter," was never sufficiently funded. Combined with the costs of the war in Vietnam, these two occurrences struck the U.S. economy hard.

By the end of the 1970s, the nation was experiencing something new and ugly: high unemployment, high inflation, and no growth. Economists christened it "stagflation," and it left the nation in a bad mood. Inflation had risen from 3.3 percent in early 1972 to 12.35 percent by late 1974. And that was only the beginning. As a result of the second oil crisis of 1979, the inflation rate reached 14.8 percent by early 1980. Unemployment, which stayed historically low throughout most the postwar period, suddenly shot up from 5 percent in 1972 to double digits for part of 1982. The danger with stagflation was that real income for the average American didn't keep up and actually fell for part of the 1970s. This was something that truly angered the public.

Later in the decade, President Jimmy Carter would speak to the American public about what was happening in the nation; it was labeled his "malaise" speech. The public blamed the politicians for their woes. Out of that emerged

221

the conservative movement of the 1970s, which eventually brought Ronald Reagan to the presidency, preaching a new sense of optimism that America's best days were ahead. The economy was fueled by the Reagan tax cuts and the ruthless cutting of inflation by the Federal Reserve Board, enabling Reagan to win reelection in 1984 on the slogan, "It's morning again in America."

A sour attitude carried over to baseball as it had on every level of American society, despite the fact that the 15 years from 1978 to 1993—there was a strike that wiped out part of the 1981 season and an even more disastrous one in 1994—were some of the most prosperous in baseball history. Despite free agency, baseball was not dominated by one or two teams. The American League prevailed in the World Series during those years, winning nine and losing six. But interestingly, nine different teams in both leagues won pennants during that period. After 1981, George Steinbrenner's Yankees were broken up and didn't win another pennant until the late 1990s.

No team dominated in the National League either. Los Angeles won three pennants and two World Series, while the Cardinals also won three pennants but only one World Series. Kansas City won its first pennant in 1980, only to lose to the Phillies, who won their first World Series. Five years later, Kansas City won it all. Minnesota, who had won nothing since 1965, won two World Series during this 15-year period. The competitive balance was better than it had ever been, and fans responded enthusiastically.

Some baseball commentators believed it was precisely free agency that had spawned this balance. That certainly was the case if one is calculating the contributions of such superstars as Reggie Jackson and Catfish Hunter to the Yankees in the 1970s, when the team became a powerhouse once again. In 1979, the Phillies benefited from signing Pete Rose, who helped them get to and win the World Series in 1980. Steve Garvey probably was a significant factor in getting San Diego to the World Series in 1984, and the Mets would not have won without Gary Carter behind the plate in 1986, and Keith Hernandez at first, although they came by way of trade. But, in general, the best teams filled in here and there with free agents but still built from their farm systems or by making shrewd trades. The Cardinals, for instance, got Willie McGee from the Yankees in a trade, and he was instrumental in helping them become one of the best teams in the National League in the early to mid-1980s. The Cubs would not have gotten to the playoffs in 1984 without Ryne Sandberg, who they stole from the Phillies in a 1982 trade, and pitcher Rick Sutcliffe, who came to them from Cleveland.

Despite this, the argument made by management was that free agency was ruining baseball, a view difficult to maintain in the face of a decade's attendance that shattered past records. Major League Baseball drew 459 million fans during the 1980s, and that includes the strike season of 1981, when they lost a third of a season. The increase over the past decade was 120 million, a record up to that time. The Dodgers were the big winners in attendance, attracting 30 million for the decade, or an average of 3 million fans a season. The Angels, Cardinals, Phillies, Mets, and Yankees together drew more than 20 million fans during the decade. The 2 million mark was no longer remarkable. Now even the 3 million mark was reached 11 times.[1]

The late 1970s and first half the 1980s saw some the most exciting baseball in years. The game was populated with great players, including such future Hall of Famers as Mike Schmidt, Steve Carlton, Tom Seaver, Andre Dawson, Gary Carter, and Eddie Murray, to note just a few. The 1980s would witness no less than five pitchers become 300-game winners, something baseball would not see again until the first decade of the twenty-first century, when Tom Glavine, Greg Maddux, and Roger Clemens joined that exclusive club. Mike Schmidt topped the 500-homer mark, a level not achieved since Willie Mays and Hank Aaron did it in the late 1960s. Moreover, as had happened in the past, baseball renewed itself, producing a handful of fresh talent. There were hitters like Wade Boggs, Don Mattingly, Darryl Strawberry, and Tony Gwynn, and pitchers like Roger Clemens, Fernando Valenzuela, and Jack Morris. There were great pennant races during these years and exciting World Series, with teams who had never won a pennant or World Series winning both.

In the game, pitching dominated, as it hadn't since the expansion of the strikezone in the early 1960s. In the 1982 World Series, Cardinals pitching shut down a great-hitting Milwaukee team. In 1988, Dodgers pitcher Orel Hershiser gave one of the most remarkable performances ever. He went 23–8 but, more impressively, broke the record for consecutive scoreless innings, with 59. He also led the league with eight shutouts and 15 complete games, topping off that incredible season by winning three games in the playoffs and World Series, while compiling an ERA of just over 1.00. He won the Cy Young Award running away.

The 1986 World Series was one of the most exciting in baseball history. The Boston Red Sox, who hadn't won a Series since 1918, seemed on their way to defeating a young New York Mets team. Leading in Game 6 of the Series with two out in the 10th, they saw the Mets rally and win the game on an easy ground ball that rolled through the legs of first baseman Bill Buckner. The next night, the Mets beat the Red Sox to win the Series. It looked like the "Curse of the Bambino" still prevailed.

The other remarkable aspect of 1980s baseball was the return of the running game. Once again, as it had when Maury Wills and Lou Brock ran wild in the 1960s, the stolen base gained in popularity. In 1980, three men stole more than 90 bases, one of whom was Rickey Henderson, who pilfered 100. That had never happened before. Henderson would exceed that total twice, including a record 130 in 1982. Tim Raines of the Expos would set a rookie record for stolen bases with 71 in 1981, during which time he played in just 88 games. Juan

Samuel of the Phillies would break that record in 1984. Raines would steal 70 or more bases for six consecutive seasons. Vince Coleman, a light-hitting outfielder with the Cardinals, would steal over 100 bases in each of his first three years in the majors. Some ballparks, especially those with AstroTurf, seemed tailored for the running game.

To some extent, this revived running game was the result of the growing use of artificial turf in the new stadiums that opened in the 1970s and 1980s. Artificial turf made for a faster game because there were none of the idiosyncrasies of the old-fashioned parks. No longer could the grounds crew doctor a field to suit a particular team, as the Dodgers had in the 1960s when they had speedsters like Willie Davis and Wills playing for them. The area around first base was kept hard so that Davis and Wills could get a quick start. With AstroTurf, that kind of thing was not possible. But as the Cardinals proved under manager Whitey Herzog, you could tailor a field to suit you and build a team to take advantage of the new, fast turf.

The Cardinals team from 1982 to 1987 featured speed at the expense of power. They were christened the "Running Redbirds." In 1982, when they won the World Series against the Milwaukee Brewers, they hit just 67 home runs, while stealing 200 bases. Milwaukee hit 216 homers, stole 84 bases, and lost. The Cardinals stole more than 300 bases when they won the National League pennant in 1985. Every team tried to duplicate the Cardinals' formula but with varying degrees of success in the 1980s. Just about every team used the stolen base to one degree or another. No other team, however, lived and died with the stolen base as had the Cardinals. In 1982, National League teams stole almost 1,800 bases, while the American League had 1,400. The stolen base was back with a vengeance, and it helped return excitement to baseball.

Home runs also were up during the decade. The 40-homer mark was topped 15 times. League totals stayed at all-time high levels of more than 1,000 per league until the remarkable 1987 season, when the National League totaled 1,800 home runs, while the American League hit an incredible 2,634. There is no simple explanation for this, although some baseball writers believed the ball was made livelier, as had been suspected in past seasons, for instance, 1930, when all kinds of hitting records were established. Others attributed the rise in home runs to the smaller stadiums, but most of them had been around for years. It is interesting that the home run totals dropped considerably in the following seasons, although they were still being slugged at a high level when compared to the past. It is also worth noting that attendance increased by almost 10 percent in 1987 compared to the previous season. Fans still loved the long ball.[2]

The 1980s also witnessed some exciting World Series. The 1986 World Series saw one of the most incredible postseason games ever played, one that rivaled Bobby Thomson's game-winning home run in the 1951 playoff. With Boston leading the Mets in the World Series three games to two, the Red Sox scored two runs to take a 5–3 lead. With two outs and no one on in the bottom of the 10th, the Mets scored three runs, the last scoring on a ground ball that went through the legs of first baseman Bill Buckner. The Mets won the title two nights later. Two years later, the Dodgers took Game 1 against the Oakland A's when the injured Kirk Gibson came off the bench to hit a game-winning, two-out home run against one of the best relief pitchers in baseball history, future Hall of Famer Dennis Eckersley. Five years later, Joe Carter of Toronto won the World Series with a ninth-inning home run off Phillies pitcher Mitch Williams.

Fans loved the game and turned out in record numbers. Baseball was gaining a wider following in the 1980s because of the greater use of television. Beginning in the 1980s, the rise of the so-called Super Stations was sending the game throughout the country. Led by Ted Turner's WTBS and Chicago's WGN, fans in every part of the country could watch games just about every day. Yankees and Mets games were also televised nationally for a time in the 1980s. This forced just about every team to systematize the televising of their games so as not to lose audiences to the Braves and Cubs. These local arrangements brought in more money for certain teams. The Yankees signed a lucrative contract to televise their games in the New York area, while the Phillies did the same for the tristate region of Pennsylvania, New Jersey, and Delaware.

In 1980, Commissioner Bowie Kuhn, in one of his last successful actions, negotiated a national television contract worth $43 million. By 1993, that figure had risen to $377 million. Everything pointed to the prosperity of baseball at record levels. The highest price paid for a baseball franchise in the past had been the $11 million CBS paid for the Yankees in 1964. It took 13 years for that figure to be topped. Then in the so-called troubled days of baseball in the 1980s, with the threat of strikes looming, the value of franchises skyrocketed. In 1991, the sale of Montreal reached the $100 million plateau, and three years later, Baltimore commanded $174 million. When the Florida Marlins and Colorado Rockies were admitted to the National League in 1993, the price of admission was $95 million.[3] Thirty years earlier, the entrance fee for the Mets and Houston in the National League had been $2 million. Baseball was rolling in money. Yet, the owners were deeply unhappy.

CIVIL WAR IN BASEBALL

What really bothered baseball management was that they had lost control of the game to the players and to Marvin Miller, who they had turned into their personal enemy. Once management had lost the argument concerning free agency, they became obsessed with trying to regain the position of dominance they had held for so long. Management was equally obsessed with winning a victory against the players. This led them to make some catastrophic decisions.

Labor relations issues after free agency saw a continued improvement of the player's position. Pension issues that had once been crucial in all player management disputes became less important as baseball salaries steadily rose. Salary questions were at the heart of baseball's labor wars now. Arbitration decisions had tended to favor the players. The minimum salary continued a slow rise throughout the late 1970s into the 1980s: The figure increased from $19,000 in the late 1970s to $35,000 by 1983. The latter would have been considered a lucrative salary before the start of free agency. Minimum salaries were elevated by the explosion of baseball salaries during these years. At the end of World War II, the average salary in baseball was about $13,000. It slowly rose during the next 25 years and, after free agency, reached $121,000 in 1979, and an incredible $1.7 million on the eve of the strike of 1994.

This improvement in the player's economic situation did not come at the expense of management profits. From the late 1970s to the strike year of 1994, management had some of its most profitable years, with gross revenue rising from $422 million in 1982 to $1,880 million just before the strike of 1994. The problem wasn't baseball's profitability. Rather, it was the owner's sense that the sport was slipping out of their control. Management acted as if the most important thing was a victory against Marvin Miller and the Players' Association. This mindset fueled their actions from baseball's first major strike of 1981 to the second disastrous one of 1994.

In 1980, the owners decided on a showdown with Miller and the Players' Union. They built up a strike fund of $30 million and forced the issue with the union by demanding major changes in the labor management agreement, especially on the question of compensation for losing free agents. Clubs that lost a player to free agency, they insisted, had to be compensated in some way for the player. Miller rejected this and saw compensation as a way of discouraging free agency. Negotiations went on through 1980 and early 1981, with neither side budging. On June 11, 1981, the players went on strike and were in decent shape financially, having collected almost half of their salary, which was paid out during a six-month period during the baseball season. At the time of the strike, slightly more than a third of the season had been played.

The strike ended when the owners' strike fund ran out of money, and the season would be renewed with about one-third left to play. Management had lost on the major issues, a result of seriously underestimating the players' unity, especially now that Miller had won their loyalty. As a result of the increase in salaries and lucrative endorsements he had won for them, the players were able to survive a strike and come away unharmed.[4]

As a result of the strike, a complicated system was set up to create a pool of players from which a team that lost someone to free agency could be compensated. An All-Star Game would open the remainder of the 1981 season, and the teams that led their divisions at the beginning of the strike would play the winners of the second half of the season before moving on to the World Series. It was an awkward solution, but it worked fairly well.

One of the first casualties of the 1981 strike was Commissioner Kuhn. He had done a good job during his first term in office, signing a lucrative television deal for baseball and modernizing the commissioner's office, but he was seen as too interfering by the owners during his second term. He had run afoul of them by interfering in what the owners believed was their prerogative. When Charlie Finley of the Oakland A's began selling off his players in the mid-1970s, Kuhn cancelled those sales as not being in the best interests of baseball. While the owners had no love for Finley, they resented Kuhn's interference in what they considered their private affairs. They were correct in one sense because in the past, owners such as Connie Mack had sold off their stars when their contracts became too costly.

Kuhn resigned in 1984, and the owners turned to a baseball outsider, as they had disastrously with General Eckert. This time they were looking for someone with a mastery of public relations, and they settled on Peter Ueberroth. Ueberroth had managed the highly successful 1984 Olympics in Los Angles. He had actually turned a profit with his ability to commercialize and merchandize just about every aspect of the Olympic Games. He was a handsome, domineering executive who knew virtually nothing about baseball. He quickly formed an opinion bordering on contempt for the baseball owners who had hired him.

Ueberroth dealt with a number of minor issues and then, with baseball thriving, negotiated a new contract with the Players' Union in 1985, avoiding another strike. He also signed an even more lucrative television deal than Kuhn had. During his tenure, the drug issue surfaced in a major way. This time the drug of choice was cocaine. Baseball had turned a blind eye to alcoholism in the past and tacitly accepted "greenies," or amphetamines, which were popular in the 1960s and 1970s. Cocaine was a raging problem not only among baseball players, but also throughout the country in the 1980s.[5]

The issue broke into the open in September 1985, as a result of a Pittsburgh grand jury investigation into the use of cocaine among a group of players. The drugs were supplied by clubhouse men for various teams. The players involved were some of the biggest names in baseball. They included future Hall of Famer Tim Raines; two former batting champs, Keith Hernandez and Willie Wilson; Mets slugger Darryl Strawberry; catcher Darrel Porter; and Dodgers relief pitcher Steve Howe. Raines admitted that he kept a vile of cocaine in his back pocket and joked that he slid headfirst to avoid breaking it.

During the grand jury investigation, in which, in return for speaking publicly, the players were granted immunity, Hernandez estimated that 40 percent of the players were using cocaine. That figure is believed to be exaggerated but is an indication of how serious the problem was. With public relations in mind, Commissioner Ueberroth suspended the players and commuted their sentences in exchange for donating 10 percent of their salaries to antidrug programs and doing major community service. The cocaine issue gradually disappeared as baseball found other drugs to flirt with.[6]

Cocaine took its toll. Steven Howe was suspended seven times for drug use, and each time the union interceded on his behalf, a mistake they would come to regret. Howe battled alcohol and drug use for the rest of his life, dying at age 48, in a car accident, while inebriated. Rod Scurry, a talented relief pitcher for the Pirates, died from a cocaine-related heart attack at 36. Darryl Porter admitted he had a $1,000-a-week cocaine habit. He died of an overdose in the front seat of his car at 50. The cocaine issue was never dealt with effectively by Major League Baseball or the Players' Union. Both, in effect, turned a blind eye to the problem. They would pay a heavier price later.

While perhaps the most devastating blow to the game was the abuse of drugs, which became commonplace from the 1970s onward, baseball players had been using some kind of artificial stimulation since the beginning of the sport. After World War II, for example, "greenies," or amphetamines, were found in every clubhouse and used by players to improve performance. But alcohol was baseball's drug of choice. There was a long line of distinguished players who were heavy drinkers and some who were confirmed alcoholics. The problem was usually winked at by management and even society. When Jim Bouton published his expose of baseball, *Ball Four*, in which he revealed that Mickey Mantle was drunk during a game, fans were outraged at the demeaning of a hero, but they weren't shocked. They knew Mantle was just one of a long line of "drinking men."

In the 1960s and 1970s, baseball players, like other young Americans, began using marijuana. Much more seriously, the spread in popularity of cocaine and other hard drugs in the 1970s and 1980s caused tremendous harm to the sport. For almost 20 years, attempts to deal with the problem rationally proved fruitless. The Players' Union, in particular, was viewed by the public as defending players who should have been disciplined for their actions. The union and management could never reach agreement on a lasting program to deal with drug abuse. The union was especially sensitive to calls for testing, which they argued was subject to abuse. Baseball had a black eye in the 1990s that it would need to treat with serious and painful medicine.

While baseball was congratulating itself for getting the cocaine issue out of the way, Ueberroth made his last and most disastrous contribution to the sport.

He advised the owners that the way to control free agency was to avoid competing for the top players. What he labeled economic restraint, the union regarded as collusion among the owners. When virtually no offers were made to those who reached free agency status in 1985, the union went to court, arguing that the owners were conspiring among themselves to control costs. According to the existing collective bargaining agreement, the issue was sent to a neutral arbitrator, who eventually ruled that the owners had colluded and assessed a fine of $280 million. That was enough to sour the owners on Ueberroth, who had lost interest in baseball. He had developed political ambitions, aiming at running for the Senate from California. That never panned out. He resigned in 1988, before the owners had a chance to fire him.

As his replacement, they chose a well-known baseball fan with impeccable credentials, A. Bartlett Giamatti, former president of Yale. Giamatti loved baseball and often rhapsodized about its role in defining American culture. He was also a fan with a limited recognition of the sordid side of baseball's economic situation. Before he had hardly settled into office, he was confronted with a major crisis. Pete Rose, one of the most popular players of his generation and now manager of the Cincinnati Reds, was accused of betting on baseball games. Rose didn't deny betting on sports but adamantly claimed that he never bet on baseball. After an investigation in the summer of 1989, Giamatti banished Rose from baseball activities ostensibly for life. Rose agreed to not appeal, and it was believed after a period of time and by expressing contrition Rose would be reinstated. But in September 1989, Giamatti died, and the commissioner's job was passed on to his assistant, a corporation lawyer, Fay Vincent.

Vincent believed he could restore confidence in baseball by acting like a stern commissioner. He ordered a further investigation, and the Rose issue only festered, with both sides denouncing one another. When Rose was later jailed for income tax evasion for not reporting money earned from signing autographs at card shows, this confirmed Vincent's determination to keep Rose out of baseball.[7] Rose didn't help matters by refusing to accept responsibility for his actions.

While the Rose issue remained unresolved, Vincent stumbled into the next great labor-management fight. He saw his role as similar to Judge Kenesaw Landis, as having the right to act in the "best interests of baseball," a phrase he liked to repeat. The owners hadn't been concerned with his actions in the Rose case, but they had no intention of letting Vincent speak for them in labor-management negotiations, especially when he showed signs of sympathy toward some of the union's demands. The baseball owners had already had one Judge Landis and didn't want another. They forced Vincent's resignation on September 8, 1992, replacing him with a committee made up of the presidents of both leagues, plus a group of owners. They named one of their own, Milwaukee's Bud Selig, as acting commissioner.

The owners, who had lost every battle with the Players' Association, were now determined to have yet another showdown. Their focus would be a demand for revenue-sharing, along with a cap on salaries, something other sports had adopted. In return, they offered the Players' Association nothing tangible. Donald Fehr, Miller's successor as head of the association, was an irascible individual and adamantly rejected these demands, arguing that they were nothing less than an attempt to roll back rights the players had won since the end of the reserve clause.

Negotiations were fruitless, and both sides prepared for a strike. Attempts at mediation, one of which was a feeble effort by President Bill Clinton, accomplished little. Well-known labor mediator William Usery met with both sides but could make no progress toward a solution. After an exciting 1993 season, which saw record-setting attendance, both sides planned for a strike in 1994. That season opened with indications of another record-breaking year. The Montreal Expos had put together one of the best teams in recent years and looked to bring a pennant, if not a World Series, to Canada. Tony Gwynn of San Diego was threatening the .400 mark in batting, and Matt Williams of the Giants was ahead of Babe Ruth's home run pace. But on August 12, the season ended. There was hope that the World Series might be played using the teams in first place when the strike began, but that proved futile. For the first time since 1904, the World Series, played even during two World Wars, was cancelled. Baseball's statistical sanctity also was shattered again. For the second time, the first being during the 1981 strike, the baseball season was not completed.

During the winter, both sides dug in their heels, although negotiations were held on an irregular basis. The owners announced if there was no agreement, they would start the 1995 season using replacement players. This was a foolhardy action given the ridicule professional football had suffered when it resorted to replacement players during the 1987 season. It seemed that management had learned nothing, not only from past strike threats, but also from a disaster in another professional sport.

The threat to use "scabs" outraged the Players' Association and was ridiculed by fans, sportswriters, and even some politicians who got into the act. In 1995, spring training opened with replacement players. Some owners were unhappy, one of whom was Baltimore's Peter Angelos, who announced he would not use replacements. According to Canadian law, strike breakers couldn't be used, so Toronto also rejected replacement players. The highly respected Sparky Anderson, manager of the Detroit Tigers, refused to report to spring training, saying he wanted no part of this brand of baseball.

In March 1995, the Players' Association took their case to the National Labor Relations Board. The board, after an investigation, filed a preliminary injunction accusing management of failing to bargain in good faith. When management appealed that decision, the case reached U.S. district judge Sonia

Sotomayor. She, in turn, upheld the injunction and excoriated management for putting the entire "concept of collective bargaining on trial." Although management appealed Judge Sotomayor's decision, it was upheld by the Court of Appeals for the Second Circuit, which also denounced management for not bargaining honestly.[8]

Baseball had survived its second strike but was left in a parlous state. The 1994 strike was a catastrophe for the sport. It showed that both sides, owners and players, were more interested in their own personal goals than the game itself. The mystique of baseball, which had survived the Black Sox Scandal, tales of alcohol and drug abuse, and now a second strike, was in danger of losing the fans' trust. If there ever was a doubt about baseball being big business, the 1994 strike ended it. Dave Anderson, sports columnist for the *New York Times*, wrote that the sense of gloom that hung over baseball was worse than during the Black Sox Scandal. He didn't see any Babe Ruth in the offing.[9]

Baseball was under a cloud after 1994. When the 1995 season started, fans stayed away. Total attendance for the season was 20 million less than the peak in 1993. It would be years before baseball would recapture the enthusiasm of the past.

THE STATE OF BASEBALL IN THE 1990S

A new basic agreement left the status of baseball basically the same as it was before the 1994 strike. Many of the major questions between the owners and the union remained unresolved. The agreement was renewed in 2000, without the threat of a strike, although some owners still sought a showdown.

As baseball entered the twenty-first century, on the surface the sport seemed to have recovered, with booming attendance figures and huge sums of money flowing in from television; however, the cloud hanging over the game since the 1970s had not dissipated. A combination of factors was robbing the sport of its luster, some of it the result of the transfer of power from the owners to the players. The emphasis on big money alienated many fans, not because they begrudged the players the huge salaries, but rather because the priority shifted from the field to off-the-field financial negotiations. Players had always made more money than the average fan, but now the gap was in the millions. It put the players on a different plane, one that few fans could fully grasp.

Free agency had been a boon to the players and was the key to the rapid rise in baseball salaries. But there was a price, as players jumped from team to team in pursuit of the best offer. Fan loyalty, often unrealistic when it came to the nature of the sport, was challenged when players frequently switched teams. One of the first things that stabilized baseball in the nineteenth century was the crackdown on jumping from team to team. The reserve clause was erected to stop that. Now the reserve clause was gone, and players took advantage of their right to pursue better financial terms. It just seemed like disloyalty to their fans.

Even the nature of sportswriting contributed to the negative attitude many fans took toward baseball and sports in general. The great writers of the past, Grantland Rice and Red Smith, were guilty of hyping sports as something almost magical. Smith, who was a tremendous admirer of Joe DiMaggio, was told by his editor when writing about him to "stop goding up the athletes."[10] In the early days of baseball, until the 1960s, the writers exaggerated the exploits of the players and covered up for their flaws and excesses. The prevailing view of the sports fraternity was to cover what happened on the field and little else about the game. It was a version of the old rule "what happens in the clubhouse, stays in the clubhouse." Fans never knew about Babe Ruth's womanizing or the drinking exploits of players in the past.

A new generation of sportswriters, reflecting the change in the nation that had emerged in the 1960s, became critics and not boosters of the game. Sportswriters, often labeled "chipmunks" by traditionalists, became more honest in their reporting, probing the private lives of the players and frequently harping on scandal, while often going to extremes. When one ballplayer mentioned that his wife just had a baby, one of the new sportswriters asked, "Breast or bottle?" It was hardly the kind of question Red Smith would have posed. Part of the price of modern journalism was to demystify the players and thereby baseball itself.

In the 1980s, just as the relationship between players and management reached new lows, Hollywood rediscovered baseball. Hollywood had made baseball-themed movies in the past, most successfully *Pride of the Yankees*, about the life of Lou Gehrig, but it had neglected the sport for years. Sport films were supposed to be poison at the box office. That changed beginning in 1984, with the filming of Bernard Malamud's *The Natural*, featuring one of Hollywood's biggest stars, Robert Redford. Not satisfied with Malamud's ending, where the hero, Roy Hobbs, strikes out, Hollywood had him hit a game-winning home run. That didn't matter, as the film had an aura of accuracy as regards the details of baseball. For the next decade, a string successful baseball films appeared. *Eight Men Out* (1988) told the story of the Black Sox Scandal in dramatic fashion. *Bull Durham*, that same year, was a hugely popular insight into life in the minor leagues and starred another hot Hollywood property, Kevin Costner.

Sports Illustrated named *Bull Durham* one of best sports movies of all time. The next year, Hollywood released two further box-office successes dealing with baseball: the comedy about the rise of a woeful Cleveland team, *Major League*, and a film that captured the mythic quality of baseball, *Field of Dreams*, which also starred Costner. *Field of Dreams* was based on W. P. Kinsella's novel *Shoeless Joe*, about the doomed great hitter of the Black Sox Scandal. The fairy tale-type fable was nominated for three Academy Awards, notably Best Picture. In 1992, a film about women's baseball during World War II, *A League of Their Own*, was a great commercial and critical success. These films were popular with the public, while *Bull Durham*, *Field of Dreams*, and *A League of Their Own* also were critical successes.

Baseball films continued to be a staple of the film industry for the next few years, although none that followed had quite the impact of the first group. Despite that, these films showed that baseball continued to have a deep hold on the imagination of the American public.

Questions for Consideration

1. How did baseball reflect conditions in the United States from 1978 to 1994?
2. Discuss some of the reasons for the transfer of power in baseball from management to labor during the years covered in this chapter.
3. Compare and contrast the baseball strikes of 1981 and 1994. What were the effects of the two strikes? In your estimate, which had the greater consequences for baseball?
4. Outside of labor problems, what were some of the outstanding developments that took place in baseball during the 15 years covered in this chapter?
5. What is the connection, if any, between pitching dominance during the 1978 and 1994 seasons and the state of baseball offense?
6. What were some of the inside-the-game changes that took place between 1978 and 1993? How did they impact the game?
7. Discuss the emergence of popular films about baseball during the 1980s. Why did this happen, and what do these films tell us about baseball?
8. Discuss baseball's experience with alcohol and drugs in the 1980s and 1990s.

Notes

1. "1980–1989 Ballpark Attendance," *Ballparksofbaseball.com*, https://www.ballparksofbaseball.com/1980-1989-mlb-attendance/.

2. Leonard Koppett, *The New Thinking Fan's Guide to Baseball* (New York: Simon & Schuster, 1991) discusses some of the reasons for the increase in baseball offense in the 1980s.

3. Leonard Koppett, *Koppett's Concise History of Major League Baseball* (Philadelphia: Temple University Press, 1998), chapter 24, analyzes the economic side of baseball from 1975 to 1995.

4. Robert F. Burk, *Much More Than a Game: Players, Owners, and American Baseball since 1921* (Chapel Hill: University of North Carolina Press, 2001) provides a good overview of the 1981 strike.

5. For the increase in baseball offense, see Leonard Koppett, *The New Thinking Fan's Guide to Baseball.*

6. Joe Kinsey, "The 1980s MLB Cocaine All-Star Team: When Baseball Was Paranoid and Addicted," *Bustedcoverage.com*, February 9, 2002, https://bustedcoverage .com/2012/02/09/the-1980s-mlb-cocaine-all-star-team-when-baseball-was-paranoid -addicted/ (accessed May 9, 2018); "30 for 30: The Pittsburgh Drug Trials," *Vimeo*, May 2016, https://vimeo.com/140446134 (accessed May 9, 2018).

7. The best treatment of the Rose case can be found in James Reston Jr., *Collision at Home Plate: The Lives of Pete Rose and Bart Giamatti* (Lincoln: University of Nebraska Press, 1997).

8. Koppett, *Koppett's Concise History of Major League Baseball* gives the best overview of the background to the 1994 strike in chapter 25.

9. Dave Anderson, "The Worst Interests of Baseball," *New York Times*, September 8, 1992.

10. Red Smith as told to Jerome Holtzman, "I'm Sure I Contributed to False Values," *Bronx Banter*, May 31, 2013.

THE QUEST OF MARVIN MILLER:
A BRIEFCASE FOR A LANCE

Lawrence Richards

On November 27, 2012, a *New York Times* article was headed, "Marvin Miller, Union Leader Who Changed Baseball, Dies at 95." A respectful, notable headline by all means, but considering Miller's transcending influence, not only on baseball, but on all professional sports, it was somewhat tepid. A few other views:

> Marvin Miller is as important in the history of baseball as Jackie Robinson.—Hank Aaron

> (After Babe Ruth), the second most influential man in the history of baseball.—Red Barber

> No man in our time had more impact on the business of baseball than Marvin Miller.—Tom Seaver

> The most important baseball figure in the last 50 years. He truly emancipated the players.—Fay Vincent

With the reader's permission, one more quote, definitely self-serving:

> The fact of so many knowing so little about Marvin Miller's accomplishments is astounding.—Lawrence Richards

The viselike grip owners maintained over their players in 1966 hadn't changed much since the 1890s. The reserve clause allowed them to keep players indefinitely.

Lawrence Richards, "The Quest of Marvin Miller: A Briefcase for a Lance," *National Pastime Museum*, November 22, 2016, http://www.thenationalpastimemuseum.com/article/quest-marvin-miller-briefcase -lance. Reprinted with the kind permission of the author.

a blatantly unconstitutional state of affairs. Negotiating power? Take the owner's contract offer or don't play. Want to be released, traded, or sold to another team? Only if the club allows. A problem with your team? Go see the commissioner—realistically, an employee of the owners.

In 1966, the minimum annual salary for ballplayers was $6,000, a $1,000 increase from 1946. The uber-rich owners exemplified the Golden Rule. They had the gold; they made the rules. Challenge or complain and face the consequences.

The Players' Union's resources were meager. Established in 1954, the union had less than $5,400 in the bank and no full-time employee. Their primary goal was a modest increase in pension benefits. Players had been told by owners for years that they were lucky to be compensated for playing "a boy's game." Collective bargaining? Huh? What were their alternatives? Return to the farm, the factory, the mine? Risk being fired? They had no negotiating power because the vast consensus was that they had no cards to play. One recalls the lyric of an old Tennessee Ernie Ford tune, "Sixteen Tons," about the plight of coal miners—"I owe my soul to the company store."

In 1966, a committee headed by Robin Roberts was given the task by the Major League Baseball Players Association (MLBPA) to screen candidates for the position of executive director. Roberts knew they needed a bargaining pro; the opposition across the table was entrenched, united, connected—very, very wealthy powerbrokers. To make matters worse, MLBPA members were largely apathetic, generally not well educated, lacking experience with unions, and somewhat suspicious of them in general. Not exactly an easy group to mobilize. Then along came Marvin Miller.

The committee kept hearing recommendations that Miller should be interviewed. His credentials and experience were lauded by many, for good reason. He worked for the National War Labor Board during World War II, negotiated contracts for the International Association of Machinists and United Auto Workers, and served as chief economist and lead negotiator for the United Steelworkers. However, even with these credentials, Roberts had trepidations. Most shared the perception that labor leaders and their minions and union officials in general didn't exactly exemplify model citizens

Let's remember that this was the heyday of John L. Lewis, United Mine Workers; George Meany, AFL-CIO; Mike Quill, NYC Transport Workers; Walter Reuther, United Automobile Workers: and—gulp—Jimmy Hoffa, International Brotherhood of Teamsters. Fiery, high-profile, bombastic men whose reputations included nefarious methods to "get their way." Their range of bargaining chips was extremely varied and persuasive. Some committee members objected: "Anyone from that ilk? C'mon, how is this gonna play from a private and public relations standpoint?" Notwithstanding these concerns, a meeting was arranged.

Miller's demeanor and appearance defied expectations. He was a slightly built man of average height with silver hair and a well-groomed mustache—conservatively dressed. He was quiet, mildmannered, soft-spoken, and listened carefully to all that was said. He seemed more suited to academia than the arena of no-holds-barred street fighters. The committee didn't know that Miller had been in training all his life.

Born in 1917, Miller was raised in the Bronx and, later, the Flatbush area of Brooklyn, New York. His father, Alexander, was a clothing salesman, active in the International Garment Workers Union; his mother, Gertrude, was a member of the New York City teachers' union. As a kid, he walked picket lines with both. The struggles to protect and further the rights of working people in all types of business enterprises, their right to work in a decent, healthy environment and be treated with respect and fairness became part of Miller's DNA. In 1938, he graduated from New York University with a degree in economics. He always looked forward but never forgot to look back.

During spring training '66, Miller conducted a mini-tour of camps in Florida and Arizona. The Roberts committee wanted him to meet the players before they voted to hire or pass. Miller thought it was an excellent idea as well; he had his own reservations. Yankee Jim Bouton remembers the visit vividly. "We were all expecting to see someone with a cigar out of the corner of his mouth, a real knuckle-dragging 'deze and doze' guy. To say we were surprised would be a great understatement! We all liked him."

Miller was hired, and he and general counsel Richard Moss began sorting out priorities. Player expectations were low; maybe a few bucks in the future for the pension fund, if that. The owners (Goliath) and Miller (David) prepared to square off—this time, no Messiah in sight. No line. 'Cause nobody put a bet on Miller—Don Quixote jousting with a briefcase. Game on!

Miller's tenure as executive director of the MLBPA (1966–1982) is notable for precedent-setting achievements—most with profound ramifications still shaping the landscape today. The reader is encouraged to pick up a copy of Miller's autobiography, *A Whole Different Ball Game*, to fully appreciate the machinations, personalities, and clash of vested interests embedded in literal game-changing negotiations—Caveat Emptor. As one would expect, there is a lot of "legalese" and much layered detail in a book written by an economist/labor negotiator. But try to get past it. There's enough drama—heroes and villains, comedy and tragedy, twists and turns—to rival the best of Elizabethan theater.

So how did "Man of La Mancha" fare? For our purposes, an abbreviated Marvin Miller highlight reel:

- Negotiates the first collective bargaining agreement in all professional sports
- Independent, impartial arbitration becomes the mechanism for resolving disputes. Greg Bouris, director of communications for the MLBPA, with whom I spoke, said: "If Marvin were here, I believe he'd say this was his biggest

achievement. Most everything flowed from there. Differences and issues became settled and monitored by outside parties."
- Adds salary grievances to the arbitration process.
- The MLBPA demonstrates solidarity by striking (1972) to increase owner pension contributions—the first major sports strike in North America. After an 86-game cancellation, the players prevail.
- Curt Flood challenges the reserve clause. Miller counsels and advises Flood, discusses the broad ramifications with union members, brings in Flood for intense question-and-answer sessions involving members. He arranges for noted labor attorney Arthur Goldberg to take the case pro bono—just expenses. The Supreme Court rules against Flood. However, this opening salvo by the courageous Flood, strongly backed by the union, sets the stage for coming free agency. (If the reader hasn't read *A Well-Paid Slave: Curt Flood's Fight for Free Agency in Professional Sports*, by Brad Snyder, Viking, 2006, secure a copy immediately. You can wait until you finish this essay.)
- Leads the union through three strikes, two lockouts—fighting and clawing to establish a fair and level playing field. These gains were akin to hand-to-hand combat. If you believe the changes were due to owner benevolence, well . . .
- Major League Baseball becomes the only U.S. pro sport without a salary cap.
- Perhaps most significantly, though amorphous, Miller's efforts result in players obtaining dignity and respect—a voice in their fate. Joe Morgan summed it up this way: "We could have searched 100 years and wouldn't have found a more perfect person for our situation." Referencing policy dispute results, Bouton being Bouton said, "I think Bowie Kuhn was 0-for-67."

It needs to be stated that Miller was aided greatly by a number of events that enabled him to maximize various negotiating positions. Seminal developments such as expansion to the West Coast and South, attendance growth, television revenue, and increasing marketing and licensing fees shifted the economic balance—moving the needle in the players' favor. But, in my view, this in no way diminishes what Miller achieved.

There are those who feel strongly that the changes Miller wrought are not positive at all. Quite the contrary, actually—detrimental to the game. Consider players with averages close to the "Mendoza Line" (.200), players with bloated ERAs, relief pitchers and closers working sporadically, throwing 15 to 30 pitches or less a week. They make millions now. Rosters change annually—during the season. It's hard to root for a particular team without continuity of personnel. Team loyalty? Fan appreciation? Players are tantamount to mercenaries, thanks to Miller. I get it.

But I would ask those who harbor such understandable feelings to view the terrain from a wider lens. There are those within any system who are the recipients of benefits accrued due to their membership. Not all are equally worthy in any profession. For every bloated salary, there are far more whose careers will be short-lived with far less compensation. Should we feel sorry for them? Of course not. But we must remember that the freedom to choose whom you work for, for how long, and where is a cornerstone of democracy. An enlightened system? No, professional ballplayers are not the same as garment workers, factory workers, farm workers. But they are responsible for bringing in vast sums of money for their employers. Their rewards are commensurate with that reality. That's what Marvin Miller was about.

Greg Bouris and I further discussed Miller's legacy. He assured me that all current MLBPA employees celebrate and are well aware of Miller's groundbreaking contributions—his role in "the birth of a union." Greg heartily agreed that advances achieved by the MLBPA affected all U.S. professional sports in profound ways in varying degrees germane to each sport.

I think I might have caught Greg a bit off balance when I asked, "Why do you think Miller hasn't been voted into the Hall of Fame? He's been on the Veterans Committee voting list five separate times. What's the union's position?"

As expected, Greg acknowledged this long-term injustice. He stated, somewhat poetically, I thought, "The Hall is emptier without him," I pressed a bit. "So, why is this still the case? Any lobbying planned on behalf of Miller?" Smart, smooth, savvy, and undoubtedly politically aware, Greg responded, "I don't want to go down that road." We left it there.

My next stop was Cooperstown. Craig Muder, Hall of Fame director of communications, was extremely helpful in providing background, He pointed out that there's a lot of material about Miller at the HOF, but election is determined by the Veterans Committee. He kindly referred me to Jon Shestakofsky, vice president of Communications and Education. Jon sent a long e-mail referencing Miller as a "polarizing figure" but mentioned that Miller never reached the requisite 75 percent of total votes cast for enshrinement.

Okay, so what's the criteria? They are: record, ability, integrity, sportsmanship, character, and—drum roll, please—contributions to the game. If someone can make a case out that Miller's rejection by five separate Veterans Committees is fair and thoughtful, I'd like to hear it.

No doubt, Miller was hurt, bitter, and felt discriminated against. In 2008, he told the *Boston Globe*, "I find myself unwilling to contemplate one more rigged Veterans Committee whose members are handpicked to reach a particular outcome while offering a pretense of a democratic vote. At the age of 91, I can do without farce." He laughed. "I've never prepared an acceptance speech."

So, what can we do? We can shake our heads in dismay, cluck sympathetically, or adopt the old Brooklyn Dodgers bromide—"Wait 'til next year." I say we take action. The next group of Veterans Committee members will be announced during the Winter Meetings, voting later in the year. Craig Muder and Jon Shestakofsky assured me all letters of support for Miller will be distributed. Please send them to:

Eras Committee
National Baseball Hall of Fame and Museum
25 Main Street
Cooperstown, NY 13326

My good friend and history professor, Joe Dorinson, shared this anecdote with me. Many years ago, he attended a rally in the South preparing for a civil rights march. He stood up and told those assembled, "I teach history. Now, I'd like to make history." Standing ovation. We at TNPM write about history; let's make some as well; right the wrong! In the words of Marvin Miller: "Organize!"

> The criteria for nonplaying personnel is the impact they made on the sport. Therefore, Marvin Miller should be in the Hall of Fame on that basis. Maybe there are not a lot of my predecessors who would agree with that, but if you're looking for people who make an impact on the sport, yes, you would have to say that.—Former MLB commissioner Bud Selig

CHAPTER 10

Late Innings: Baseball Enters the New Century, 1995–2017

The Steroid Crisis

Baseball entered the new century seemingly fully recovered from the terrible strike of 1994. The McGwire–Sosa pursuit of Roger Maris's home run record had generated tremendous interest in baseball. Attendance figures reflected that as the game slowly recovered from the low point of the 1995 season. Television revenues and ratings also were up. There was even relative harmony between labor and management, as Don Fehr, head of the Players' Union, and the new commissioner, Bud Selig, recognized that another confrontation like 1994 could ruin the game.

The new century opened with the revived New York Yankees winning their fourth World Series in 2000, against their rival New Yorkers, the Mets. The Yankees dynasty was denied a fifth World Series title the next year when the Arizona Diamondbacks surprised everyone by winning the National League pennant and then beating the Yankees in a tough best-of-seven series. In 2004, the Boston Red Sox put an end to the "Curse of the Bambino" by beating the Yankees in a playoff where they were down three games to none and then went on to win the World Series by sweeping four-consecutive games from a very good Cardinals team. It was their first World Series victory since 1918. The next season, the Chicago White Sox, long a testament to futility, won their first pennant since 1959 and their first World Series in 88 years. Baseball was back and exciting.

Major League Baseball also played a significant role in healing the nation after the attack on the Twin Towers on 9/11. Out of respect, Commissioner Bud Selig postponed all baseball games for a week. When the season resumed, the games were surrounded by patriotic displays. President George Bush, who had roots in baseball as an owner of the Texas team, agreed to throw out the first ball in New York. The game also honored the police and fire personnel who did so much to help the survivors of the collapse of the Twin Towers. September 11 gave baseball an opportunity to do what the sport was good at: uniting the nation in a time of crisis.

The quality of play remained high in the majors as the new decade opened. Such new players such as Jimmy Rollins, Ichiro Suzuki, Alex Rodriguez, Ken Griffey Jr., Vladimir Guerrero, Derek Jeter, Larry Walker, Todd Helton, and Jim Thome brought excitement to the game. Three years after Mark McGwire had set a new home run record, Barry Bonds shocked the baseball world when he hit 73 homers. It seemed like better times ahead for America's game.

However, there was a cloud hovering over professional baseball. For some time in the 1990s, baseball writers and fans began to talk about the use of illegal drugs to improve performance. The word "steroid," or PED (performance-enhancing drugs), began to enter baseball parlance. During the "love fest" following the McGwire–Sosa home run race in 1998, a sportswriter noted that McGwire was using androstenedione, or andro, a well-known anabolic steroid, with potentially dangerous side effects. Andro, which was supposed to massively boost testosterone levels, was legal, although the NFL, the NCAA, and the International Olympic Committee had banned it because of its potentially dangerous side effects.

McGwire shrugged off his use of andro as insignificant, saying it helped him overcome some minor injuries that had developed during the course of his career. In the middle of the 1999 season, growing tired of questions about his use of the drug, McGwire told reporters he was giving it up because he didn't want to have a bad influence on youngsters.[1] But the issue was now out in the open.

The steroid issue did not lay dormant for long. When Commissioner Selig called for some form of testing to remove questions about drug use, the Players' Union adamantly refused. For the first time since Marvin Miller made the Players' Union a powerhouse, the public showed sympathy for management on a major issue. During Bonds's pursuit of McGwire's home run record, it was noted that he had grown massive and didn't physically resemble the player of the 1990s. The same was noted for other players, including Sosa, Lenny Dykstra, and Rafael Palmeiro, who were said to resemble the balloons in the Macy's Thanksgiving Day Parade. What forced the steroid issue to the surface was a shocking revelation in 2002. Respected baseball writer Tom Verducci, in *Sports Illustrated*, published a well-documented article entitled "Totally Juiced," about National League third baseman Ken Caminiti's use of steroids to improve his performance.[2]

Caminiti had entered the majors in 1987 with the Houston Astros. He was a solid, if unspectacular, player through the early part of his career. When he was traded to San Diego in 1995, he suddenly began to put up offensive numbers that had no relation to those of his early career. In 1996, he batted .326, hit 40 homers, and drove in 130 runs, well beyond his career averages. In his interview with *Sports Illustrated*, Caminiti documented his use—one could say abuse—of steroids. He admitted to having an addictive personality and using alcohol and illegal drugs, as well as steroids. He didn't blame anyone but himself for his drug use and didn't accuse others of imitating him. Two years later, he died alone in a rundown apartment in New York, of a drug overdose, at age 41.

The steroid issue dominated baseball talk for the next few years. Initially, Major League Baseball enacted a weak ban on steroids in 2002, which made testing purely voluntary. The next year, Jason Giambi admitted to taking steroids and also mentioned that he had used human growth hormones (HGH), for which at the time there was no test. Giambi was contrite, and no action was taken against him. The next year, the story only grew worse.

In 2005, Jose Canseco, a power-hitting outfielder and former teammate of McGwire on the Oakland A's, published a more lurid version of Caminiti's confession. Canseco's book, *Juiced: Wild Times, Rampant 'Roids, Smash Hits, and How Baseball Got Big*, discussed in detail his use of steroids.[3] More importantly, he blew the whistle by naming other players, including his teammate McGwire, Juan Gonzalez, Rafael Palmeiro, and Ivan Rodriquez, as well as Giambi, as steroid users. Unlike Caminiti, Canseco wasn't contrite but bragged about his steroid use. During his time in the major leagues, Canseco wrote, steroids were as common "as a cup of coffee."[4]

Canseco's book, although a bestseller, was dismissed by baseball management and the Players' Union as the work of a disgruntled player whose career had petered out and was seeking publicity; however, it was difficult to completely reject his charges, even if unproven, against the background of the events of the previous seasons. Baseball stats, especially power stats, had risen dramatically in the late 1990s. In 1996, Eddie Murray hit the 500th home run of his career. He was the 15th member of that celebrated group and the first to join since Mike Schmidt hit his 500th home run nine years earlier. During the next few years, 10 other players reached that level. Of the 10, six were linked to steroid use—McGwire, Palmeiro, Manny Ramirez, Gary Sheffield, Alex Rodriguez, and Barry Bonds. Another disturbing sign of steroid use was the number of players hitting 40 or more home runs in a season. Normally between two to four players would reach this figure. Between 1996 and 2001, the number was in double figures, with 17 players reaching that mark in 1996.

The press became suspicious of this power surge and took up the issue of steroid use as a major factor in explaining what was happening in the game. While blaming management for its inaction or weak response to drug problems, the press also took the Players' Union to task for opposing testing. The constant harping on the issue had a major side effect: It was demeaning the very essence of baseball—that there was no cheating allowed. In an interesting way, the press was damaging baseball's image in front of the public. The publicity surrounding the drug issue was harming baseball and soon grew worse.

In early 2002, the federal government launched an investigation into a company named Balco in the San Francisco area that manufactured various drugs. The results of the investigation became public in 2005, through the work of two enterprising San Francisco reporters, Mark Fainaru-Wada and Lance Williams. Using secret grand jury testimony, which was leaked to them, they accused Barry Bonds of steroid use dating back to the late 1990s. They wrote that Bonds was jealous of the recognition given to McGwire and Sosa in 1998, and decided to resort to steroids also. Bonds already had posted Hall of Fame-quality numbers early in his career, but beginning in the 2000 season, at the age of 36, which was old for baseball, he produced unheard-of offensive numbers—five consecutive seasons of 40 or more homers, including a record 73 in 2001, along with batting averages of .370 at age 38 and .362 at 40. No player in the history of baseball had ever posted comparable figures late in his career. In 2006, Fainaru-Wada and Williams published a book, *Game of Shadows*, which told the story in detail of the corruption of baseball by steroid use. It was an immediate bestseller in sports circles.[5]

In 2005, Congress decided to take up an issue that had captured the public's interest. In March, congressional hearings were held in which those players prominently mentioned as using steroids were ordered to appear. Their testimony was terribly damaging to baseball despite Selig and Fehr for once agreeing to do everything they could to end the abuse. An uncomfortable McGwire refused to discuss the issue or say whether he used steroids. Palmeiro absolutely denied ever using any artificial product, while Sosa was not pressed on the issue. In August, Major League Baseball announced that Palmeiro had been suspended for using an illegal substance, stanozolol. He was accused of hypocrisy, especially when it was revealed that the test he had failed was given less than two months after his adamant denial of steroid use to Congress. To put pressure on baseball, Senator Jim Bunning of Kentucky, a Hall of Fame pitcher, was given the floor to demand that baseball take action. Something had to be done, Bunning said. Baseball doesn't belong to the players or the owners, he declared, adding, "It's ours. They're just enjoying the privilege of playing it for a short time. . . . They all need to protect the integrity of the greatest game ever."[6]

Selig realized he had to somehow seize control of the issue or it would destroy the game, which was prospering as never before. In March 2006, a year after the disastrous congressional hearings, Selig asked former senator George Mitchell of Maine to carry out a thorough investigation of the steroid problem. Mitchell, fresh from his role of ending the intractable Northern Irish problem and a baseball fan, agreed, but with the proviso that he would have a free hand. The results of his investigation changed baseball forever.

Mitchell's investigation lasted a year. He had the full cooperation of Selig's office, but Fehr initially was reluctant to discuss the names of any players charged with steroid use. It didn't matter. Mitchell met with and interviewed hundreds of players from all 30 major-league teams. During his investigation, he drew on information from individuals who admitted that they supplied players with drugs of various kinds. This included Kirk Radomski of the Mets; Brian McNamee, a personal trainer with the Yankees; and Larry Starr, for 30 years a trainer with the Reds.

Mitchell issued a final report in December 2007, which was harshly critical of both players and management. The report made a number of recommendations, of which the most important was to demand that baseball use an independent body to carry out future tests. The tests also should be random to guarantee accuracy. Mitchell also wanted baseball to begin an education program to warn players, especially minor leaguers, of the dangers of steroid use. Baseball had done so successfully with the use of chewing tobacco in the past. Finally, Mitchell strongly recommended that the Players' Association cooperate with Major League Baseball in policing the program.[7]

The Mitchell Report galvanized both players and management. Testing became more stringent. In 2014, the penalties for failing a drug test were made severe. Instead of weak punishment for failing a drug test, it would be 80 games for a first failure and the entire season for failing a second time. A suspended player would not to be able to collect his salary while sidelined. Also, a player suspended for the entire season would not be allowed to take part in postseason play. Finally, players who failed three drug tests would be banned from baseball for life.

The combination of the Caminiti story, Canseco's book, the congressional hearings, and especially the Mitchell investigation finally brought the steroid issue under control. Baseball slowly began to restore the confidence of the fans in the game's exploits. They no longer would have to be suspicious of a player's performances. As in the past, baseball was late to deal with a significant problem but it ultimately summoned enough common sense to do so.

In its first year of implementation, 2005, 12 players were suspended for steroid use. The number slowly dropped throughout the years. One study carried out by *Forbes* found that just 1.4 percent of players in the major leagues, the minors, as well as the Dominican and Venezuelan summer leagues, were using steroids. The total number of major leaguers found to have used steroids or other PEDs since 2005 was 62, with just one being suspended for life.[8] As a result of these actions, fewer and fewer players tested positive, and the issue, if not disappearing, seemed under control by the second decade of the century. It was a crisis that had the potential to destroy the game, and baseball only brought it under control when pushed by outside forces.

One by-product of the steroid problem was the impact it had on players' chances of election to the Hall of Fame. The statistics of players in the 1990s and early 2000s are viewed with great skepticism by the voters for the Hall of Fame. Some of the most prominent players caught up in the scandal had put up numbers that were clearly worthy of the Hall of Fame. Barry Bonds, who broke the single-season home run record, as well as Hank Aaron's career home run record, should be a shoo-in. The same is true of McGwire; Roger Clemens, with his impressive career stats; and Palmeiro, whose 569 homers and 3,000 hits are worthy of enshrinement. So far, the electors have shown no sign of letting them in the Hall. They remain outcasts in the sport that they once dominated. Unless matters change, it is unlikely these players will ever reach the Hall of Fame.

BASEBALL FACES THE FUTURE

Despite its problem with drugs and steroids, the game of baseball has thrived in the new century. Given the poor record of labor-management relations in the past, it is noteworthy that the four most recent collective bargaining agreements have been negotiated without a strike. Attendance reached new levels, peaking at 79 million fans in 2007. There was a leveling off after that year, but attendance has remained above the 70 million mark for every season since 2007. In 2016, the last season for which we have detailed records, attendance reached 73.2 million. The small decline is worrisome and one for which there is no clear explanation. Is baseball losing its luster and appeal? It is possible, as there are more options for fans to watch other sports.

One major factor could be the cost of attending a game. Once the cheapest sport to watch, it has become an expensive proposition to go to a game. Ticket prices also have risen during the last 30 years to the point where attending a Major League Baseball game, along with parking and food, could easily top $100—a far cry from the days of the 50-cent bleacher seat. Some baseball teams have found the creation of communal spaces in the park for dining while watching the game has attracted fans. Almost every ballpark now has such a fan-friendly space, usually in a walkway around the stands. Another potential problem for baseball in the future is the length of the games. In recent seasons, games typically have averaged almost three hours. Factor in travel time, parking charges, and other incidentals, and going to a baseball game is no longer always a pleasant experience. For some fans, sitting in front of their 50-inch flat screen television is preferable to attending a game in person.

Another worrisome issue facing baseball is that its most talented players, Miguel Cabrera, Mike Trout, Clayton Kershaw, Bryce Harper, and Giancarlo Stanton, lack the appeal of some of the greats of the past. Cabrera is past his peak, and only Trout and perhaps Harper and Stanton have the charisma to be superstars like Hank Aaron, Willie Mays, or Mickey Mantle. One thing is clear: Baseball is not losing fans to other sports. In fact, Major League Baseball's attendance figure is greater than the combined total of all other major professional sports—professional football, basketball, and hockey. Baseball's average attendance has remained above 30,000 since the beginning of the 1990s. In 2016, seven teams attracted 3 million fans, and one, the Red Sox, narrowly missed that mark. Whatever else happens, baseball is not going to disappear in the future.

Since 2000, part of the reason for baseball's continuing popularity is its competitive balance. Unlike so often in the past, there is no team that dominates for long—no Yankees, Dodgers, or Braves dynasty. Free agency and the draft have produced a tendency to equalize talent. Teams have placed a renewed emphasis on building a strong farm system. One result is that competition has leveled among the teams and between the two leagues. In recent years, of the 30 teams in the majors, 18 have reached the World Series, and only four have been able to do so in consecutive seasons. No team has won back-to-back World Series since the Yankees team of the 1990s. In league terms, the National League has won nine World Series, the American eight. Baseball's balance has never been better.

The recent success of Kansas City, Houston, and the Chicago Cubs, teams that seemed doomed to mediocrity, is a sign of baseball's competitive health. It used to be argued that baseball's fans liked a dynasty if only to have a team to root against, as was the case with the great Yankees teams of 1947–1964, of whom it was said rooting for them was like rooting for U.S. Steel. That is no longer the case. The Yankees, despite spending enormous sums of money for free agents, haven't won anything since 2010.

One disturbing sign of imbalance is the All-Star Game. The All-Star Game has been dominated by the American League since 1997, perhaps because of the designated hitter rule, but the overall record of All-Star Games in 43–42, in favor of the National League.

A development in baseball in recent years that has grown powerful is the emphasis on statistics, called advanced analytics, to understand and measure the game. With the growing use of computers, more and more baseball executives are resorting to sophisticated statistical measures to evaluate talent. It is no longer enough to have a high batting average. Rather, the emphasis is on your OPS, on-base average plus slugging. That stat is giving way to a new one, WOBA, or weighted on-base average. That seeks to measure the total value of the hit that adds up to a player's on-base average. Players are also evaluated based on their

WAR, wins above replacement, which seeks to measure a player's value based on the quality of a replacement player for him. These new stats are particularly appealing to young fans and will probably continue to develop in the future. At the same time, Major League Baseball executives are placing more and more emphasis on these types of statistics to develop their teams. At least in this area, baseball is not lagging behind other sports.

Along with the strong competitive nature of recent baseball, another interesting trend is the growing influence of Latin players. Once a rarity, they now constitute one of the most important factors in shaping the modern game of baseball. There have been Latin players in baseball's past, usually white Cubans, but they made little impact. Latin numbers only began to rise in the 1950s, with the emergence of black Latins, for example, Minnie Minoso, Roberto Clemente, and Vic Power. Their numbers only became significant in the early 1970s, when they consistently produced more than 10 percent of major-league players.

In 1993, for the first time, there were more Latins on major-league rosters than African Americans. That trend continues to the present. During the 2015 season, for which there are accurate numbers, Latins, whether black or white, constituted 29.3 percent of the players on major-league rosters. The figure for African Americans is at a historic low, at 8.3 percent.[9] The most common name in the 2016 edition of *Who's Who in Baseball*, which listed the players on the major-league rosters, was not Jones or Williams, but Martinez, with Rodriguez not far behind.[10]

There a number of possible explanations for this phenomenon. Latin players can play baseball year-round. Aside from soccer, there is no other sport with great popularity in the Caribbean and other parts of Central and South America. The best athletes in those areas would naturally drift toward baseball if they have sporting skills. Latin players would find the financial rewards, even if only in minor league baseball, powerfully attractive. There has been a change in the area providing Latin players. Cuba as a source dried up for years because of political problems between the United States and Fidel Castro. Recently, Cuban players like dominant reliever Aroldis Chapman and power-hitting outfielders Yoenis Cespedes and Jose Abreu have found their way to the United States. More will follow in the next few years. In 2016, however, the main supplier of Latin talent to the majors was the Dominican Republic, with 83 players on various team rosters. Venezuela ranked second among Latin nations, with 65 players, including future Hall of Fame candidate Miguel Cabrera.

While it is difficult to predict trends, it is safe to assume that Latin America will continue to supply professional baseball with players for the foreseeable future. Asia as a supplier of major-league talent has begun to make a mark during the last 20 years. But the impact remains small, with just 1.2 percent of the players on major-league rosters in recent seasons hailing from there. Japan and South Korea, two countries where American cultural influence was, and remains, strong, have produced the most major leaguers. It is possible these numbers will continue to grow as the major leagues look abroad for polished talent. The impact of Ichiro Suzuki, by far the best Asian player in the past 17 seasons, opened the eyes of major-league talent evaluators to the possibilities of exploiting the Japanese baseball pool.

While Major League Baseball is happy with its diversity and global reach, there is considerable concern about the decline in numbers of African American players. For the last half-dozen years, their numbers have remained in the single digits. Their numbers peaked in 1981, and then began a steady decline. While there are still great African American players, no one other than Barry Bonds and perhaps Derek Jeter approached the stature of Willie Mays or Hank Aaron. The explanations given for this lack of African American talent have focused on the appeal of other sports, especially basketball and football, for African American players. Major League Baseball has tried in recent years to find a way to make baseball an attractive sport for children in urban areas, especially African American youth. Baseball has promoted the sport through its Urban Youth Academy program, and various teams have set up RBI programs, aimed at reviving baseball in urban areas. Both these programs are new and have yet to show any significant impact.

On another level, baseball has made great strides in improving its hiring practices. According to one source, it had an A– grade for its racial hiring practices. Four general managers are either African American or Latin, while there are two African American managers. Of major-league coaching ranks, 10 percent are African American, while 26 percent are Latin. The only area in which baseball lags badly is the hiring of women, but even here in recent years attempts have been made to compensate for past failures and show that baseball is no longer the "Old Boys Club." It makes sense for baseball to try to bring in more women since studies show that women prefer baseball to all other sports by a 2–1 ratio.

Women have been playing baseball in some form since the 1860s. They have had intimate contact with the sport in various capacities throughout the years. A woman named Helene Britton owned the St. Louis team in the early twentieth century. One of the most influential figures in Negro League baseball circles was a woman by the name of Effa Manley. Along with her husband, she owned and managed the popular Newark Eagles team of the Negro Leagues. She was an imaginative owner and a hard bargainer who tried to keep the Negro Leagues afloat after baseball integrated in 1946. She was the first woman elected to the Hall of Fame.

In 1999, the commissioner's office created a program known as the Initiative on Women in Baseball to prepare and train women for roles in baseball management. Progress has been slow, but the number of women in top executive positions is growing. There have been two women who have served as assistant general managers, and one of them, Kim Ng, is considered a likely candidate for a future position as GM. An even more unusual innovation for professional baseball was the hiring by the Los Angeles Dodgers of the first Muslim, Fahan Zaidi, to a high executive office. He was named GM of the Dodgers, meaning he runs all aspects of the Dodgers baseball program.

The question arises: What is the future of baseball? Financially, it has never been more secure. Baseball revenue topped the $10 billion mark in 2016, the highest in the sport's history. There is no franchise in economic difficulties today. Television revenue has made the sport financially stable even with the rise in costs, especially player contracts. In the early 2000s, there were just two players making $20 million a year. Now there are more than a dozen, with the first $30 million contracts belonging to Giancarlo Stanton, formerly of Miami and now with the Yankees. Big contracts await Mike Trout, Bryce Harper, and Clayton Kershaw.

Expansion doesn't seem to be in the offing. Most of the large urban areas have teams. The nation is balanced in the placement of the major-league franchises, with almost every part of the country represented by a team. It is possible that Montreal, despite its failure to sustain a team in the past, will again get a chance. For a time, the Expos drew well and put together a solid National League team. They were a victim of the 1994 strike, when they had possibly the best team in their history. A second franchise in Canada is not out of the question.

A bigger question is the possible expansion outside the United States to the south, to Mexico and the Caribbean. Mexico has had a strong baseball tradition, and Mexico City would be a natural site for a major-league franchise, especially with the proliferation of Latin players in the game. Havana would be another potential major-league location given the fanatical baseball tradition in Cuba. It is possible that in the future you might see the emergence of a third major league, not in Latin America, but in Asia. The Japanese are mad about baseball, and the game has caught on in South Korea and Taiwan. Given the huge potential audience, it is possible that an Asia major league may emerge. Already, the quality of play is high, as is evident from the caliber of players entering the majors from Asia. Some baseball experts rank the Japanese game on par with Triple-A baseball in the United States.

With all its troubles, baseball's future seems secure. It will continue to play a significant role in American culture. Baseball continues to touch a deep nerve in the American psyche, perhaps because it resonates with the nation's longing for a lost age of innocence. The popularity of such baseball films as *Bull Durham*, *Field of Dreams*, and *Angels in the Outfield* testifies to America's belief that the game represents a purer time in American life. Baseball's roots remain deep in the nation and are signs of the game's vitality.

Baseball has survived its continuing crises, most of which have been self-inflicted. Bismarck once remarked that God watches over drunkards, children, and the United States of America. He could have added baseball to his list. Baseball may never recover its position as America's premier sport. That position has been lost for the foreseeable future to football, unless the concussion issue, which has emerged in recent years, becomes more serious. It also will be a misnomer to call baseball America's game as more and more outsiders begin to play baseball at a sophisticated level. Non-Americans already constitute approximately 30 percent of the players in the majors, a figure that should continue to grow. It is difficult to see any areas other than those already playing baseball adopting the sport in the near future. It is played in parts of Europe, but not seriously, and baseball is not a threat to the dominance of European football.

No African country has shown any interest in baseball. In Asia, its appeal is strongest in precisely those places where American influence has been greatest in the past: Japan, South Korea, and Taiwan. Some Chinese players have emerged, but they are Taiwanese, not from mainland China. Australia has produced a couple of major leaguers, and the game could take hold there. But for the foreseeable future, it will be confined to those areas where it has already taken root.

Baseball has survived as one of the distinguishing features of American life. The game, with all its troubles, with the continuing differences between management and labor, has thrived in recent years. Its hold on the public is a powerful one, and whatever the game's difficulties, they seem to disappear once the new season rolls around.

Questions for Consideration

1. Discuss the impact of the steroid problem for baseball in the first years of the new century. Why was it so dangerous for the future of the game?
2. How did labor and management confront the steroid issue when it first surfaced? Why did it take them so long to seriously deal with the issue? Consider the history of labor–management relations in baseball in your answer.
3. Why was the Mitchell Report so significant for the future of baseball?
4. Discuss the possibilities of baseball expansion outside the United States and Canada. Is such expansion feasible or realistic?

5. Analyze the current state of African Americans in baseball. What are some of the reasons for the decline of their numbers in recent years?
6. Reflecting on baseball's past, what are some of the possibilities for the sport in the near future?

Notes

1. George Vecsey, "Baseball Must Listen to McGwire," *New York Times*, August 6, 1992.

2. Tom Verducci, "Totally Juiced: Confessions of a Former MVP," *Sports Illustrated*, June 2, 2002.

3. Jose Canseco, *Juiced: Wild Times, Rampant 'Roids, Smash Hits, and How Baseball Got Big* (New York: It Books, 2005).

4. Laura Fitzpatrick, "A Brief History of Steroids," *Time*, November 13, 2010.

5. Mark Fainaru-Wada and Lance Williams, *Game of Shadows* (New York: Books on Tape, 2006).

6. Maria Newman, "Congress Opens Hearings on Steroid Use in Baseball," *New York Times*, March 18, 2005, https://archive.nytimes.com/www.nytimes.com/learning/teachers/featured_articles/20050318friday.html (accessed May 9, 2018); "McGwire Admits Nothing; Sosa and Palmeiro Deny Use," *ESPN.com*, March 18, 2005, http://www.espn.com/mlb/news/story?id=2015420 (accessed May 9, 2018).

7. There is a summary of the Mitchell Report at http://mlb.mlb.com/mlb/news/mitchell/.

8. Fitzpatrick, "A Brief History of Steroids"; Miriam Brown, "List of Every MLB and Minor League Drug Suspension," *Forbes*, November 11, 2015.

9. Howard Bloom, *Sports Business News*, April 15, 2015; Mark Armour and Daniel R. Levitt, "Baseball Demographics, 1947–2012," *Society for American Baseball Research*, https://sabr.org/bioproj/topic/baseball-demographics-1947-2012 (accessed May 9, 2018).

10. Pete Palmer, *Who's Who in Baseball* (New York: Example Product Manufacturer, 2016).

TOTALLY JUICED: CONFESSIONS OF A FORMER MVP

Tom Verducci

Steroid use, which a decade ago was considered a taboo violated by a few renegade sluggers, is now so rampant in baseball that even pitchers and wispy outfielders are juicing up—and talking openly among themselves about it. According to players, trainers, and executives interviewed by *SI* over the last three months, the game has become a pharmacological trade show. What emerges from dozens of interviews is a portrait of baseball's intensifying reliance on steroids and other performance-enhancing drugs. These drugs include not only human growth hormone (HGH), but also an array of legal and illegal stimulants, ranging from amphetamines to Ritalin to ephedrine-laced dietary supplements, that many big leaguers pop to get a jolt of pregame energy and sharpen their focus. But it is the use of illegal steroids that is growing fastest and having a profound impact on the game.

The surest sign that steroids are gaining acceptance in baseball: the first public admission of steroid use—without remorse—by a prominent former player. Ken Caminiti, whose 15-year big-league career ended after a stint with the Atlanta Braves last season, revealed to *SI* that he won the 1996 National League Most Valuable Player Award while on steroids he purchased from a pharmacy in Tijuana, Mexico. Spurred to try the drugs by concern over a shoulder injury in early '96, Caminiti said that his steroid use improved his performance noticeably and became more sophisticated over the next five seasons. He told *SI* that he used steroids so heavily in '96 that by the end of that season, his testicles shrank and retracted; doctors found that his body had virtually stopped producing testosterone and that the level of the hormone had fallen to 20 percent of normal. "It took four months to get my nuts to drop on their own," he said of the period after he stopped taking the drugs.

Tom Verducci, "Totally Juiced: Confessions of a Former MVP," *Sports Illustrated*, June 2, 2002.

Yet Caminiti, a recovering alcoholic and former drug user, defended his use of steroids and said he would not discourage others from taking them because they have become a widely accepted—even necessary—choice for ballplayers looking for a competitive edge and financial security. "I've made a ton of mistakes," said Caminiti.

> I don't think using steroids is one of them.
>
> It's no secret what's going on in baseball. At least half the guys are using steroids. They talk about it. They joke about it with each other. The guys who want to protect themselves or their image by lying have that right. Me? I'm at the point in my career where I've done just about every bad thing you can do. I try to walk with my head up. I don't have to hold my tongue. I don't want to hurt teammates or friends. But I've got nothing to hide.

If a young player were to ask me what to do," Caminiti continued,

> I'm not going to tell him it's bad. Look at all the money in the game. You have a chance to set your family up, to get your daughter into a better school. . . . So I can't say, "Don't do it," not when the guy next to you is as big as a house and he's going to take your job and make the money.

Anabolic steroids elevate the body's testosterone level, increasing muscle mass without changes in diet or activity, though their effect is greatly enhanced in conjunction with proper nutrition and strength training. Steroids are illegal in the U.S. unless prescribed by a physician for medical conditions, such as AIDS and hypogonadism (an inability to produce enough testosterone). Studies have shown that the side effects from steroids can include heart and liver damage, persistent endocrine-system imbalance, elevated cholesterol levels, strokes, aggressive behavior, and the dysfunction of genitalia. Doctors suspect that steroid use is a major factor in the recent increase in baseball injuries, especially severe injuries such as complete muscle tears.

Unlike the NFL and NBA, both of which ban and test for steroid use—the NHL does neither—Major League Baseball has no steroid policy or testing program for big leaguers. (Baseball does test minor-league players, but violators are neither penalized nor required to undergo counseling.) Any such program would have to be collectively bargained with the Major League Baseball Players Association, which traditionally has resisted any form of drug testing but now faces a division in its membership over the issue. "Part of our task is to let a consensus emerge," says Gene Orza, the associate counsel for the Players' Union.

"No one denies that it is a problem," says Commissioner Bud Selig. "It's a problem we can and must deal with now, rather than years from now when the public says, 'Why didn't you do something about it?' I'm very worried about this."

But it is also true that fans have become more accepting of steroids as part of the game. Fourteen years ago the crowd at Fenway Park in Boston chided Oakland A's outfielder Jose Canseco during the American League Championship Series with damning chants of, "Ster-oids! Ster-oids!" The game had never before seen a physical marvel such as Canseco, a 240-pound hulk who could slug a baseball 500 feet and still be swift enough to steal 40 bases. Upon retiring last month after failing to catch on with a major-league team, Canseco, while not admitting steroid use himself, said that steroids have "revolutionized" the game and that he would write a tell-all book blowing the lid off drug use in the majors. Canseco estimated that 85 percent of major leaguers use steroids.

Heavily muscled bodies like Canseco's have now become so common that they no longer invite scorn. Players even find dark humor in steroid use. One American League outfielder, for instance, was known to be taking a steroid typically given by veterinarians to injured, ill, or overworked horses and readily available in Latin America. An opposing player pointed to him and remarked, "He takes so much of that horse stuff that one day we're going to look out in the outfield and he's going to be grazing. . . ."

The first generation of ballplayers who have grown up in the steroid culture is only now arriving. . . . The acceptance level of steroids in the game may very well continue rising until . . . until what? A labor deal that includes a comprehensive testing policy? Such a plan, unlikely as it is, given the union's resistance, might deter some players, but even baseball officials concede that the minor-league testing program in place gives players the green light to shoot up in the offseason. And athletes in other sports subject to testing have stayed one step ahead of enforcement with tactics such as using so-called "designer drugs," steroids that are chemically altered to mask the unique signature of that drug that otherwise would show on a urine test.

So even with testing, will it take something much darker for steroids to fall from favor? Renowned sports orthopedist James Andres recalled the impact of two prominent deaths on the drug culture in football. "Major League Baseball can't continue to leave this door open," says Andrews. "Steroids became a big deal in football after Lyle Alzado [died], and ephedrine became a big deal after Korey Stringer. You don't want to see it get to that [in baseball] before someone says stop. But, unfortunately, that's what it seems to take to wake people up."

Bibliography

General Studies

Alexander, Charles. *Our Game: An American Baseball History*. New York: MJF Books, 1991.

James, Bill. *The New Bill James Historical Baseball Abstract*. New York: Free Press, 2001.

Koppett, Leonard. *Koppett's Concise History of Major League Baseball*. Philadelphia: Temple University Press, 1998.

Porter, David L., ed. *Biographical Dictionary of American Sports: Baseball*. 3 vols. Westport, CT: Greenwood Press, 2000.

Rader, Benjamin. *Baseball: A History of America's Game*. Urbana: University of Illinois Press, 2008.

Seymour, Harold. *Baseball: The Early Years*. 3 vols. New York: Oxford University Press, 1960, 1989, 1990.

Ward, Geoffrey. *Baseball: An Illustrated History*. New York: Alfred A. Knopf, 2001.

Special Studies

Baldassaro, Lawrence, and Richard Johnson, eds. *The American Game: Baseball and Ethnicity*. Carbondale: Southern Illinois University Press, 2002.

The Baseball Encyclopedia, 9th ed. New York: Macmillan, 1993.

Koppett, Leonard. *The New Thinking Fan's Guide to Baseball*. New York: Simon & Schuster, 1991.

Ritter, Lawrence. *The Glory of Their Times: The Story of the Early Days of Baseball Told by the Men Who Played It*. New York: Harper Perennial, 2010.

Schwarz, Alan. *The Numbers Game: Baseball's Lifelong Fascination with Statistics*. New York: Thomas Dunne, 2004.

Thorn, John, and Peter Palmer. *The Hidden Game of Baseball.* Garden City, NY: Doubleday/Dolphin, 1985.

Thorn, John, and Peter Palmer, with Michael Gershman. *Total Baseball: The Official Encyclopedia of Major League Baseball,* 8th ed. New York: Warner Books, 1989.

Early History of Baseball

Adelman, Melvin. *A Sporting Time: New York City and the Rise of Modern Athletics, 1820–1870.* Urbana: University of Illinois Press, 1986.

Casway, Jerrold. *Ed Delahanty in the Emerald Age of Baseball.* Notre Dame, IN: University of Notre Dame Press, 2004.

Frommer, Harvey. *Old-Time Baseball: America's Pastime in the Gilded Age.* Guilford, CT: Globe Pequot, 2016.

Ivor-Campbell, Frederick. *Baseball's First Stars.* Cleveland, OH: Society for American Baseball Research, 1996.

Levine, Peter. *A. G. Spalding and the Rise of Baseball: The Promise of American Sport.* New York: Oxford University Press, 1986.

Malloy, Jerry, ed. *Sol White's History of Colored Baseball.* Lincoln: University of Nebraska Press, 1995.

Nemec, David. *The Beer and Whiskey League.* Guilford, CT: Lyons Press, 1994.

Peterson, Harold. *The Man Who Invented Baseball.* New York: Scribner, 1973.

Selzer, Jack. *Baseball in the Nineteenth Century: An Overview.* Phoenix, AZ: Society of American Baseball Research, 1988.

Sullivan, Dean, ed. *Early Innings: A Documentary History of Baseball, 1825–1908.* Lincoln: University of Nebraska Press, 1995.

Thorn, John. *Baseball in the Garden of Eden: The Secret History of the Early Game.* New York: Simon & Schuster, 2011.

Zeiler, Thomas. *Ambassadors in Pinstripes: The Spalding World Tour and the Birth of the American Empire.* Lanham, MD: Rowman & Littlefield, 2006.

Baseball History in the Twentieth Century

Abrams, Roger. *The First World Series and the Baseball Fanatics of 1903.* Boston: Northeastern University Press, 2003.

Alexander, Charles. *John McGraw.* Lincoln: University of Nebraska Press, 1995.

Asinof, Eliot. *Eight Men Out.* New York: Henry Holt, 2000.

Burk, Robert F. *Much More Than A Game: Players, Owners, and American Baseball since 1921.* Chapel Hill: University of North Carolina Press, 2001.

———. *Never Just a Game: Players, Owners, and American Baseball to 1920.* Chapel Hill: University of North Carolina Press, 1994.

Cramer, Richard Ben. *Joe DiMaggio: The Hero's Life.* New York: Simon & Schuster, 2000.

Gerlach, Larry. *The Men in Blue: Conversations with Umpires*. Lincoln: University of Nebraska Press, 1994.

Halberstam, David. *The Summer of '49*. New York: Harper Perennial Modern Classics, 2006.

Hittner, Arthur. *Honus Wagner: The Life of Baseball's Flying Dutchman*. Jefferson, NC: McFarland, 1996.

Honig, Donald. *Baseball When the Grass Was Real*. New York: Coward, McCann & Geoghegan, 1975.

Kahn, Roger. *The Boys of Summer*. New York: Harper & Row, 1972.

Kerrane, Kevin. *Dollar Sign on the Muscle: The World of Baseball Scouting*. Palmer, AK: Fireside Books, 1989.

Korr, Charles. *The End of Baseball as We Knew It: The Players' Union, 1960–1981*. Urbana: University of Illinois Press, 2002.

Kuhn, Bowie. *Hardball: The Education of a Baseball Commissioner*. Lincoln, NE: Bison Books, 1997.

Kuklick, Bruce. *To Every Thing a Season: Shibe Park and Urban Philadelphia, 1909–1976*. Princeton, NJ: Princeton University Press, 1991.

Lowenfish, Lee. *Branch Rickey: Baseball's Ferocious Gentleman*. Lincoln: University of Nebraska Press, 2007.

————. *The Imperfect Diamond: A History of Baseball's Labor Wars*. Lincoln, NE: Bison Books, 2010.

Miller, Marvin. *A Whole Different Ball Game: The Sport and Business of Baseball*. New York: Birch Lane Press, 1991.

Montville, Leigh. *The Big Bam: The Life and Times of Babe Ruth*. New York: Anchor, 2007.

————. *Ted Williams*. New York: Doubleday, 2004.

Morris, Peter. *A Game of Inches: The Stories behind the Innovations That Shaped Baseball*. Chicago: Ivan R. Dee, 2006.

Murdoch, Eugene. *Baseball between the Wars: Memories of the Game by the Men Who Played It*. Westport, CT: Greenwood Press, 1993.

Noll, Roger, ed. *Government and the Sports Business*. Washington, DC: Brookings Institution, 1974.

Peary, Daniel, ed. *We Played the Game: Sixty-Five Players Remember Baseball's Greatest Era, 1947–1964*. New York: Hyperion, 1994.

Peterson, Robert. *Only the Ball Was White: A History of Legendary Black Players and All-Black Professional Teams*. New York: Oxford University Press, 1992.

Pietrusza, David. *Judge and Jury: The Life and Times of Judge Kenesaw Mountain Landis*. South Bend, IN: Diamond Communications, 1998.

Quirk, James, and Rodney Fort. *Pay Dirt: The Business of Professional Sports*. Princeton, NJ: Princeton University Press, 1992.

Riess, Steven. *Touching Base: Professional Baseball and American Culture in the Progressive Era*. Urbana: University of Illinois Press, 1999.

Rossi, John. *The 1964 Phillies: The Story of Baseball's Most Memorable Collapse*. Jefferson, NC: McFarland, 2005.

Shapiro, Michael. *Bottom of the Ninth: Branch Rickey, Casey Stengel, and the Daring Scheme to Save Baseball from Itself.* New York: Henry Holt, 2009.

Smith, Curt. *Voices of the Game.* New York: Fireside Press, 1992.

Smith, Red. *Red Smith on Baseball.* Chicago: Ivan R. Dee, 2000.

Tygiel, Jules. *Baseball's Great Experiment: Jackie Robinson and His Legacy.* New York: Oxford University Press, 1983.

————. *Past Time: Baseball as History.* New York: Oxford University Press, 2000.

Warfield, Don. *The Roaring Redhead: Larry MacPhail, Baseball's Great Innovator.* South Bend, IN: Diamond Communications, 1987.

Weingardner, Mark. *Prophet of the Sandlots: Journeys with a Major-League Scout.* New York: Atlantic Monthly Press, 1990.

Weintraub, Robert. *The Victory Season: The End of World War II and the Birth of Baseball's Golden Age.* New York: Little, Brown, 2013.

White, G. Edward. *Creating the National Pastime: Baseball Transforms Itself, 1903–1953.* Princeton, NJ: Princeton University Press, 1996.

Zimbalist, Andrew. *Baseball and Billions.* New York: Basic Books, 1992.

Index

About the Author

John P. Rossi was born in Philadelphia in 1936. He graduated from La Salle College, earned a M.A. in history from Notre Dame, and acquired a Ph.D. in 1965 from the University of Pennsylvania. He has taught at La Salle, where he has been professor emeritus of history since 2006. Rossi is author of seven books and more than 200 articles, essays, and reviews. Along with the history of baseball, his other interests include the writings of George Orwell, about whom he has written extensively.